the BOOKS of MAGIC
Transformations

John Ney Rieber
Writer

Peter Gross
Artist

Sherilyn van Valkenburgh ❧ **Nathan Eyring**
Colorists

Richard Starkings and Comicraft
Letterer

Sherilyn van Valkenburgh ❧ **Michael Kaluta**
August Hall ❧ **Chris Bachalo**
Original Covers

Neil Gaiman
Consultant

Timothy Hunter & The Books of Magic
created by
Neil Gaiman & John

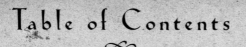

Table of Contents

Dramatis Personae

Timothy Hunter
An average teenager whose greatest aspiration was a perfect skateboard run...
until he learned that he had the potential to become the most powerful magician
in history. Tim has yet to accept his destiny, and it's uncertain he will survive
to claim it. But all around him, powerful forces have emerged — some seemingly
content to watch and wait to see what form his magical heritage will take,
others seeking a more direct role in Tim's ultimate fate.

Molly
Tim's classmate and girlfriend. Her relationship with Tim has been
tested by a recent trip to Hell, where she learned disquieting
things about him.

William Hunter
Tim's father — or is he? — who must endure not only the trials
of raising a teenager alone, but the perils of magic as well.

Gwendolyn
A young lady from Victorian times, whose skill with a needle
and thread is but one of her gifts.

Marya
A girl from the mystical realm called Free Country,
haven for abused and unwanted children.

Daniel
A child banished from Free Country, tortured
by his unrequited love for Marya and transformed
by Reverend Slaggingham into the
Climbing Boy.

Reverend Slaggingham
Originally from Victorian England,
the Reverend's head is all that
remains of this scheming cyborg.

The Amadan
Fool, jester, and string-puller par
excellence of the Faerie realm.

Death
One of the Endless.
Sister to Dream.

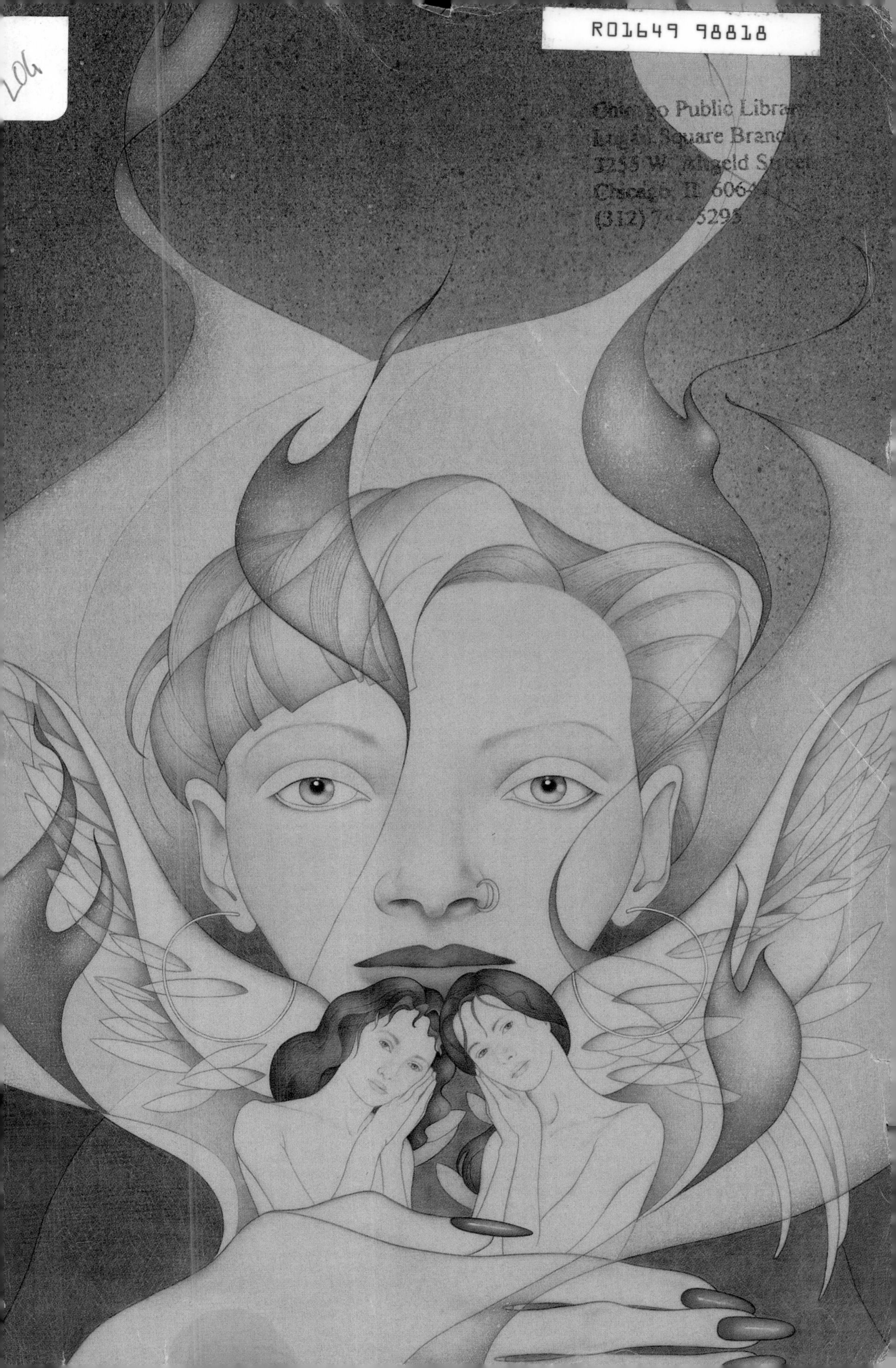

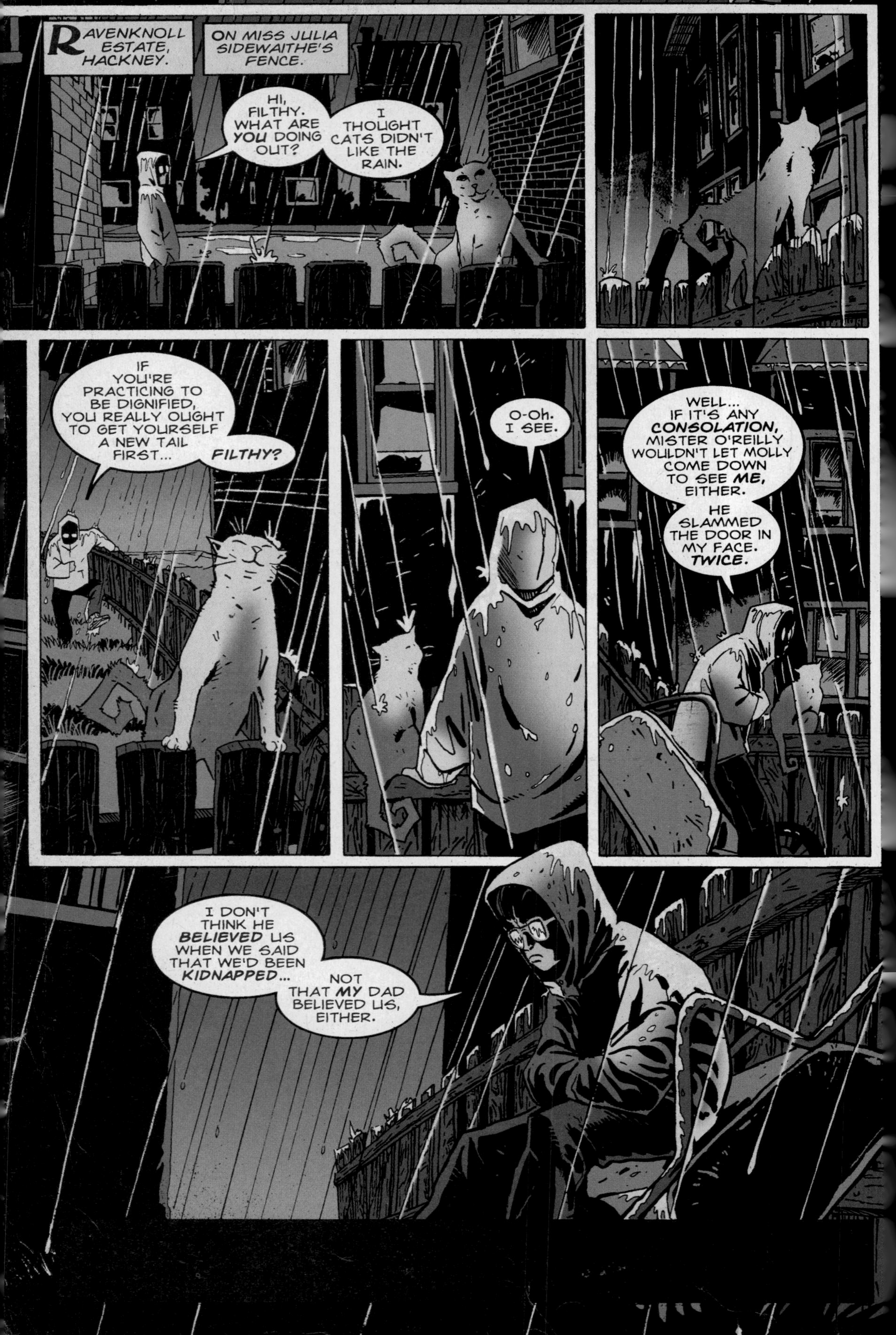
RAVENKNOLL ESTATE, HACKNEY.
ON MISS JULIA SIDEWAITHE'S FENCE.
HI, FILTHY. WHAT ARE YOU DOING OUT?
I THOUGHT CATS DIDN'T LIKE THE RAIN.
IF YOU'RE PRACTICING TO BE DIGNIFIED, YOU REALLY OUGHT TO GET YOURSELF A NEW TAIL FIRST... FILTHY?
O-OH. I SEE.
WELL... IF IT'S ANY CONSOLATION, MISTER O'REILLY WOULDN'T LET MOLLY COME DOWN TO SEE ME, EITHER.
HE SLAMMED THE DOOR IN MY FACE. TWICE.
I DON'T THINK HE BELIEVED US WHEN WE SAID THAT WE'D BEEN KIDNAPPED...
NOT THAT MY DAD BELIEVED US, EITHER.

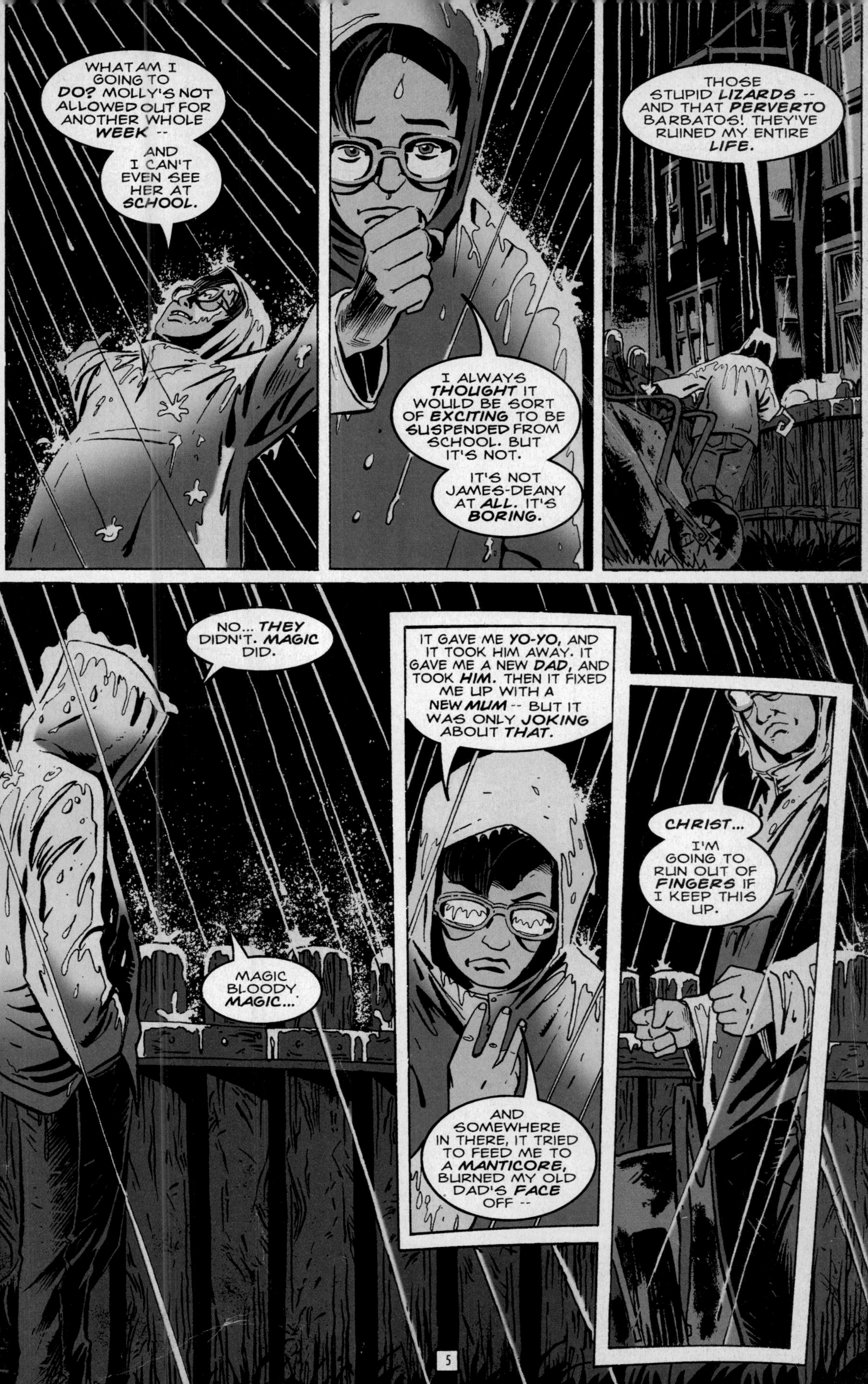
WHAT AM I GOING TO DO? MOLLY'S NOT ALLOWED OUT FOR ANOTHER WHOLE WEEK --
AND I CAN'T EVEN SEE HER AT SCHOOL.
I ALWAYS THOUGHT IT WOULD BE SORT OF EXCITING TO BE SUSPENDED FROM SCHOOL. BUT IT'S NOT.
IT'S NOT JAMES-DEANY AT ALL. IT'S BORING.
THOSE STUPID LIZARDS -- AND THAT PERVERTO BARBATOS! THEY'VE RUINED MY ENTIRE LIFE.
NO... THEY DIDN'T. MAGIC DID.
MAGIC BLOODY MAGIC...
IT GAVE ME YO-YO, AND IT TOOK HIM AWAY. IT GAVE ME A NEW DAD, AND TOOK HIM. THEN IT FIXED ME UP WITH A NEW MUM -- BUT IT WAS ONLY JOKING ABOUT THAT.
AND SOMEWHERE IN THERE, IT TRIED TO FEED ME TO A MANTICORE, BURNED MY OLD DAD'S FACE OFF --
CHRIST...
I'M GOING TO RUN OUT OF FINGERS IF I KEEP THIS UP.

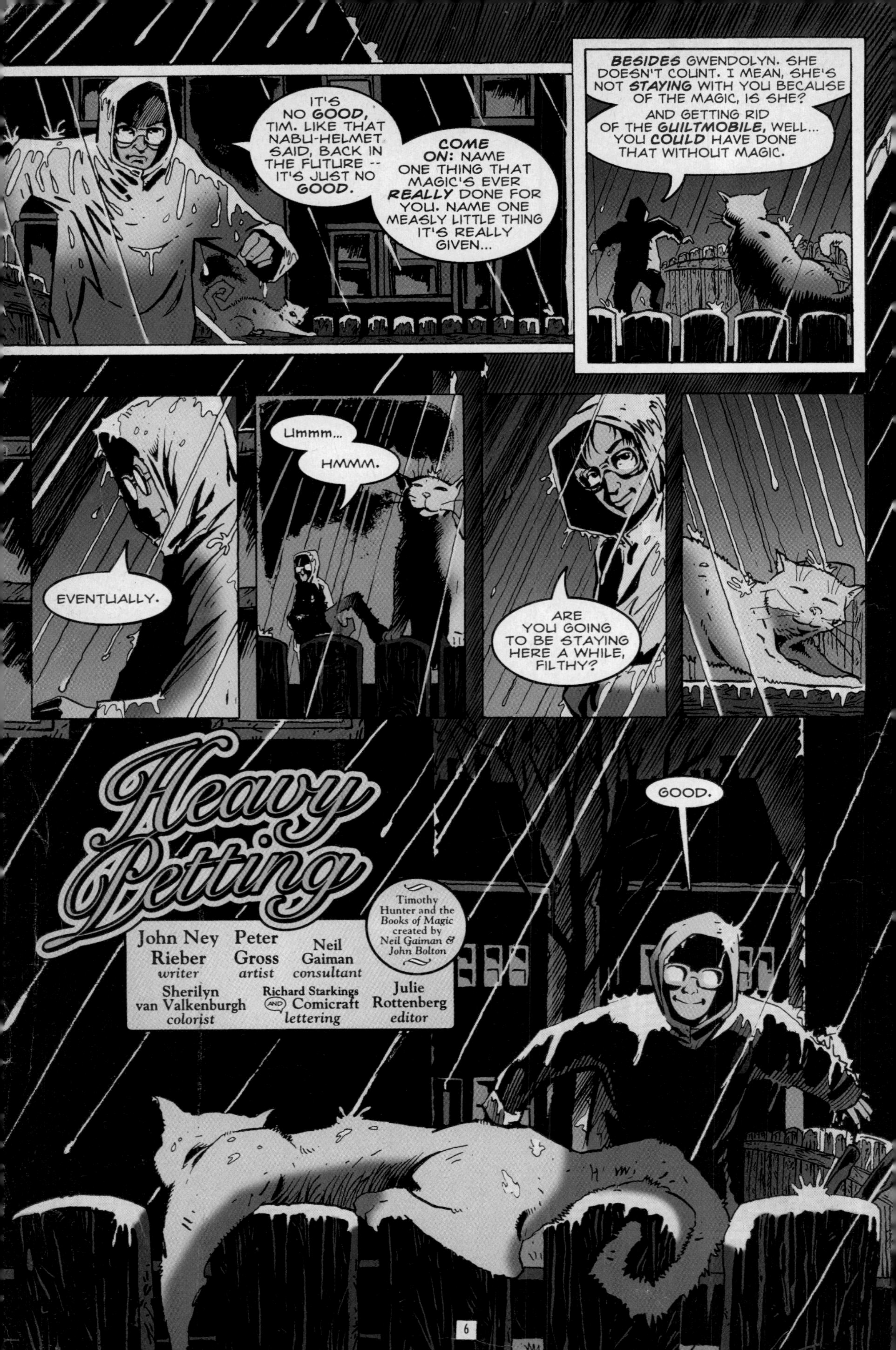
IT'S NO GOOD, TIM. LIKE THAT NABU-HELMET SAID, BACK IN THE FUTURE -- IT'S JUST NO GOOD.
COME ON: NAME ONE THING THAT MAGIC'S EVER REALLY DONE FOR YOU. NAME ONE MEASLY LITTLE THING IT'S REALLY GIVEN...
BESIDES GWENDOLYN. SHE DOESN'T COUNT. I MEAN, SHE'S NOT STAYING WITH YOU BECAUSE OF THE MAGIC, IS SHE?
AND GETTING RID OF THE GUILTMOBILE, WELL... YOU COULD HAVE DONE THAT WITHOUT MAGIC.
EVENTUALLY.
Ummm...
HMMM.
ARE YOU GOING TO BE STAYING HERE A WHILE, FILTHY?
GOOD.
Heavy Petting
John Ney Rieber writer
Peter Gross artist
Neil Gaiman consultant
Timothy Hunter and the Books of Magic created by Neil Gaiman & John Bolton
Sherilyn van Valkenburgh colorist
Richard Starkings AND Comicraft lettering
Julie Rottenberg editor

Soho.

A FEW BLOCKS AWAY FROM HYDE PARK.

GO AHEAD, RAIN ON ME.

SEE IF I CARE.

M-mm...

CIRC
TATTOOING & OTHER A

NICE. VERY NICE.

EVENING, MISS... DON'T I KNOW YOU FROM SOMEWHERE?

YEAH, RIGHT. BUZZ OFF.

NO SWEET NOTHINGS FOR YOU, EH, DARLING? WELL, I'M RIGHT WITH YOU, THERE --

-- SO HOW DO YOU LIKE IT? YOUR PLACE, MY PLACE? CASH OR PLASTIC?

YOU'RE INTERRUPTING A GOOD CIGARETTE.

SOME PEOPLE JUMP TO THE MOST INTERESTING CONCLUSIONS.

THE
I LI
I LI
WAL
GOD
CI

BUT I'M NOT ADVERTISING ANYTHING.

SO GO *AWAY*, LOVERBOY. FLY AWAY *HOME* --

--OR COME INSIDE.

CIRCE'S
TATTOOING • PIERCING & OTHER ALTERATIONS

YOU KNOW, YOU'VE GOT A LOVELY VOICE, DARLING... BUT I CAN'T QUITE PLACE YOUR *ACCENT*...

NOT FROM AROUND HERE, ARE YOU?

CIRCE'S
TATTOOING • PIERCING & OTHER ALTERATIONS

CIRCE'S
TATTOOING • PIERCING & OTHER ALTERATIONS

CIRCE'S
TATTOOING • PIERCING & OTHER ALTERATIONS

CLOSED

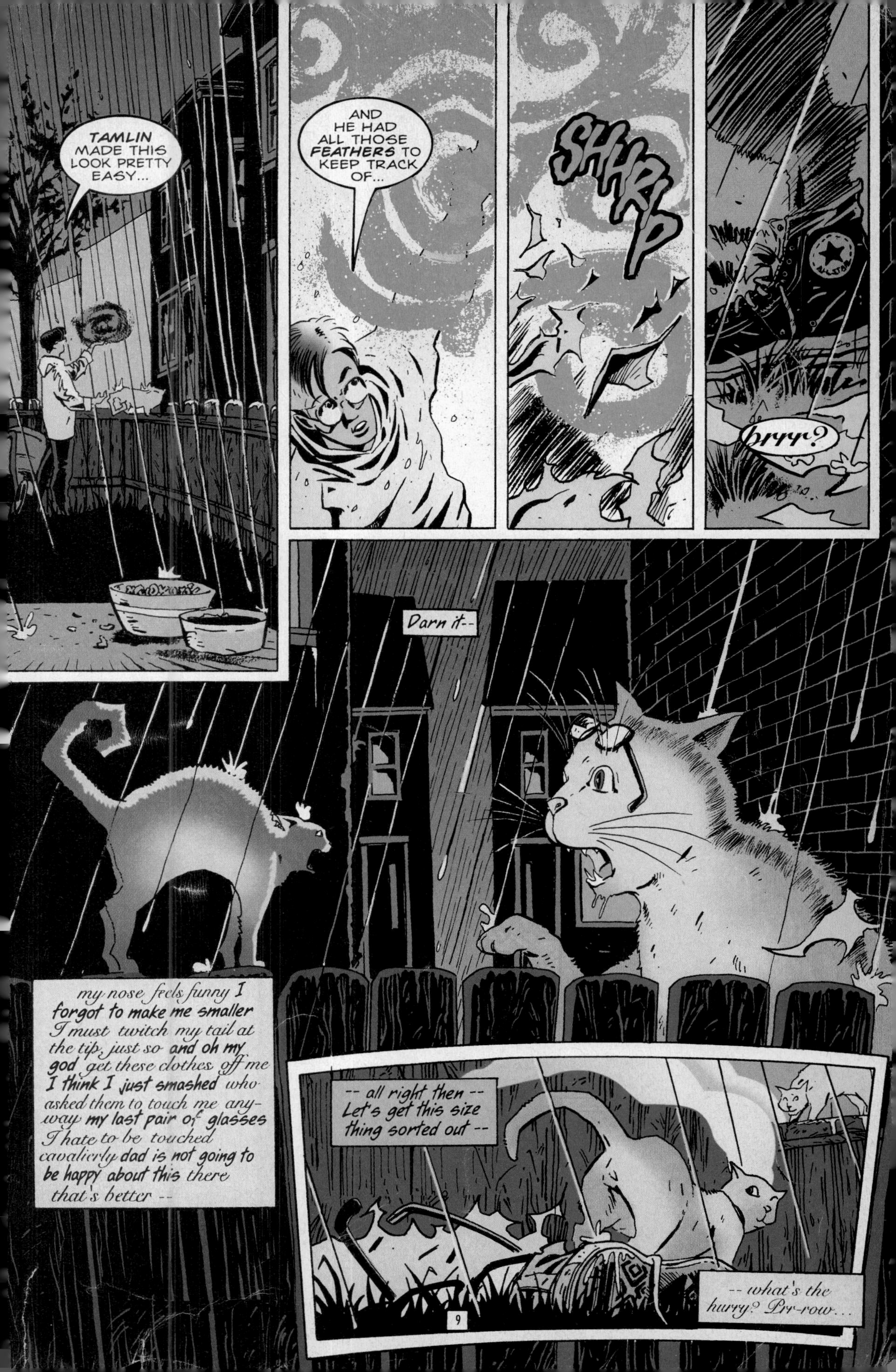
TAMLIN MADE THIS LOOK PRETTY EASY...
AND HE HAD ALL THOSE FEATHERS TO KEEP TRACK OF...
SHHRP
hrrr?
Darn it--
my nose feels funny I forgot to make me smaller I must twitch my tail at the tip, just so and oh my god get these clothes off me I think I just smashed who asked them to touch me any-way my last pair of glasses I hate to be touched cavalierly dad is not going to be happy about this there that's better --
-- all right then -- Let's get this size thing sorted out --
-- what's the hurry? Prr-row...

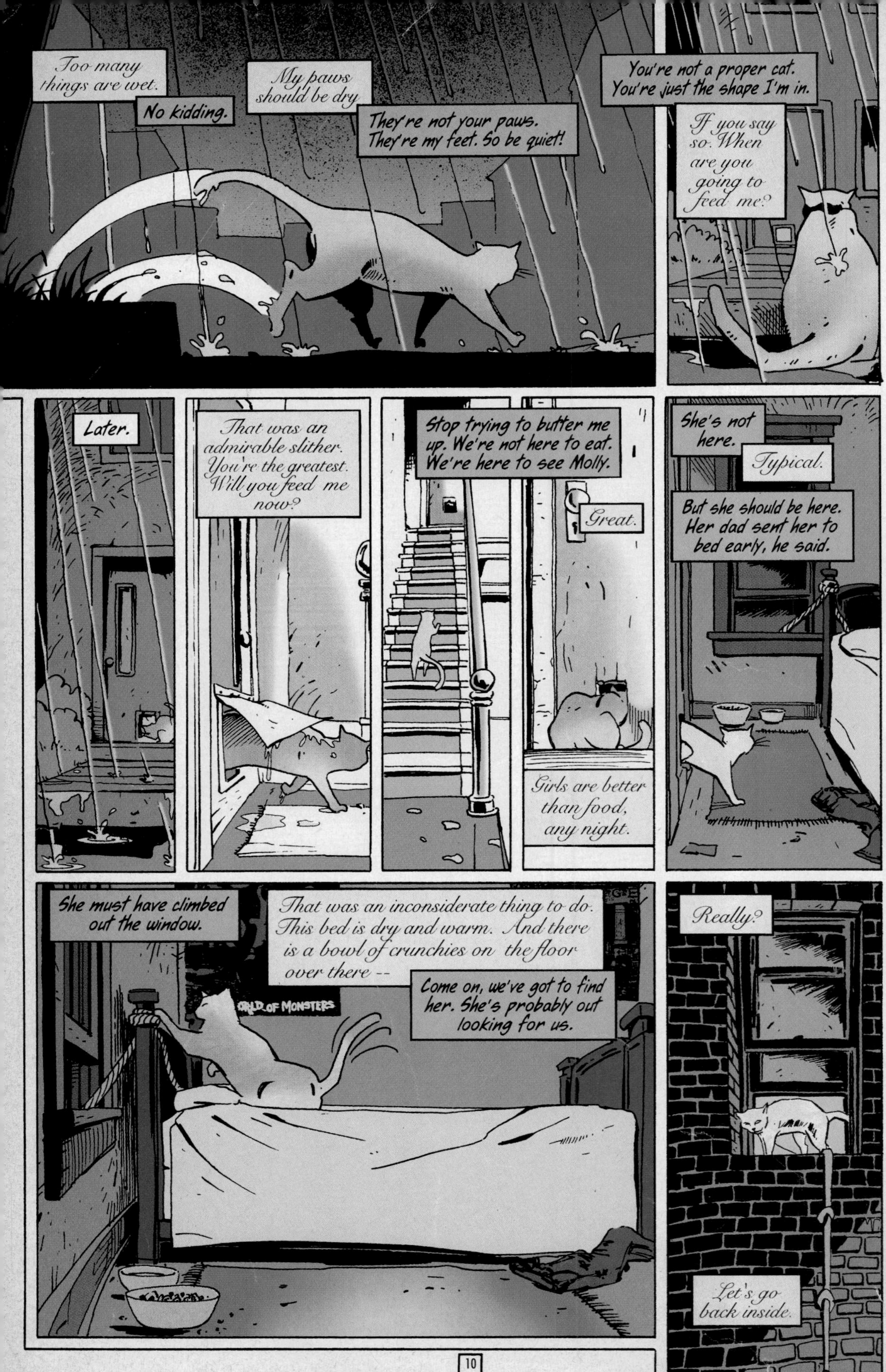
Too many things are wet.
No kidding.
My paws should be dry
They're not your paws. They're my feet. So be quiet!
You're not a proper cat. You're just the shape I'm in.
If you say so. When are you going to feed me?
Later.
That was an admirable slither. You're the greatest. Will you feed me now?
Stop trying to butter me up. We're not here to eat. We're here to see Molly.
Great.
Girls are better than food, any night.
She's not here.
Typical.
But she should be here. Her dad sent her to bed early, he said.
She must have climbed out the window.
That was an inconsiderate thing to do. This bed is dry and warm. And there is a bowl of crunchies on the floor over there --
Come on, we've got to find her. She's probably out looking for us.
Really?
Let's go back inside.

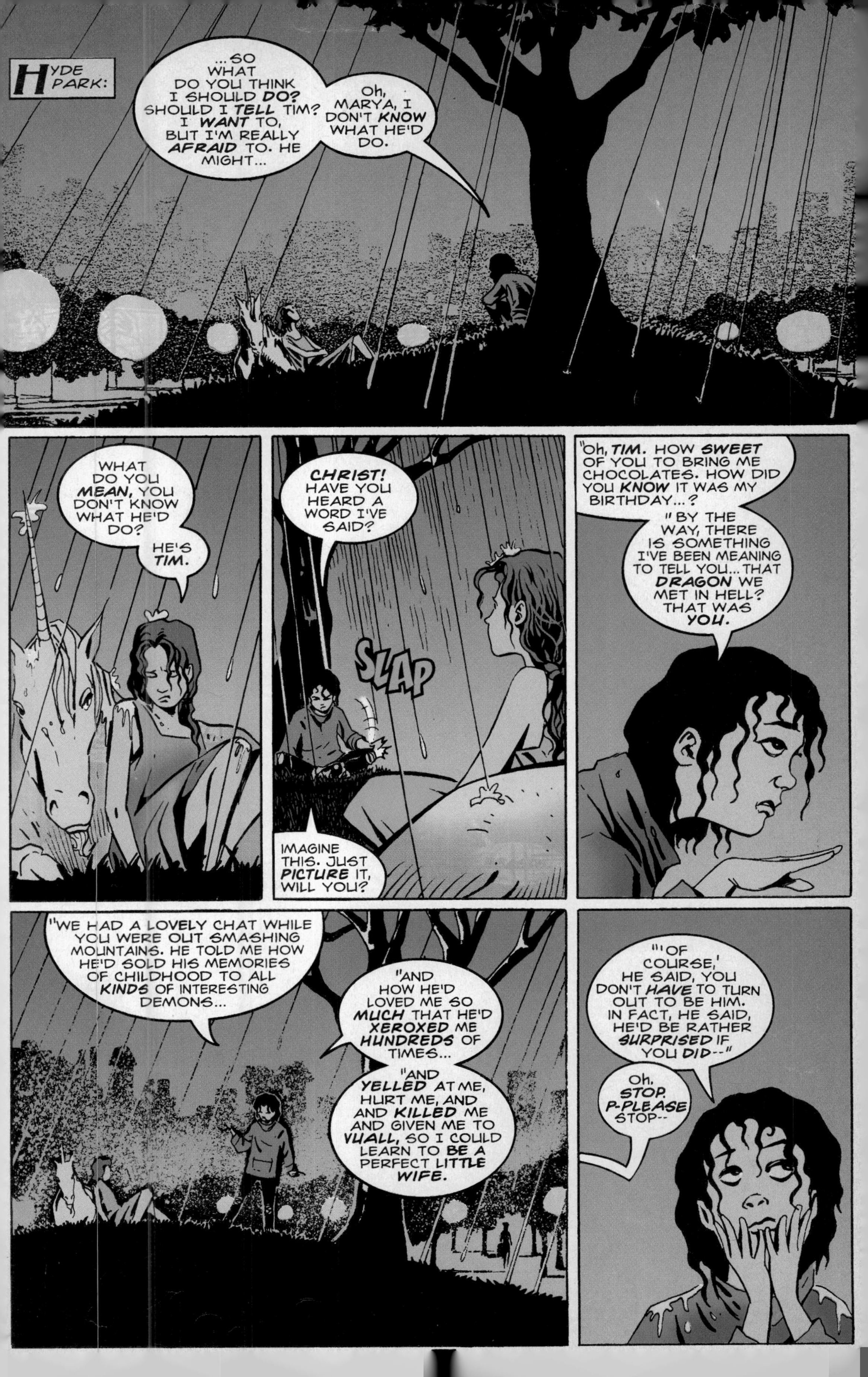
HYDE PARK:
...SO WHAT DO YOU THINK I SHOULD DO? SHOULD I TELL TIM? I WANT TO, BUT I'M REALLY AFRAID TO. HE MIGHT...
Oh, MARYA, I DON'T KNOW WHAT HE'D DO.
WHAT DO YOU MEAN, YOU DON'T KNOW WHAT HE'D DO?
HE'S TIM.
CHRIST! HAVE YOU HEARD A WORD I'VE SAID?
SLAP
IMAGINE THIS. JUST PICTURE IT, WILL YOU?
"Oh, TIM. HOW SWEET OF YOU TO BRING ME CHOCOLATES. HOW DID YOU KNOW IT WAS MY BIRTHDAY...?
"BY THE WAY, THERE IS SOMETHING I'VE BEEN MEANING TO TELL YOU... THAT DRAGON WE MET IN HELL? THAT WAS YOU.
"WE HAD A LOVELY CHAT WHILE YOU WERE OUT SMASHING MOUNTAINS. HE TOLD ME HOW HE'D SOLD HIS MEMORIES OF CHILDHOOD TO ALL KINDS OF INTERESTING DEMONS...
"AND HOW HE'D LOVED ME SO MUCH THAT HE'D XEROXED ME HUNDREDS OF TIMES...
"AND YELLED AT ME, HURT ME, AND AND KILLED ME AND GIVEN ME TO VUALL, SO I COULD LEARN TO BE A PERFECT LITTLE WIFE.
"'OF COURSE,' HE SAID, YOU DON'T HAVE TO TURN OUT TO BE HIM. IN FACT, HE SAID, HE'D BE RATHER SURPRISED IF YOU DID--"
Oh. STOP. P-PLEASE STOP--

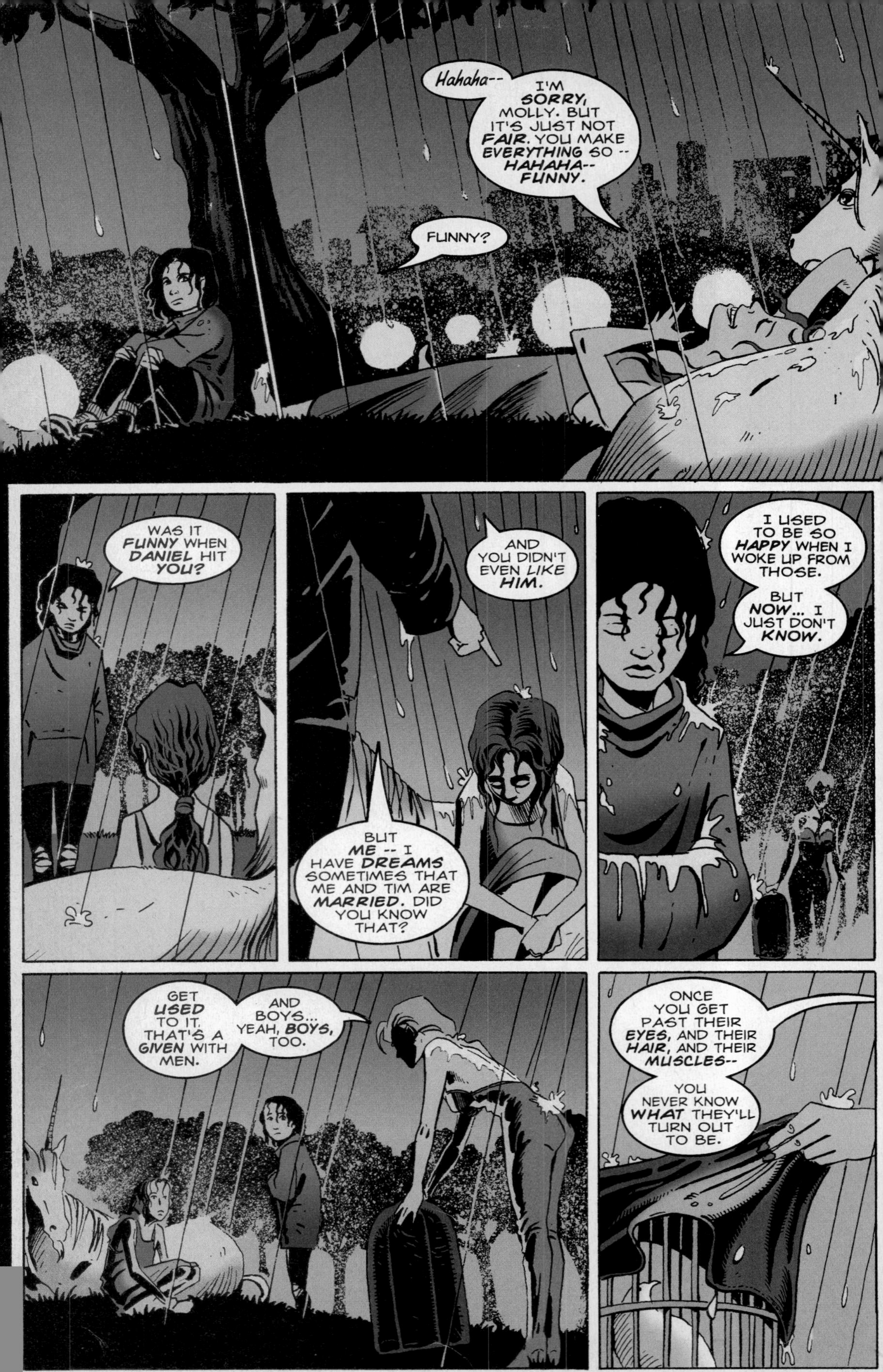
Hahaha-- I'M SORRY, MOLLY. BUT IT'S JUST NOT FAIR. YOU MAKE EVERYTHING SO -- HAHAHA-- FUNNY.
FUNNY?
WAS IT FUNNY WHEN DANIEL HIT YOU?
AND YOU DIDN'T EVEN LIKE HIM.
BUT ME -- I HAVE DREAMS SOMETIMES THAT ME AND TIM ARE MARRIED. DID YOU KNOW THAT?
I USED TO BE SO HAPPY WHEN I WOKE UP FROM THOSE.
BUT NOW... I JUST DON'T KNOW.
GET USED TO IT. THAT'S A GIVEN WITH MEN.
AND BOYS... YEAH, BOYS, TOO.
ONCE YOU GET PAST THEIR EYES, AND THEIR HAIR, AND THEIR MUSCLES--
YOU NEVER KNOW WHAT THEY'LL TURN OUT TO BE.

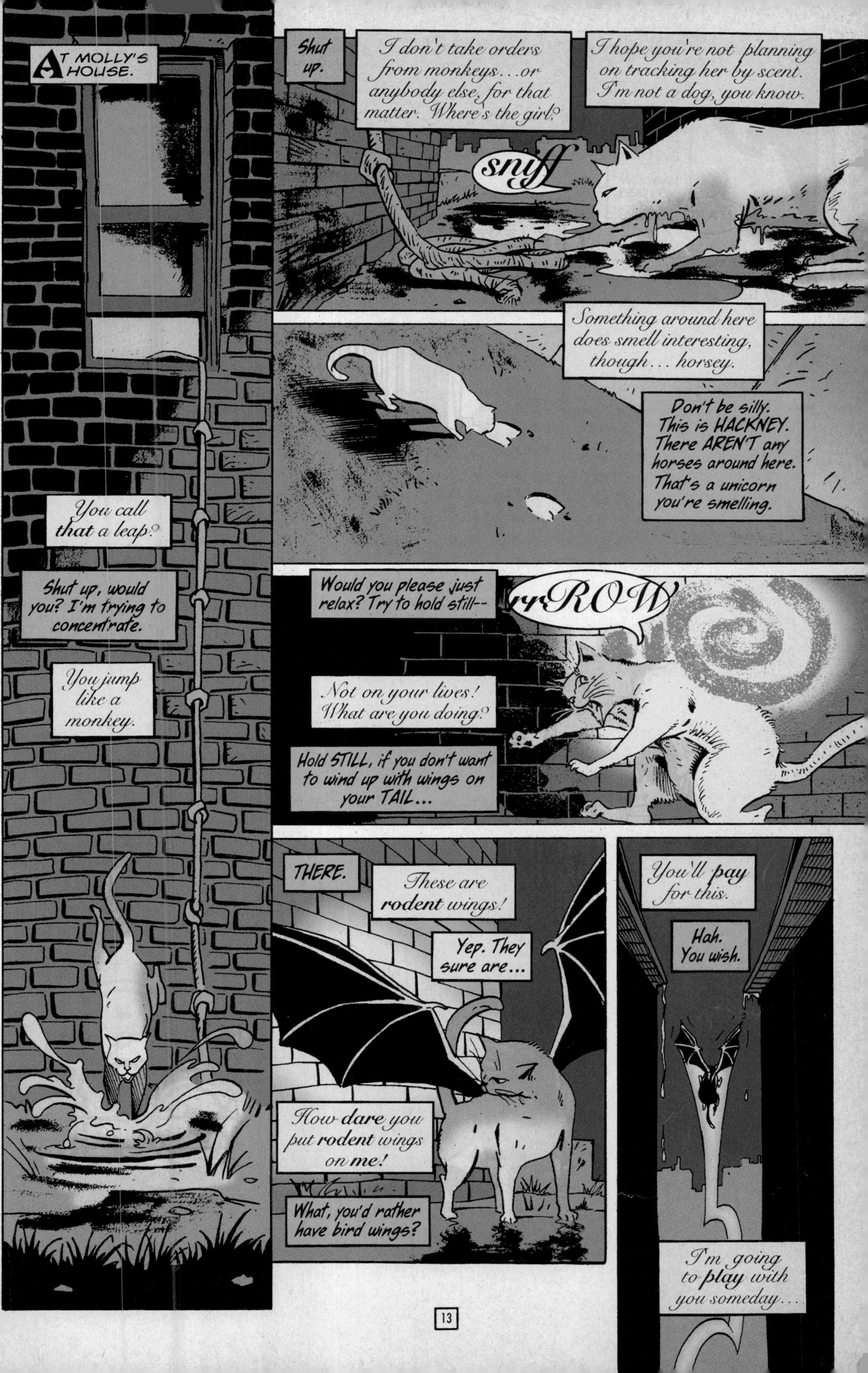
AT MOLLY'S HOUSE.
You call that a leap?
Shut up, would you? I'm trying to concentrate.
You jump like a monkey.
Shut up.
I don't take orders from monkeys...or anybody else, for that matter. Where's the girl?
I hope you're not planning on tracking her by scent. I'm not a dog, you know.
sniff
Something around here does smell interesting, though... horsey.
Don't be silly. This is HACKNEY. There AREN'T any horses around here. That's a unicorn you're smelling.
Would you please just relax? Try to hold still--
rrROW
Not on your lives! What are you doing?
Hold STILL, if you don't want to wind up with wings on your TAIL...
THERE.
These are rodent wings!
Yep. They sure are...
How dare you put rodent wings on me!
What, you'd rather have bird wings?
You'll pay for this.
Hah. You wish.
I'm going to play with you someday...

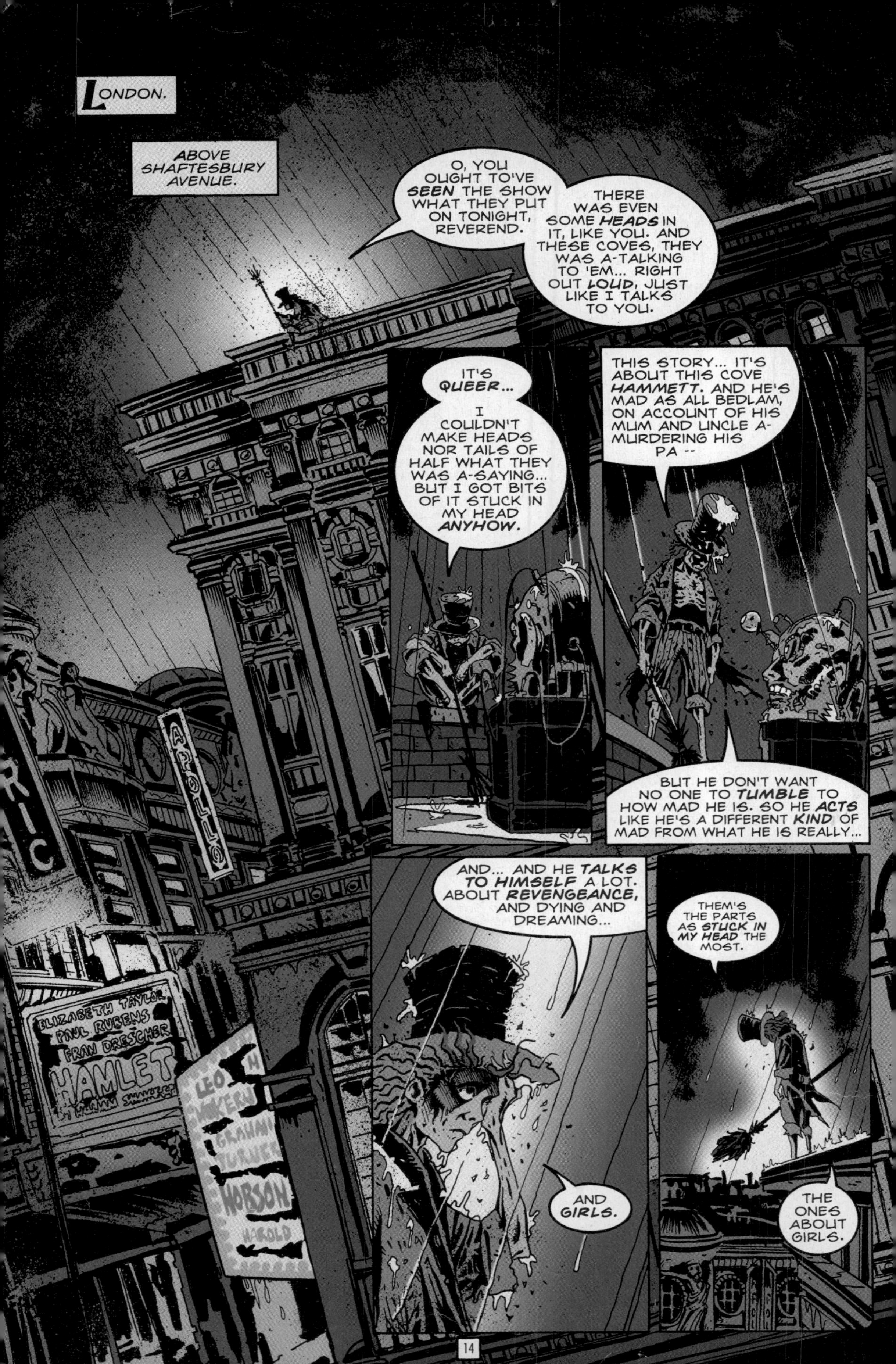
LONDON.
ABOVE SHAFTESBURY AVENUE.
O, YOU OUGHT TO'VE SEEN THE SHOW WHAT THEY PUT ON TONIGHT, REVEREND.
THERE WAS EVEN SOME HEADS IN IT, LIKE YOU. AND THESE COVES, THEY WAS A-TALKING TO 'EM... RIGHT OUT LOUD, JUST LIKE I TALKS TO YOU.
IT'S QUEER...
I COULDN'T MAKE HEADS NOR TAILS OF HALF WHAT THEY WAS A-SAYING... BUT I GOT BITS OF IT STUCK IN MY HEAD ANYHOW.
THIS STORY... IT'S ABOUT THIS COVE HAMMETT. AND HE'S MAD AS ALL BEDLAM, ON ACCOUNT OF HIS MUM AND UNCLE A-MURDERING HIS PA --
BUT HE DON'T WANT NO ONE TO TUMBLE TO HOW MAD HE IS. SO HE ACTS LIKE HE'S A DIFFERENT KIND OF MAD FROM WHAT HE IS REALLY...
APOLLO
ELIZABETH TAYLOR
PAUL RUBENS
FRAN DRESCHER
HAMLET
AND... AND HE TALKS TO HIMSELF A LOT. ABOUT REVENGEANCE, AND DYING AND DREAMING...
AND GIRLS.
THEM'S THE PARTS AS STUCK IN MY HEAD THE MOST.
THE ONES ABOUT GIRLS.

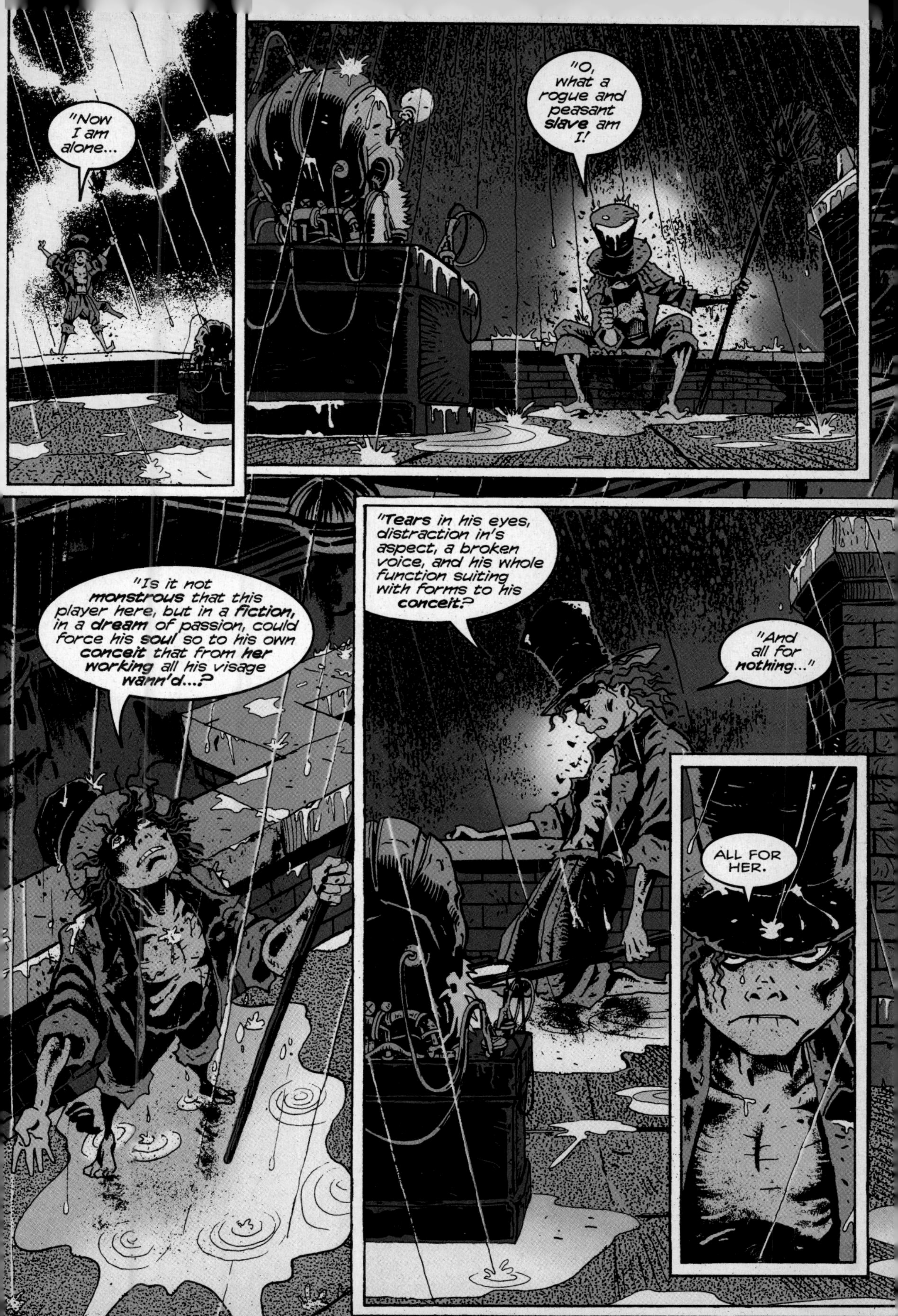
"Now I am alone...
"O, what a rogue and peasant slave am I!
"Is it not monstrous that this player here, but in a fiction, in a dream of passion, could force his soul so to his own conceit that from her working all his visage wann'd...?
"Tears in his eyes, distraction in's aspect, a broken voice, and his whole function suiting with forms to his conceit?
"And all for nothing..."
ALL FOR HER.

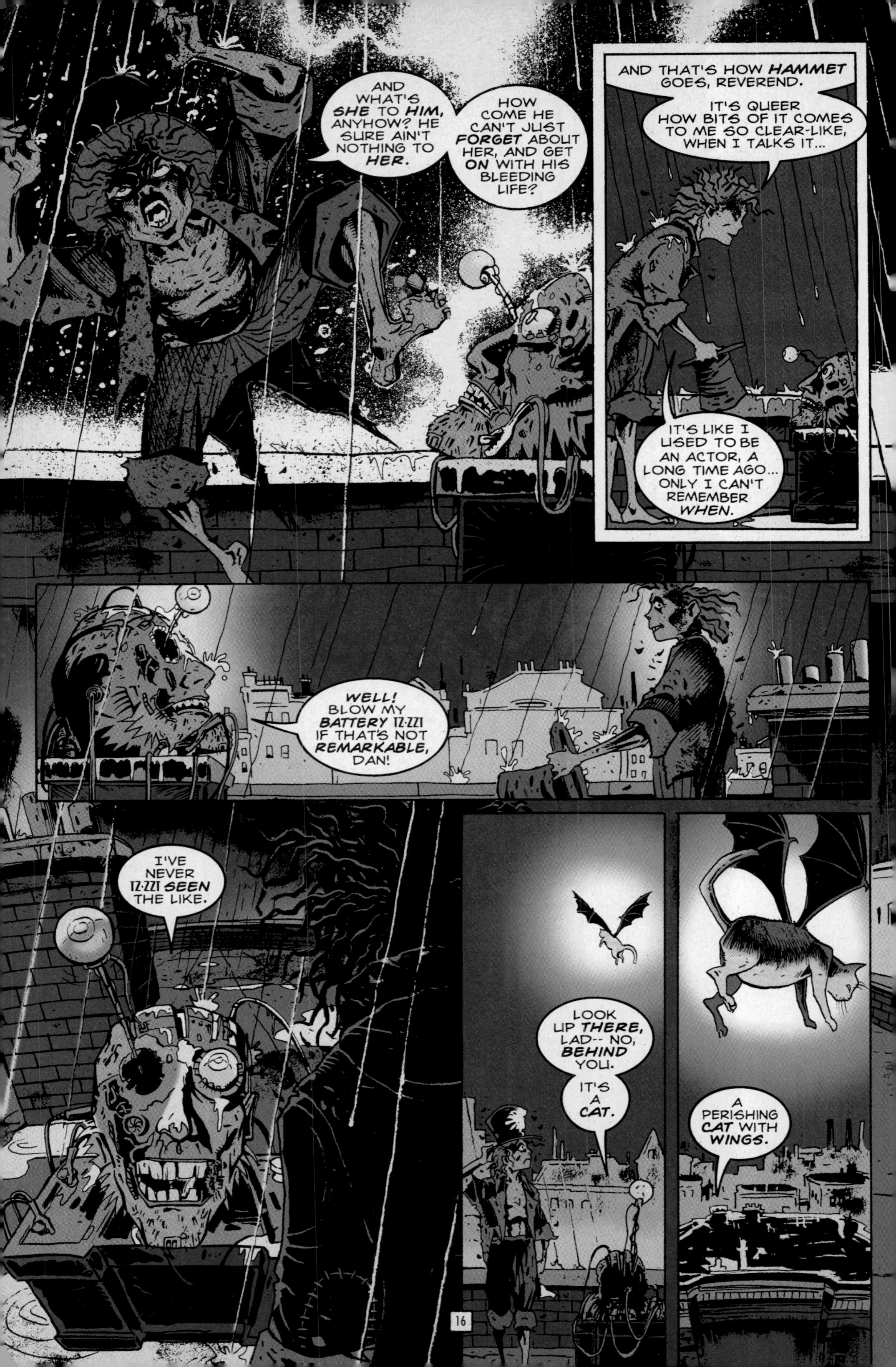
AND WHAT'S SHE TO HIM, ANYHOW? HE SURE AIN'T NOTHING TO HER.
HOW COME HE CAN'T JUST FORGET ABOUT HER, AND GET ON WITH HIS BLEEDING LIFE?
AND THAT'S HOW HAMMET GOES, REVEREND.
IT'S QUEER HOW BITS OF IT COMES TO ME SO CLEAR-LIKE, WHEN I TALKS IT...
IT'S LIKE I USED TO BE AN ACTOR, A LONG TIME AGO... ONLY I CAN'T REMEMBER WHEN.
WELL! BLOW MY BATTERY IZ-ZZT IF THAT'S NOT REMARKABLE, DAN!
I'VE NEVER IZ-ZZT SEEN THE LIKE.
LOOK UP THERE, LAD-- NO, BEHIND YOU.
IT'S A CAT.
A PERISHING CAT WITH WINGS.

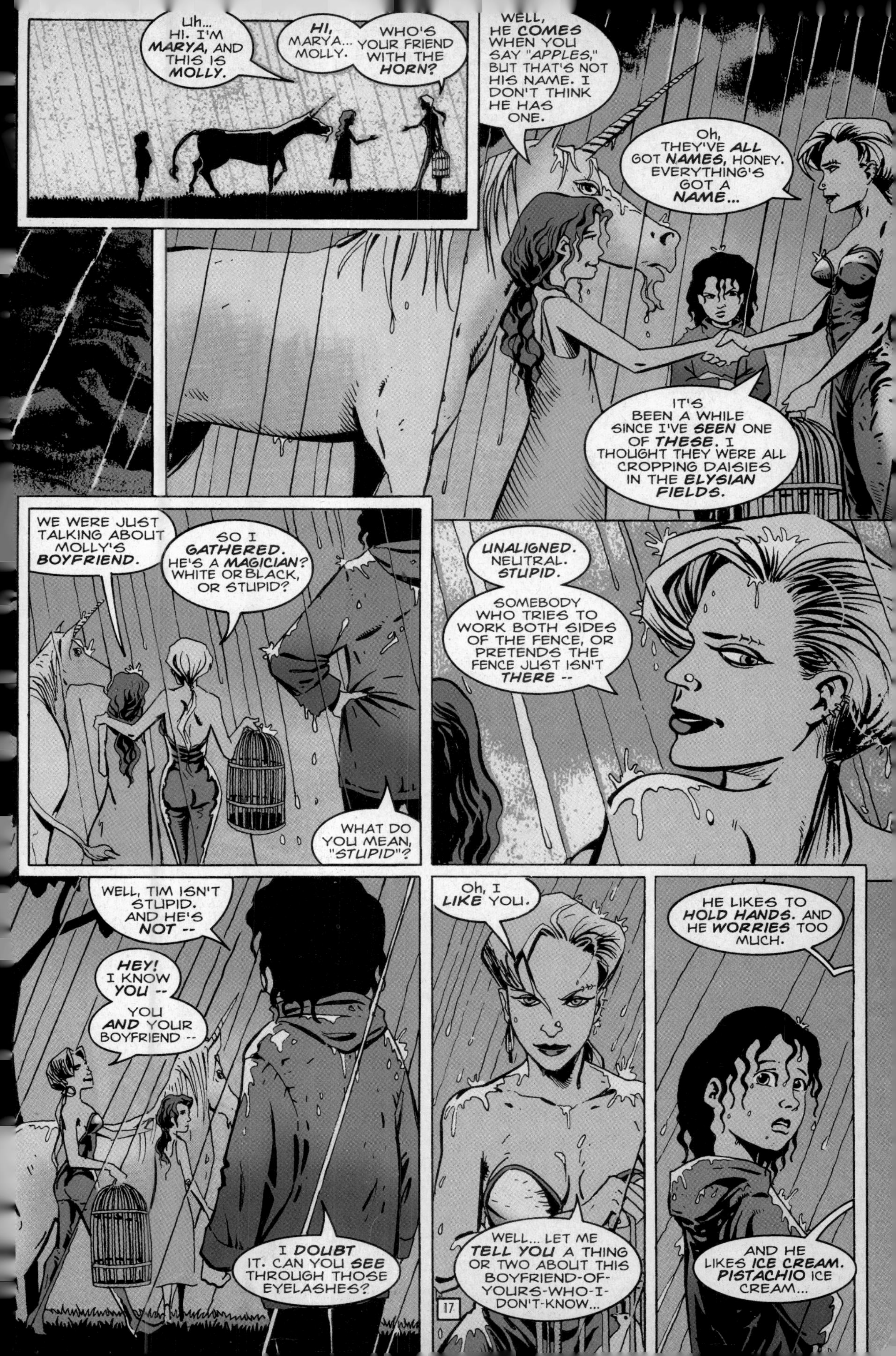

UH... HI. I'M MARYA, AND THIS IS MOLLY.
HI, MARYA... MOLLY.
WHO'S YOUR FRIEND WITH THE HORN?
WELL, HE COMES WHEN YOU SAY "APPLES," BUT THAT'S NOT HIS NAME. I DON'T THINK HE HAS ONE.
Oh, THEY'VE ALL GOT NAMES, HONEY. EVERYTHING'S GOT A NAME...
IT'S BEEN A WHILE SINCE I'VE SEEN ONE OF THESE. I THOUGHT THEY WERE ALL CROPPING DAISIES IN THE ELYSIAN FIELDS.
WE WERE JUST TALKING ABOUT MOLLY'S BOYFRIEND.
SO I GATHERED. HE'S A MAGICIAN? WHITE OR BLACK, OR STUPID?
WHAT DO YOU MEAN, "STUPID"?
UNALIGNED. NEUTRAL. STUPID.
SOMEBODY WHO TRIES TO WORK BOTH SIDES OF THE FENCE, OR PRETENDS THE FENCE JUST ISN'T THERE --
WELL, TIM ISN'T STUPID. AND HE'S NOT --
HEY! I KNOW YOU --
YOU AND YOUR BOYFRIEND --
I DOUBT IT. CAN YOU SEE THROUGH THOSE EYELASHES?
Oh, I LIKE YOU.
WELL... LET ME TELL YOU A THING OR TWO ABOUT THIS BOYFRIEND-OF-YOURS-WHO-I-DON'T-KNOW...
HE LIKES TO HOLD HANDS. AND HE WORRIES TOO MUCH.
AND HE LIKES ICE CREAM. PISTACHIO ICE CREAM...

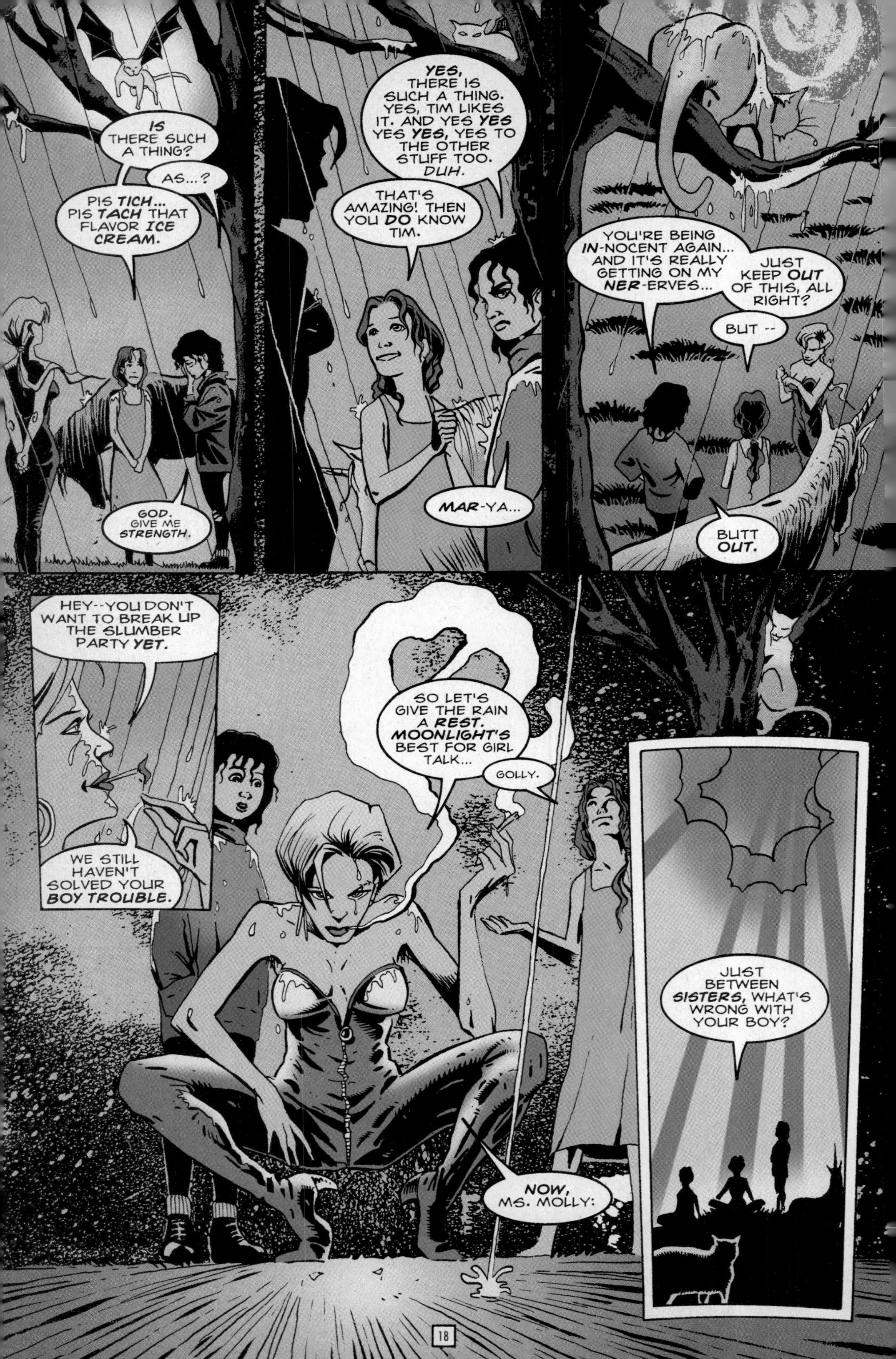
IS THERE SUCH A THING?
AS...?
PIS TICH... PIS TACH THAT FLAVOR ICE CREAM.
GOD. GIVE ME STRENGTH.
YES, THERE IS SUCH A THING. YES, TIM LIKES IT. AND YES YES YES YES, YES TO THE OTHER STUFF TOO. DUH.
THAT'S AMAZING! THEN YOU DO KNOW TIM.
MAR-YA...
YOU'RE BEING IN-NOCENT AGAIN... AND IT'S REALLY GETTING ON MY NER-ERVES...
JUST KEEP OUT OF THIS, ALL RIGHT?
BUT --
BUTT OUT.
HEY--YOU DON'T WANT TO BREAK UP THE SLUMBER PARTY YET.
WE STILL HAVEN'T SOLVED YOUR BOY TROUBLE.
SO LET'S GIVE THE RAIN A REST. MOONLIGHT'S BEST FOR GIRL TALK...
GOLLY.
NOW, MS. MOLLY:
JUST BETWEEN SISTERS, WHAT'S WRONG WITH YOUR BOY?

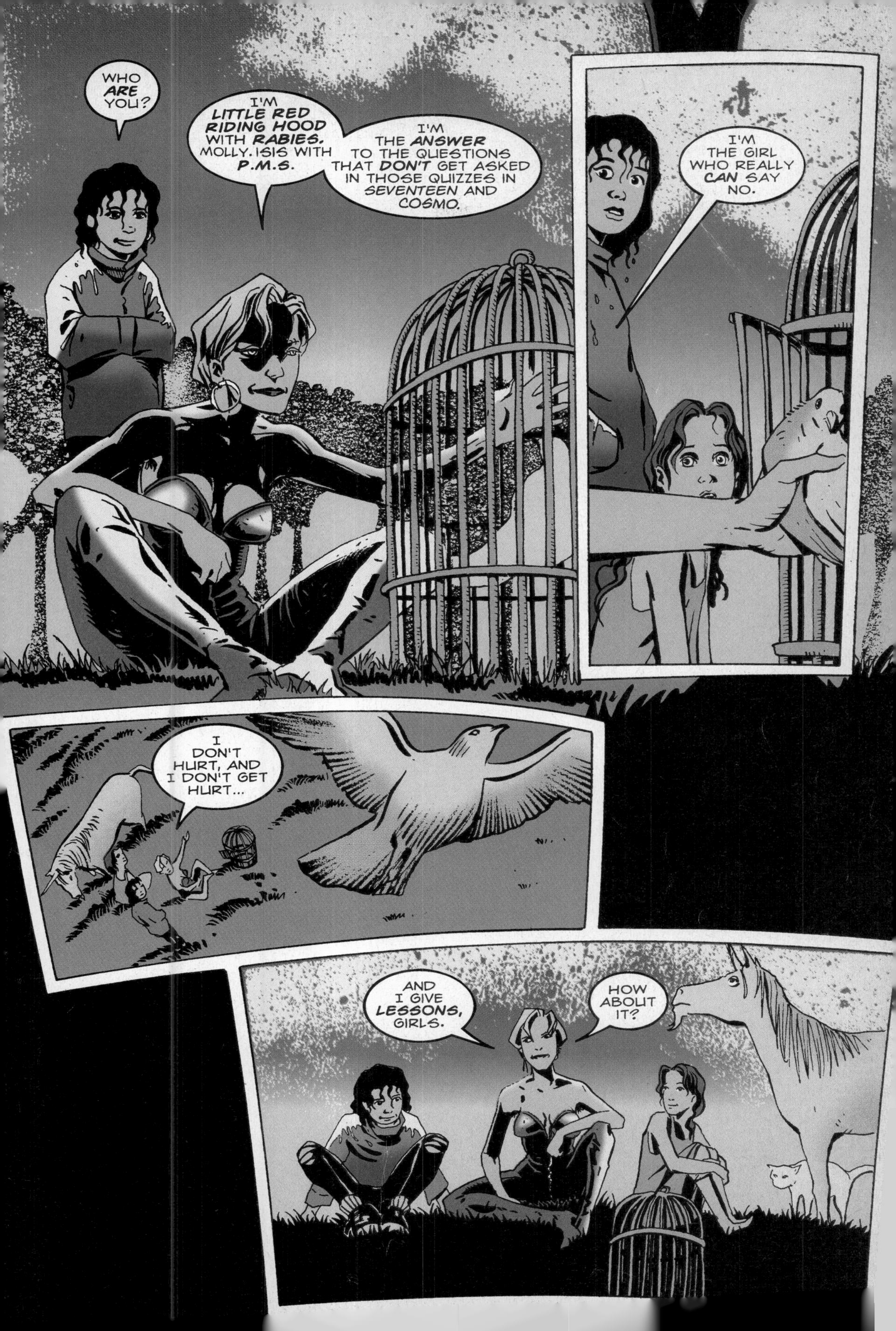
WHO ARE YOU?
I'M LITTLE RED RIDING HOOD WITH RABIES. MOLLY. ISIS WITH P.M.S.
I'M THE ANSWER TO THE QUESTIONS THAT DON'T GET ASKED IN THOSE QUIZZES IN SEVENTEEN AND COSMO.
I'M THE GIRL WHO REALLY CAN SAY NO.
I DON'T HURT, AND I DON'T GET HURT...
AND I GIVE LESSONS, GIRLS.
HOW ABOUT IT?

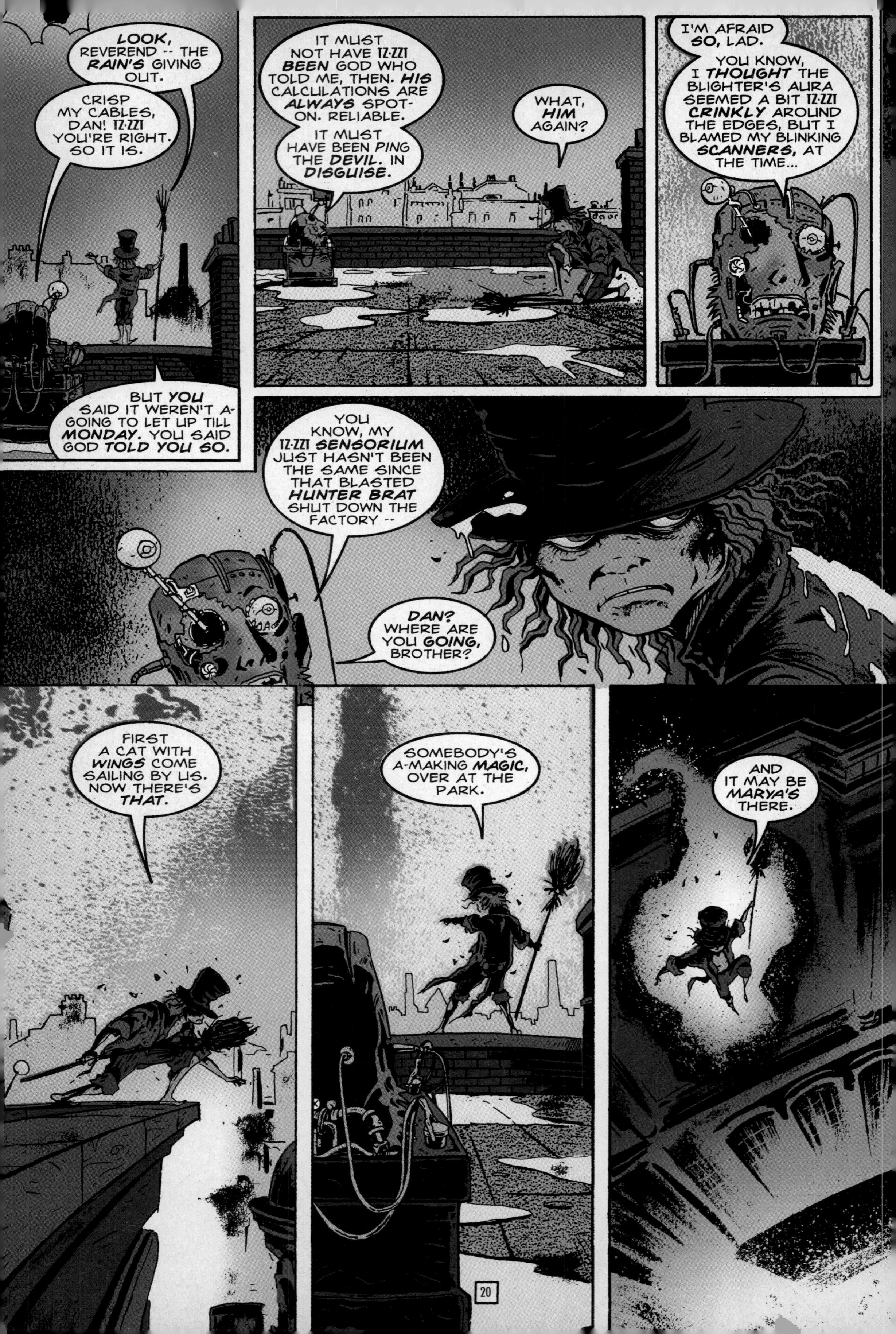
LOOK, REVEREND -- THE RAIN'S GIVING OUT.
CRISP MY CABLES, DAN! TZ-ZZT YOU'RE RIGHT. SO IT IS.
BUT YOU SAID IT WEREN'T A-GOING TO LET UP TILL MONDAY. YOU SAID GOD TOLD YOU SO.
IT MUST NOT HAVE TZ-ZZT BEEN GOD WHO TOLD ME, THEN. HIS CALCULATIONS ARE ALWAYS SPOT-ON. RELIABLE.
IT MUST HAVE BEEN PING THE DEVIL. IN DISGUISE.
WHAT, HIM AGAIN?
I'M AFRAID SO, LAD.
YOU KNOW, I THOUGHT THE BLIGHTER'S AURA SEEMED A BIT TZ-ZZT CRINKLY AROUND THE EDGES, BUT I BLAMED MY BLINKING SCANNERS, AT THE TIME...
YOU KNOW, MY TZ-ZZT SENSORIUM JUST HASN'T BEEN THE SAME SINCE THAT BLASTED HUNTER BRAT SHUT DOWN THE FACTORY --
DAN? WHERE ARE YOU GOING, BROTHER?
FIRST A CAT WITH WINGS COME SAILING BY US. NOW THERE'S THAT.
SOMEBODY'S A-MAKING MAGIC, OVER AT THE PARK.
AND IT MAY BE MARYA'S THERE.

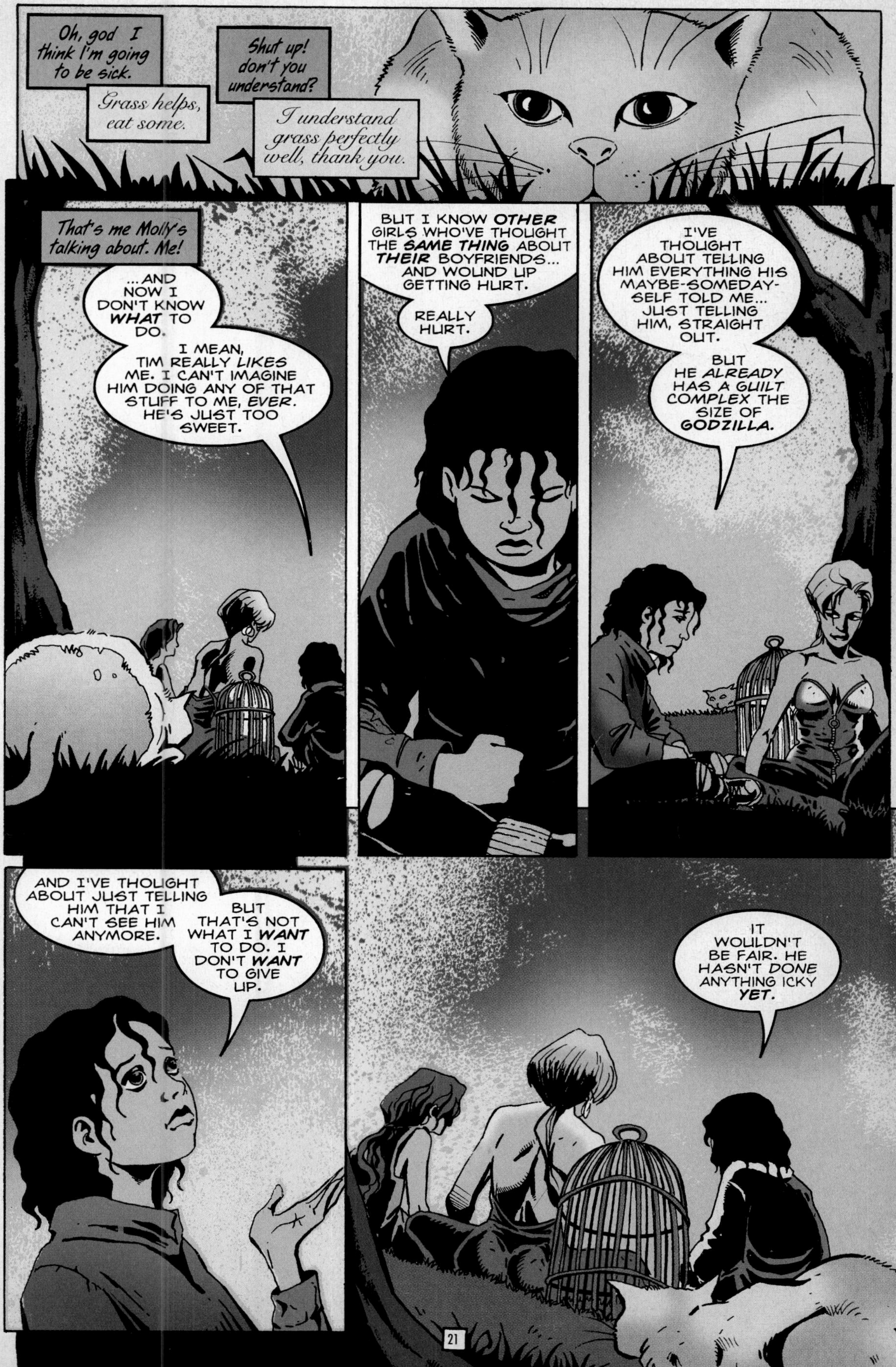

Oh, god I think I'm going to be sick.
Grass helps, eat some.
Shut up! don't you understand?
I understand grass perfectly well, thank you.
That's me Molly's talking about. Me!
...AND NOW I DON'T KNOW WHAT TO DO.
I MEAN, TIM REALLY LIKES ME. I CAN'T IMAGINE HIM DOING ANY OF THAT STUFF TO ME, EVER. HE'S JUST TOO SWEET.
BUT I KNOW OTHER GIRLS WHO'VE THOUGHT THE SAME THING ABOUT THEIR BOYFRIENDS... AND WOUND UP GETTING HURT.
REALLY HURT.
I'VE THOUGHT ABOUT TELLING HIM EVERYTHING HIS MAYBE-SOMEDAY-SELF TOLD ME... JUST TELLING HIM, STRAIGHT OUT.
BUT HE ALREADY HAS A GUILT COMPLEX THE SIZE OF GODZILLA.
AND I'VE THOUGHT ABOUT JUST TELLING HIM THAT I CAN'T SEE HIM ANYMORE.
BUT THAT'S NOT WHAT I WANT TO DO. I DON'T WANT TO GIVE UP.
IT WOULDN'T BE FAIR. HE HASN'T DONE ANYTHING ICKY YET.

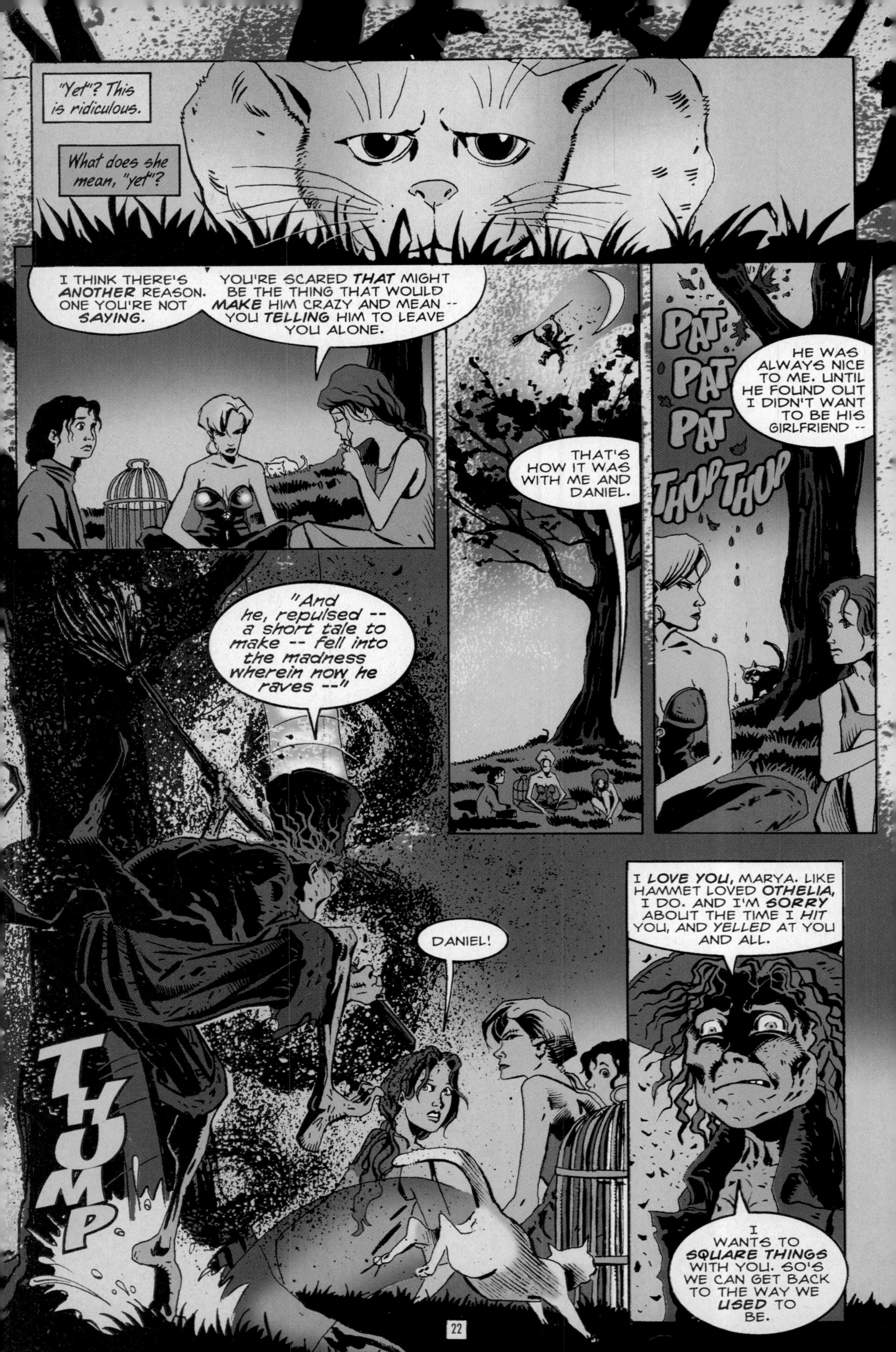
"Yet"? This is ridiculous.
What does she mean, "yet"?
I THINK THERE'S ANOTHER REASON. ONE YOU'RE NOT SAYING.
YOU'RE SCARED THAT MIGHT BE THE THING THAT WOULD MAKE HIM CRAZY AND MEAN -- YOU TELLING HIM TO LEAVE YOU ALONE.
THAT'S HOW IT WAS WITH ME AND DANIEL.
PAT PAT PAT
HE WAS ALWAYS NICE TO ME. UNTIL HE FOUND OUT I DIDN'T WANT TO BE HIS GIRLFRIEND --
THUP THUP
"And he, repulsed -- a short tale to make -- fell into the madness wherein now he raves --"
THUMP
DANIEL!
I LOVE YOU, MARYA. LIKE HAMMET LOVED OTHELIA, I DO. AND I'M SORRY ABOUT THE TIME I HIT YOU, AND YELLED AT YOU AND ALL.
I WANTS TO SQUARE THINGS WITH YOU. SO'S WE CAN GET BACK TO THE WAY WE USED TO BE.

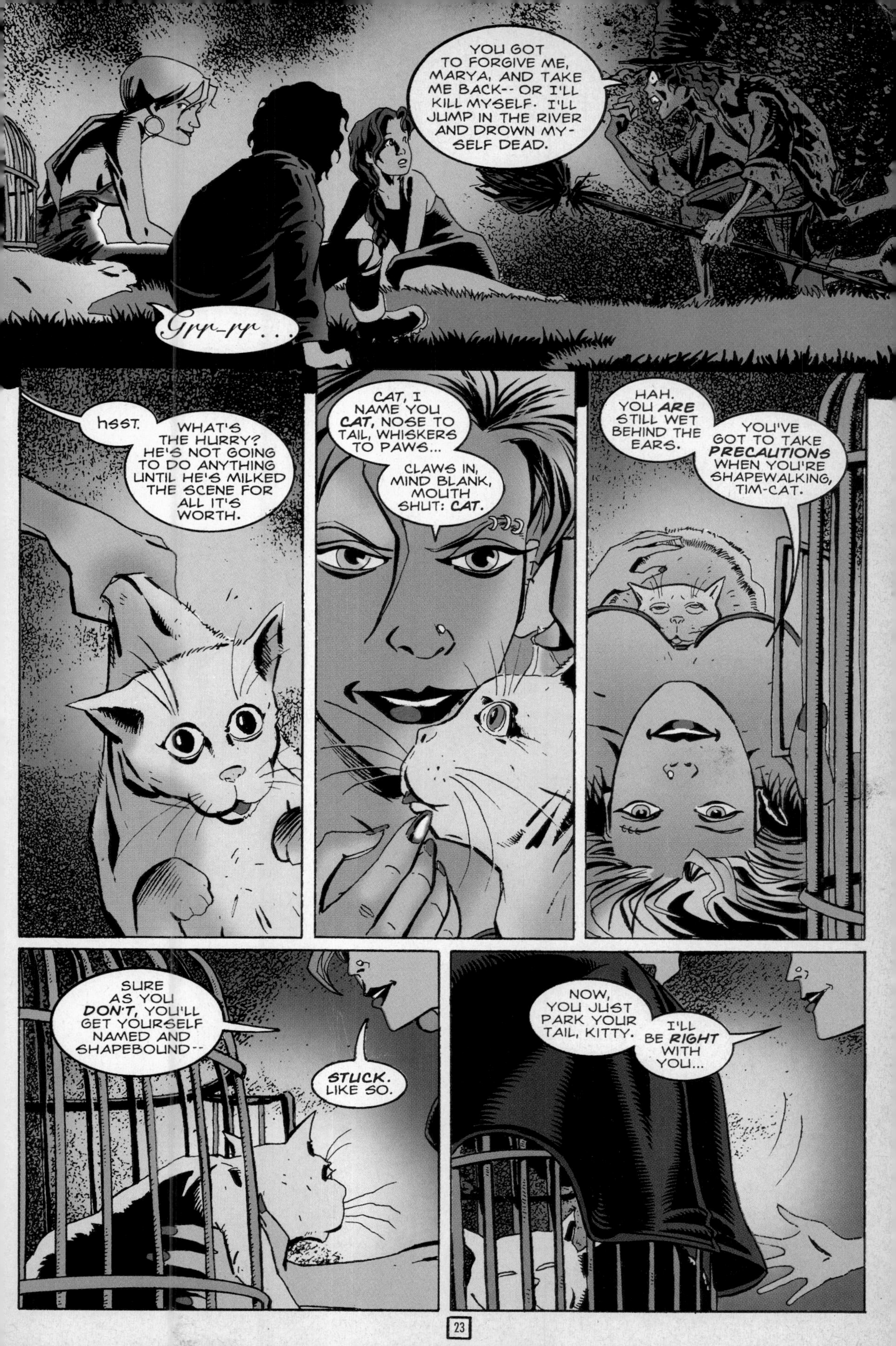
YOU GOT TO FORGIVE ME, MARYA, AND TAKE ME BACK-- OR I'LL KILL MYSELF. I'LL JUMP IN THE RIVER AND DROWN MY-SELF DEAD.
Grr-rr...
hsst.
WHAT'S THE HURRY? HE'S NOT GOING TO DO ANYTHING UNTIL HE'S MILKED THE SCENE FOR ALL IT'S WORTH.
CAT, I NAME YOU CAT, NOSE TO TAIL, WHISKERS TO PAWS...
CLAWS IN, MIND BLANK, MOUTH SHUT: CAT.
HAH. YOU ARE STILL WET BEHIND THE EARS.
YOU'VE GOT TO TAKE PRECAUTIONS WHEN YOU'RE SHAPEWALKING, TIM-CAT.
SURE AS YOU DON'T, YOU'LL GET YOURSELF NAMED AND SHAPEBOUND--
STUCK. LIKE SO.
NOW, YOU JUST PARK YOUR TAIL, KITTY.
I'LL BE RIGHT WITH YOU...

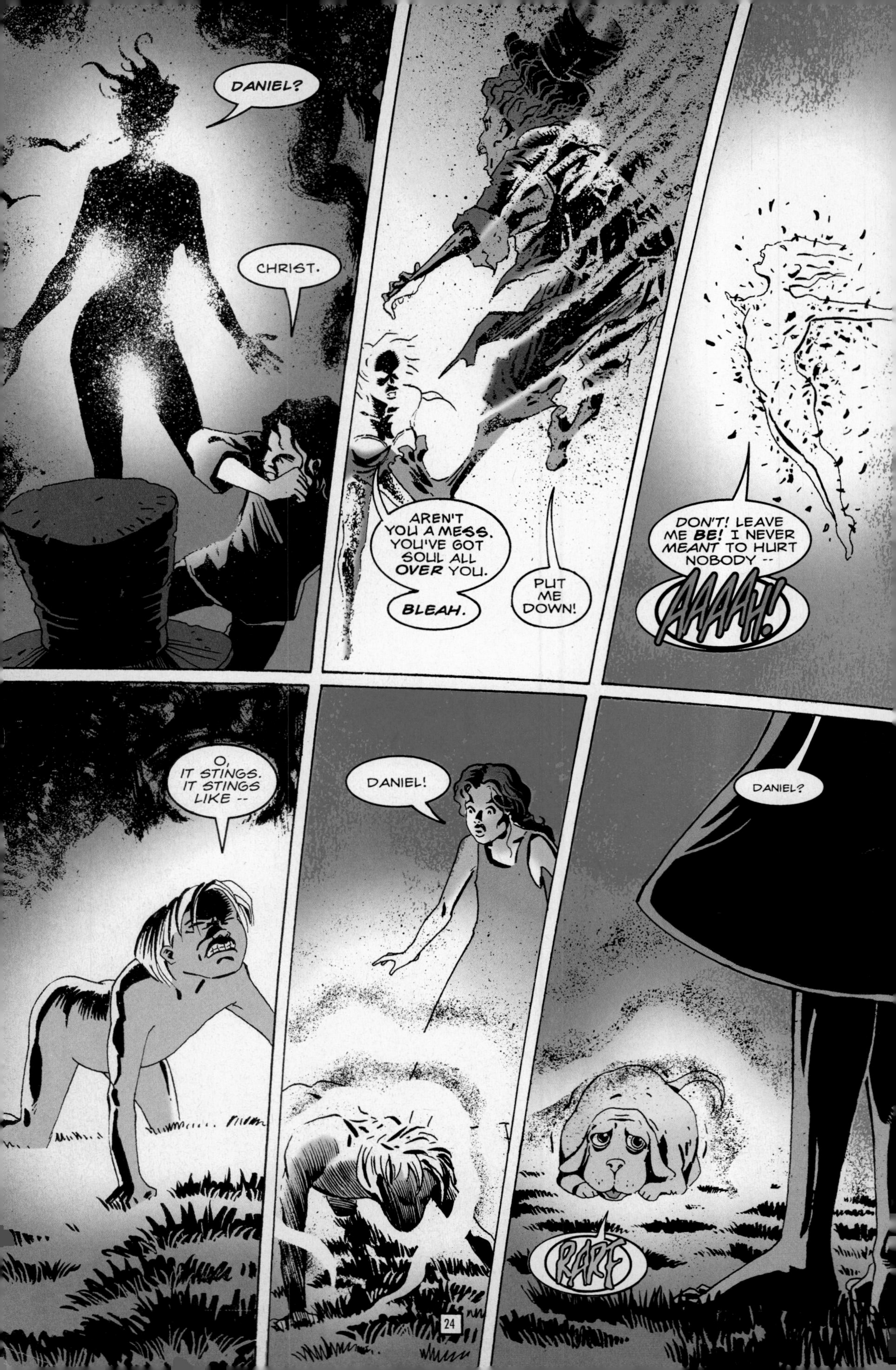
DANIEL?
CHRIST.
AREN'T YOU A MESS. YOU'VE GOT SOUL ALL OVER YOU.
BLEAH.
PUT ME DOWN!
DON'T! LEAVE ME BE! I NEVER MEANT TO HURT NOBODY --
AAAAH!
O, IT STINGS. IT STINGS LIKE --
DANIEL!
DANIEL?
RARF

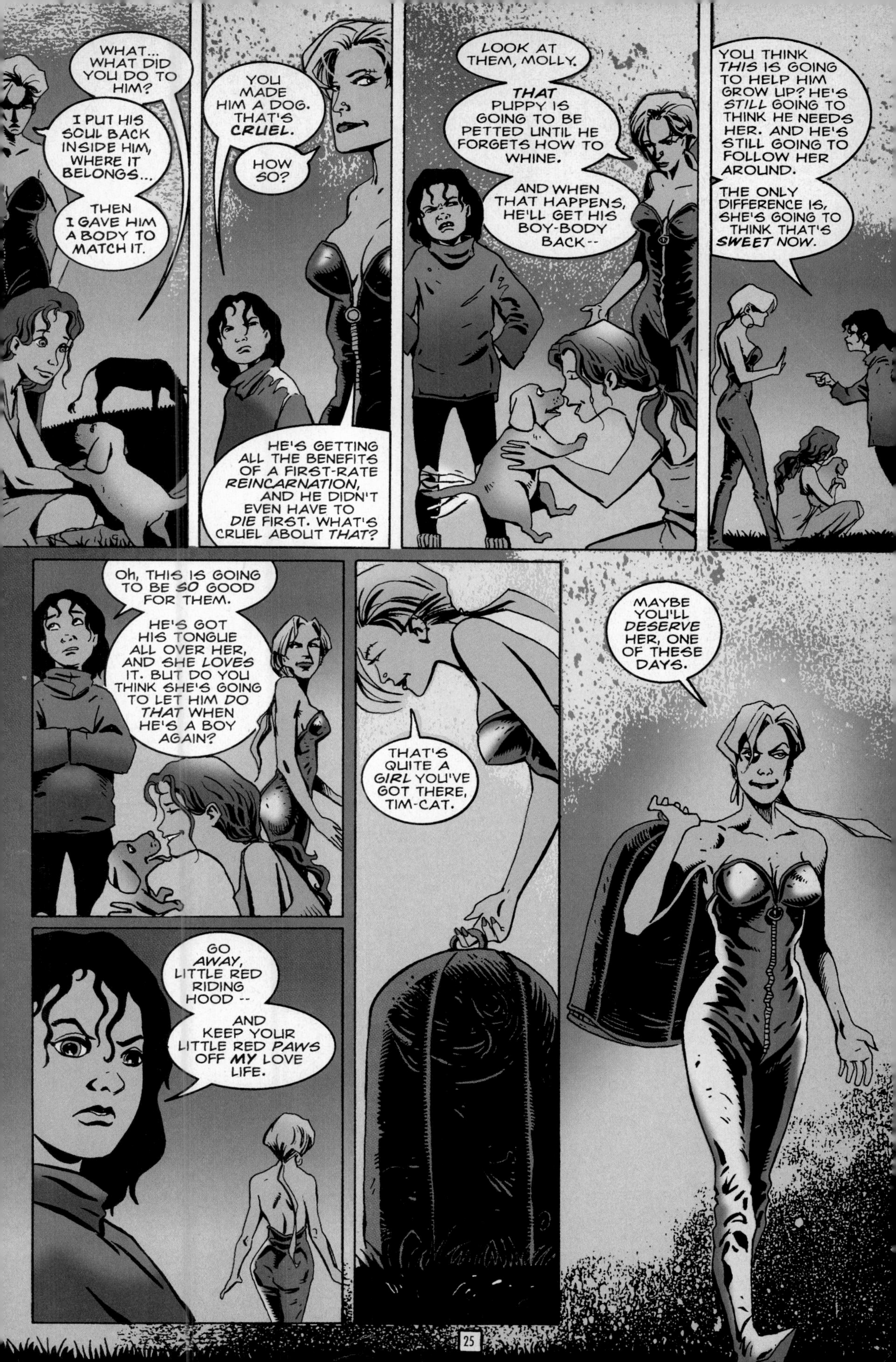
WHAT... WHAT DID YOU DO TO HIM?
I PUT HIS SOUL BACK INSIDE HIM, WHERE IT BELONGS...
THEN I GAVE HIM A BODY TO MATCH IT.
YOU MADE HIM A DOG. THAT'S CRUEL.
HOW SO?
HE'S GETTING ALL THE BENEFITS OF A FIRST-RATE REINCARNATION, AND HE DIDN'T EVEN HAVE TO DIE FIRST. WHAT'S CRUEL ABOUT THAT?
LOOK AT THEM, MOLLY.
THAT PUPPY IS GOING TO BE PETTED UNTIL HE FORGETS HOW TO WHINE.
AND WHEN THAT HAPPENS, HE'LL GET HIS BOY-BODY BACK--
YOU THINK THIS IS GOING TO HELP HIM GROW UP? HE'S STILL GOING TO THINK HE NEEDS HER. AND HE'S STILL GOING TO FOLLOW HER AROUND.
THE ONLY DIFFERENCE IS, SHE'S GOING TO THINK THAT'S SWEET NOW.
Oh, THIS IS GOING TO BE SO GOOD FOR THEM.
HE'S GOT HIS TONGUE ALL OVER HER, AND SHE LOVES IT. BUT DO YOU THINK SHE'S GOING TO LET HIM DO THAT WHEN HE'S A BOY AGAIN?
GO AWAY, LITTLE RED RIDING HOOD --
AND KEEP YOUR LITTLE RED PAWS OFF MY LOVE LIFE.
THAT'S QUITE A GIRL YOU'VE GOT THERE, TIM-CAT.
MAYBE YOU'LL DESERVE HER, ONE OF THESE DAYS.

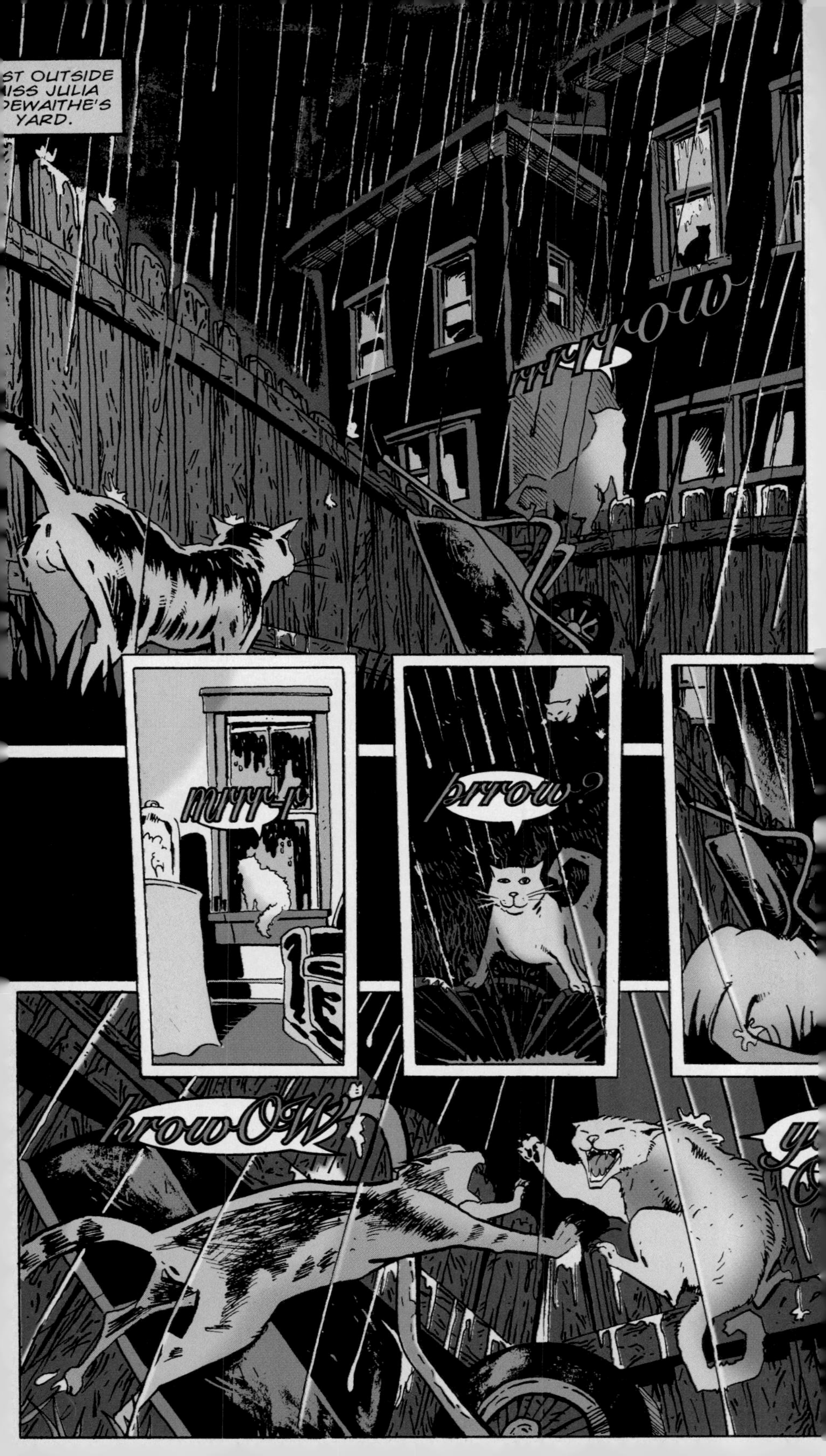

ST OUTSIDE
ISS JULIA
DEWAITHE'S
YARD.
rrrrrow
mrrr-p
prrow?
hrowOW

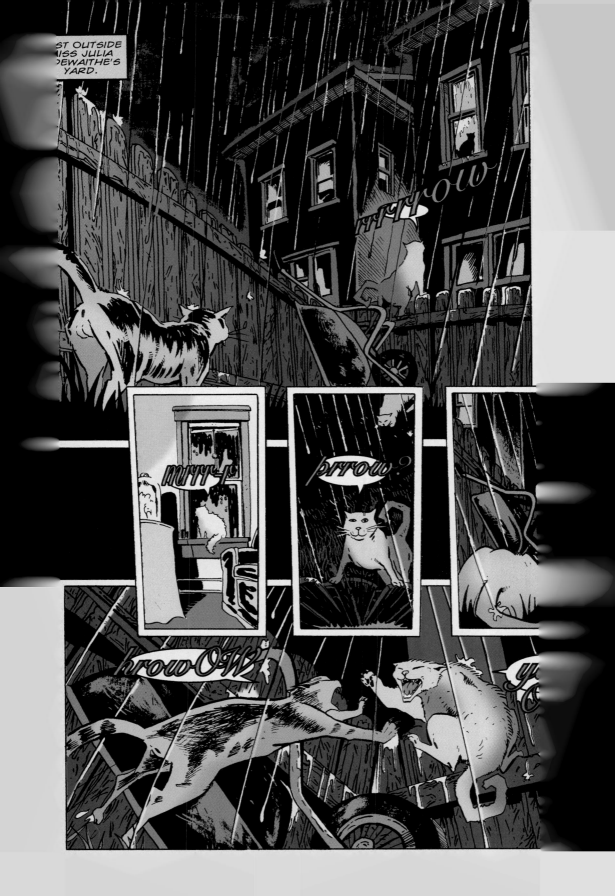

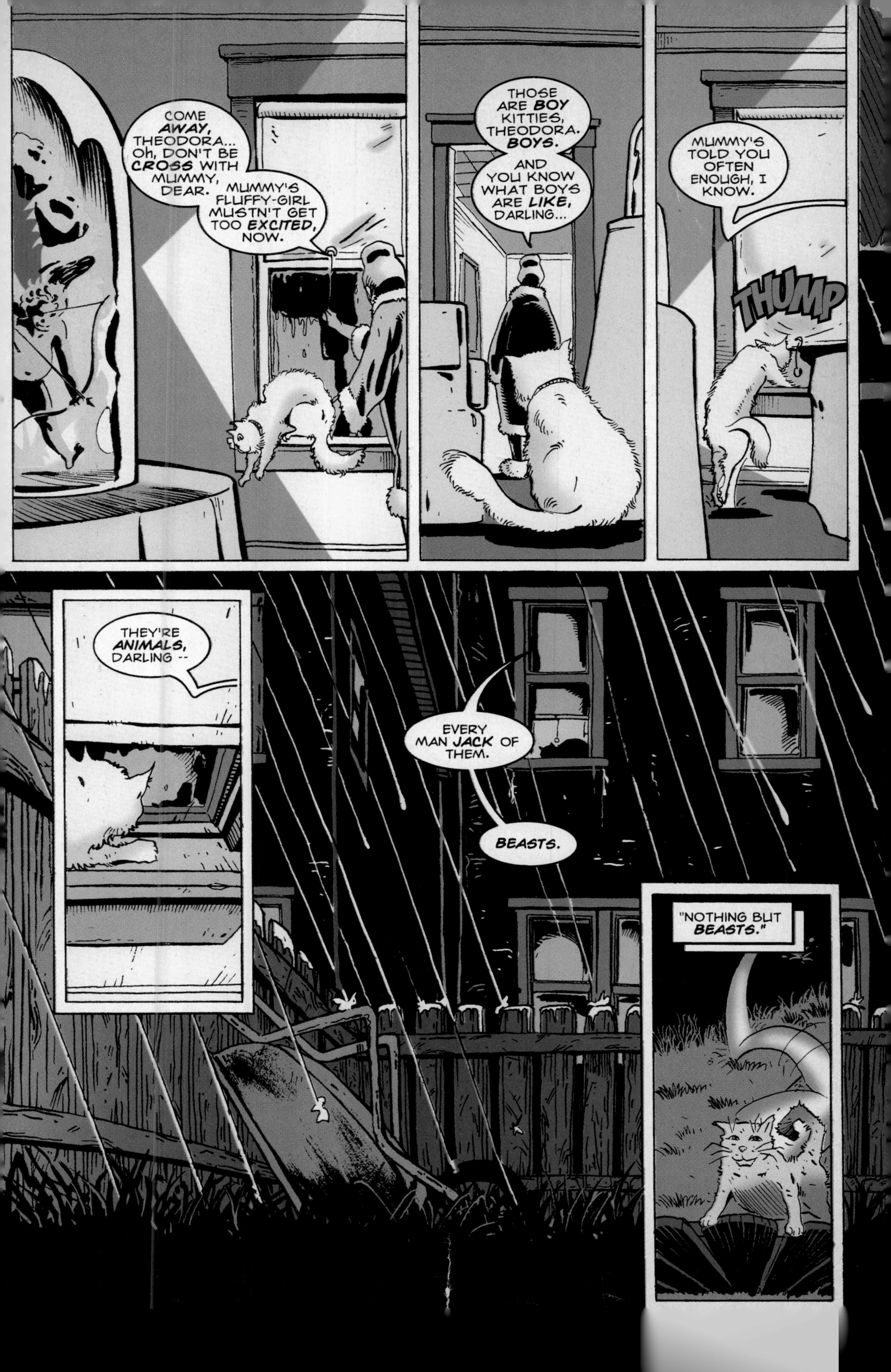
COME AWAY, THEODORA... Oh, DON'T BE CROSS WITH MUMMY, DEAR.
MUMMY'S FLUFFY-GIRL MUSTN'T GET TOO EXCITED, NOW.
THOSE ARE BOY KITTIES, THEODORA. BOYS.
AND YOU KNOW WHAT BOYS ARE LIKE, DARLING...
MUMMY'S TOLD YOU OFTEN ENOUGH, I KNOW.
THUMP
THEY'RE ANIMALS, DARLING --
EVERY MAN JACK OF THEM.
BEASTS.
"NOTHING BUT BEASTS."

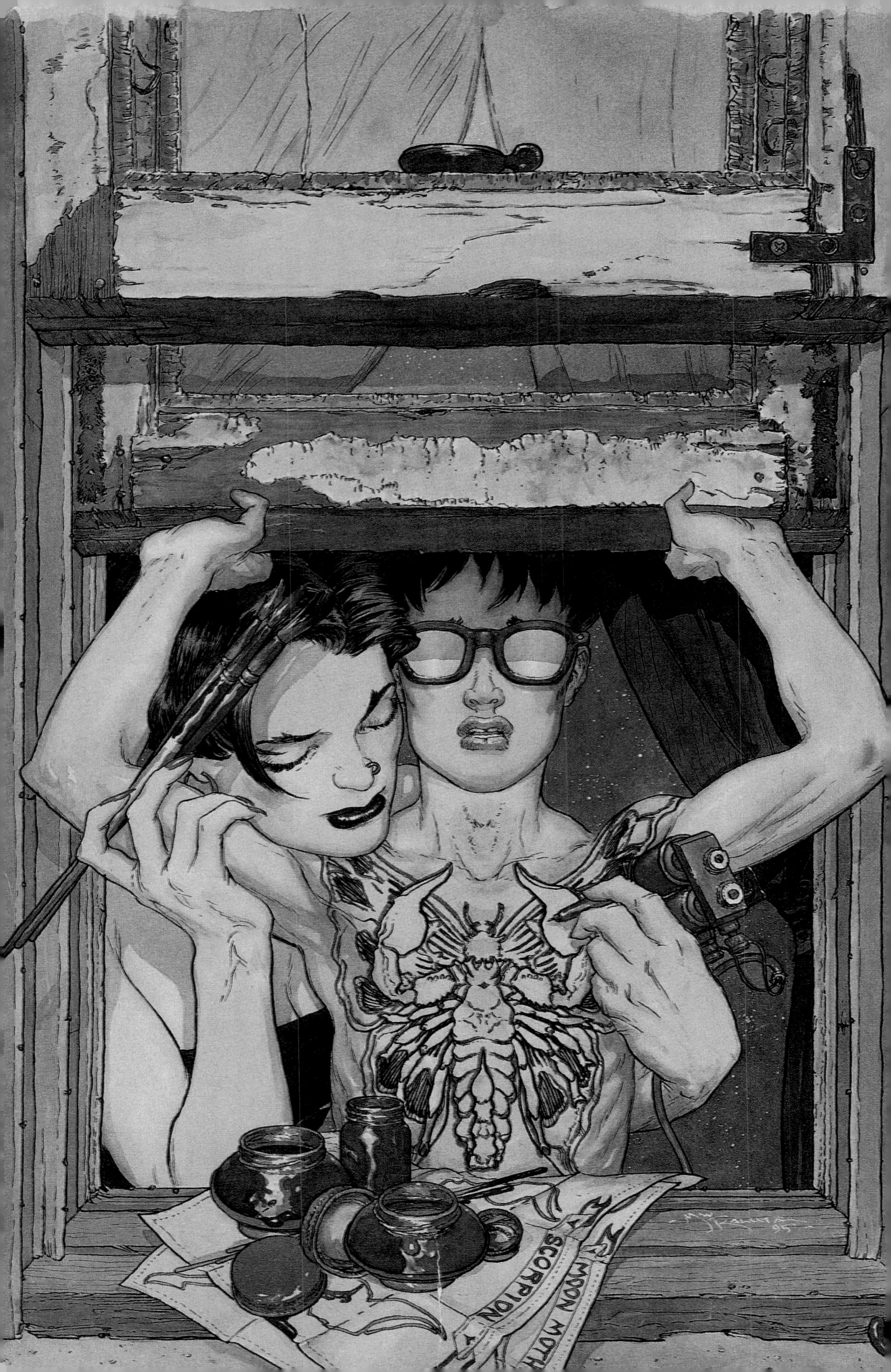
SCORPION
MOON MOTH
MW KALUTA 95

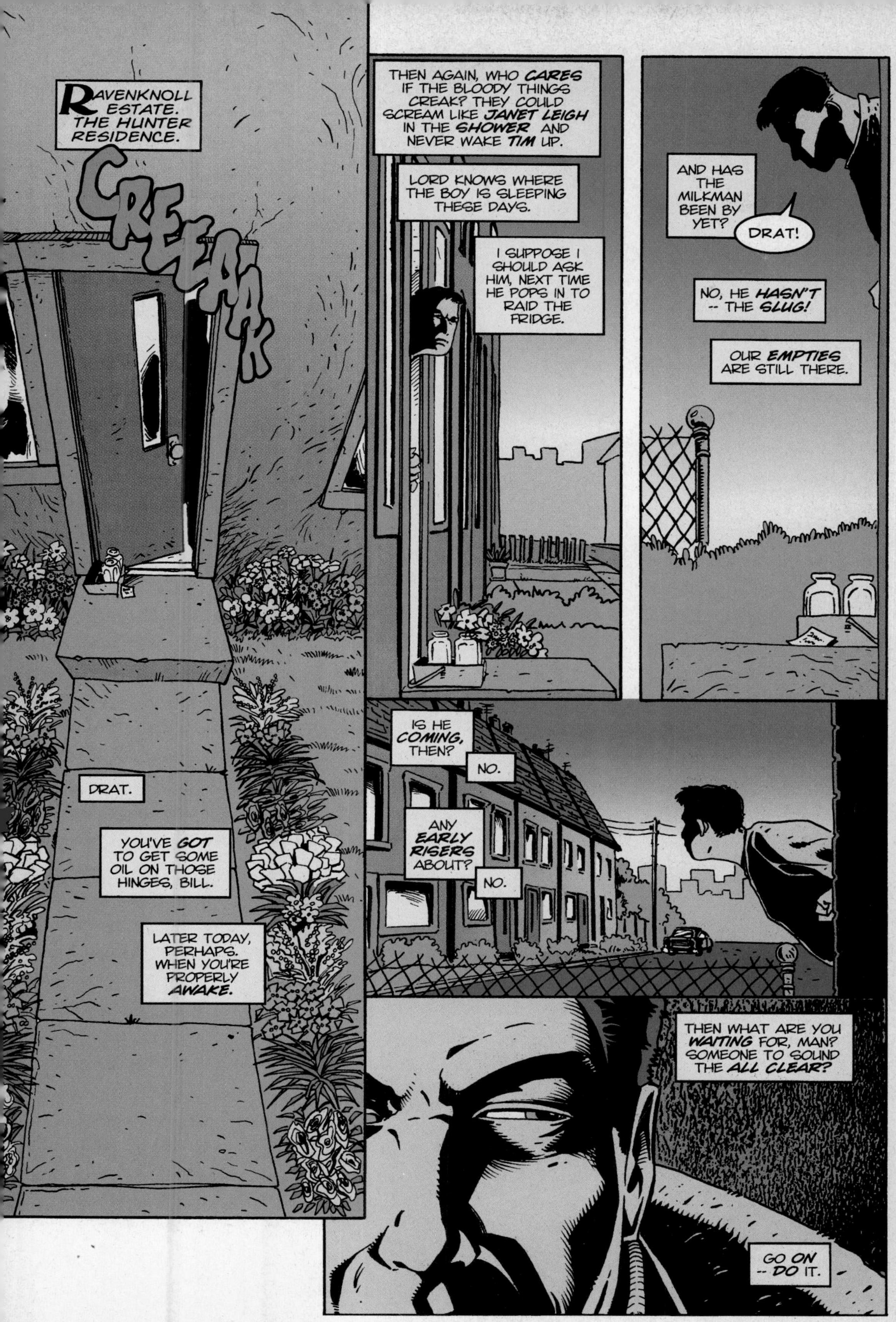
RAVENKNOLL ESTATE. THE HUNTER RESIDENCE.
CREEAAAK
DRAT.
YOU'VE GOT TO GET SOME OIL ON THOSE HINGES, BILL.
LATER TODAY, PERHAPS. WHEN YOU'RE PROPERLY AWAKE.
THEN AGAIN, WHO CARES IF THE BLOODY THINGS CREAK? THEY COULD SCREAM LIKE JANET LEIGH IN THE SHOWER AND NEVER WAKE TIM UP.
LORD KNOWS WHERE THE BOY IS SLEEPING THESE DAYS.
I SUPPOSE I SHOULD ASK HIM, NEXT TIME HE POPS IN TO RAID THE FRIDGE.
AND HAS THE MILKMAN BEEN BY YET?
DRAT!
NO, HE HASN'T -- THE SLUG!
OUR EMPTIES ARE STILL THERE.
IS HE COMING, THEN?
NO.
ANY EARLY RISERS ABOUT?
NO.
THEN WHAT ARE YOU WAITING FOR, MAN? SOMEONE TO SOUND THE ALL CLEAR?
GO ON -- DO IT.

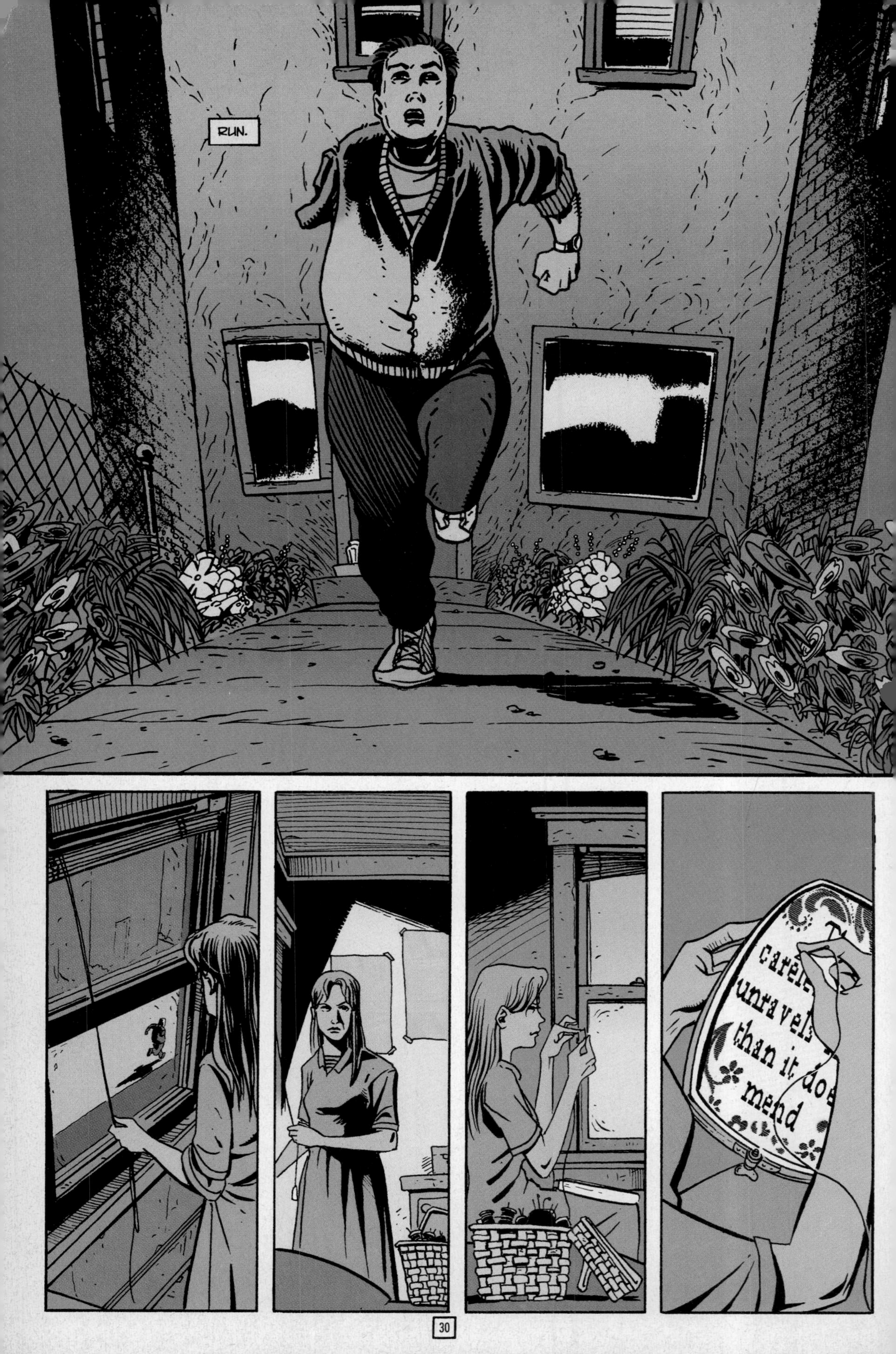
RUN.
than it
mend

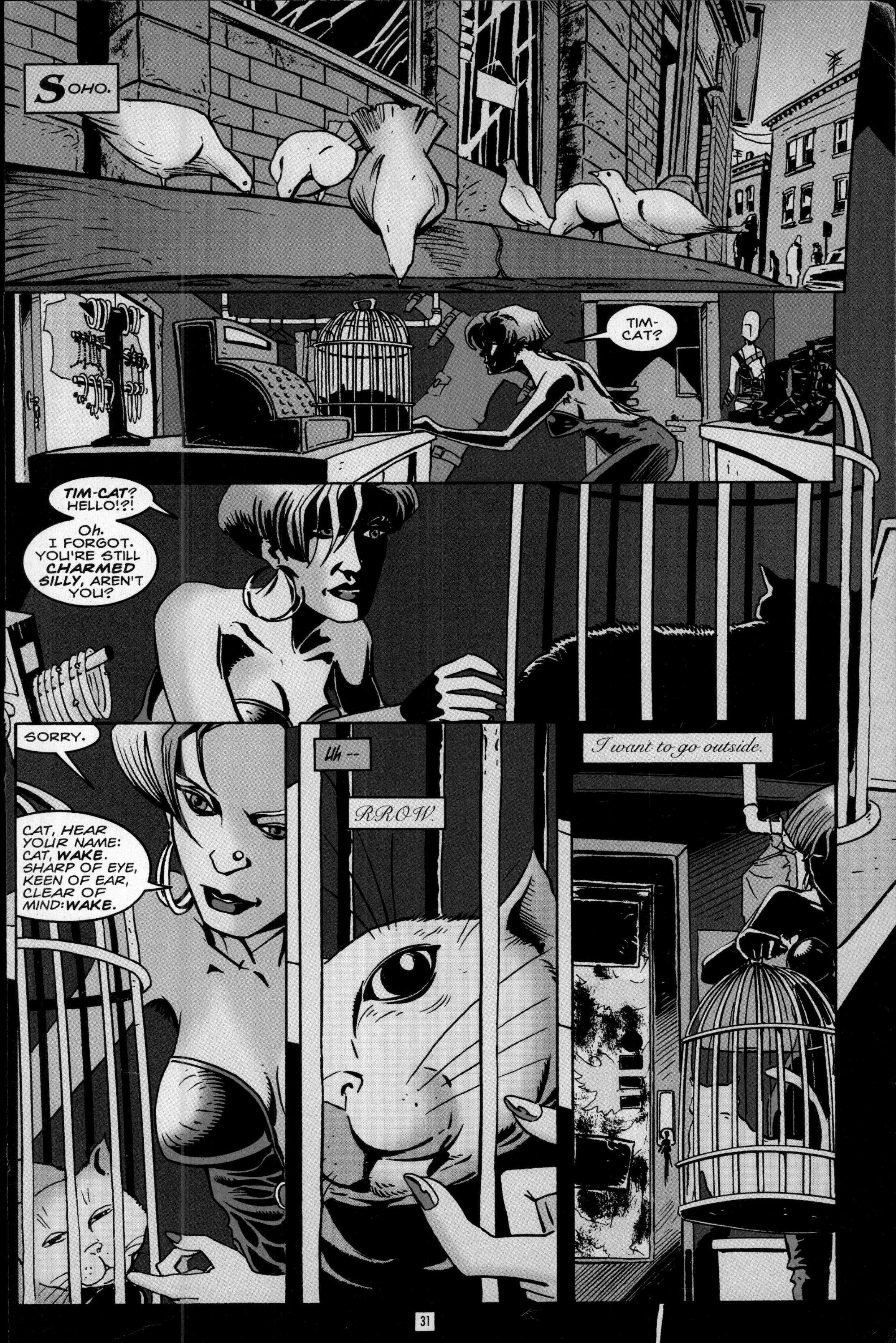
SOHO.
TIM-CAT?
TIM-CAT? HELLO!?!
Oh. I FORGOT. YOU'RE STILL CHARMED SILLY, AREN'T YOU?
SORRY.
CAT, HEAR YOUR NAME: CAT, WAKE. SHARP OF EYE, KEEN OF EAR, CLEAR OF MIND: WAKE.
Uh --
RROW.
I want to go outside.

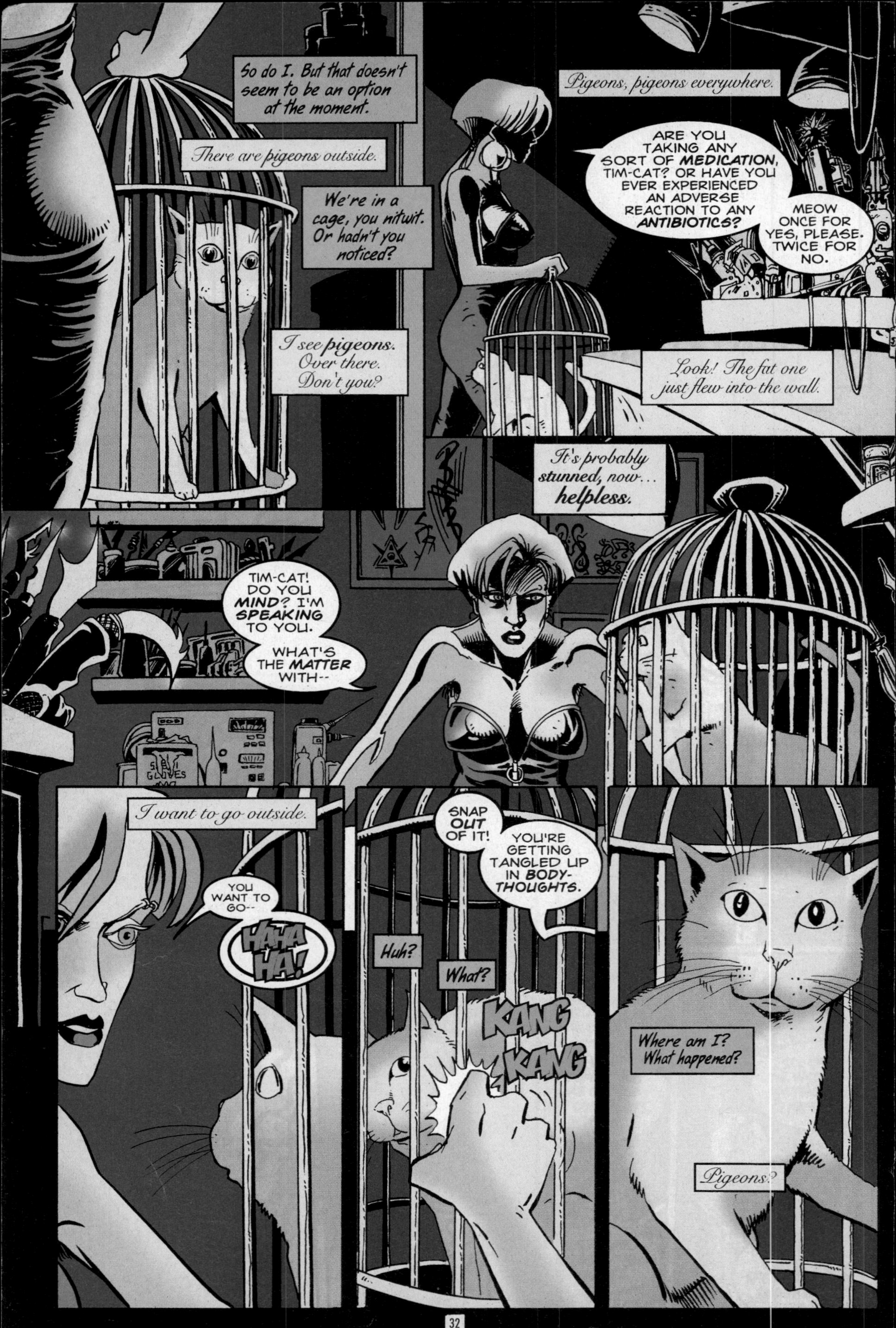
So do I. But that doesn't seem to be an option at the moment.
There are pigeons outside.
We're in a cage, you nitwit. Or hadn't you noticed?
I see pigeons. Over there. Don't you?
Pigeons, pigeons everywhere.
ARE YOU TAKING ANY SORT OF MEDICATION, TIM-CAT? OR HAVE YOU EVER EXPERIENCED AN ADVERSE REACTION TO ANY ANTIBIOTICS?
MEOW ONCE FOR YES, PLEASE. TWICE FOR NO.
Look! The fat one just flew into the wall.
It's probably stunned, now... helpless.
TIM-CAT! DO YOU MIND? I'M SPEAKING TO YOU.
WHAT'S THE MATTER WITH--
I want to go outside.
YOU WANT TO GO--
HAHA HA!
SNAP OUT OF IT!
YOU'RE GETTING TANGLED UP IN BODY-THOUGHTS.
Huh?
What?
KANG
KANG
Where am I? What happened?
Pigeons?

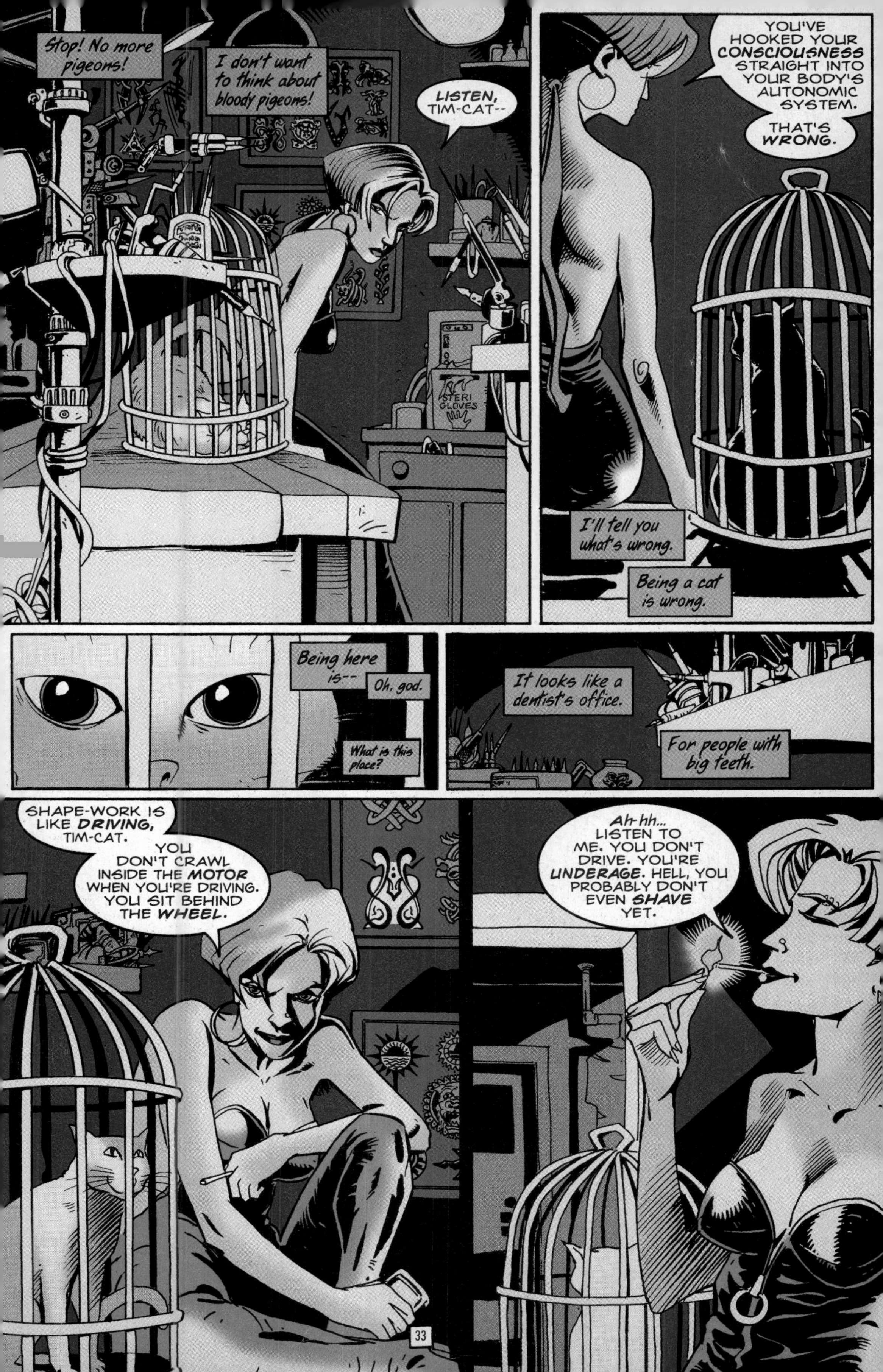
Stop! No more pigeons!
I don't want to think about bloody pigeons!
LISTEN, TIM-CAT--
STERI GLOVES
YOU'VE HOOKED YOUR CONSCIOUSNESS STRAIGHT INTO YOUR BODY'S AUTONOMIC SYSTEM.
THAT'S WRONG.
I'll tell you what's wrong.
Being a cat is wrong.
Being here is--
Oh, god.
What is this place?
It looks like a dentist's office.
For people with big teeth.
SHAPE-WORK IS LIKE DRIVING, TIM-CAT.
YOU DON'T CRAWL INSIDE THE MOTOR WHEN YOU'RE DRIVING. YOU SIT BEHIND THE WHEEL.
Ah-hh... LISTEN TO ME. YOU DON'T DRIVE. YOU'RE UNDERAGE. HELL, YOU PROBABLY DON'T EVEN SHAVE YET.

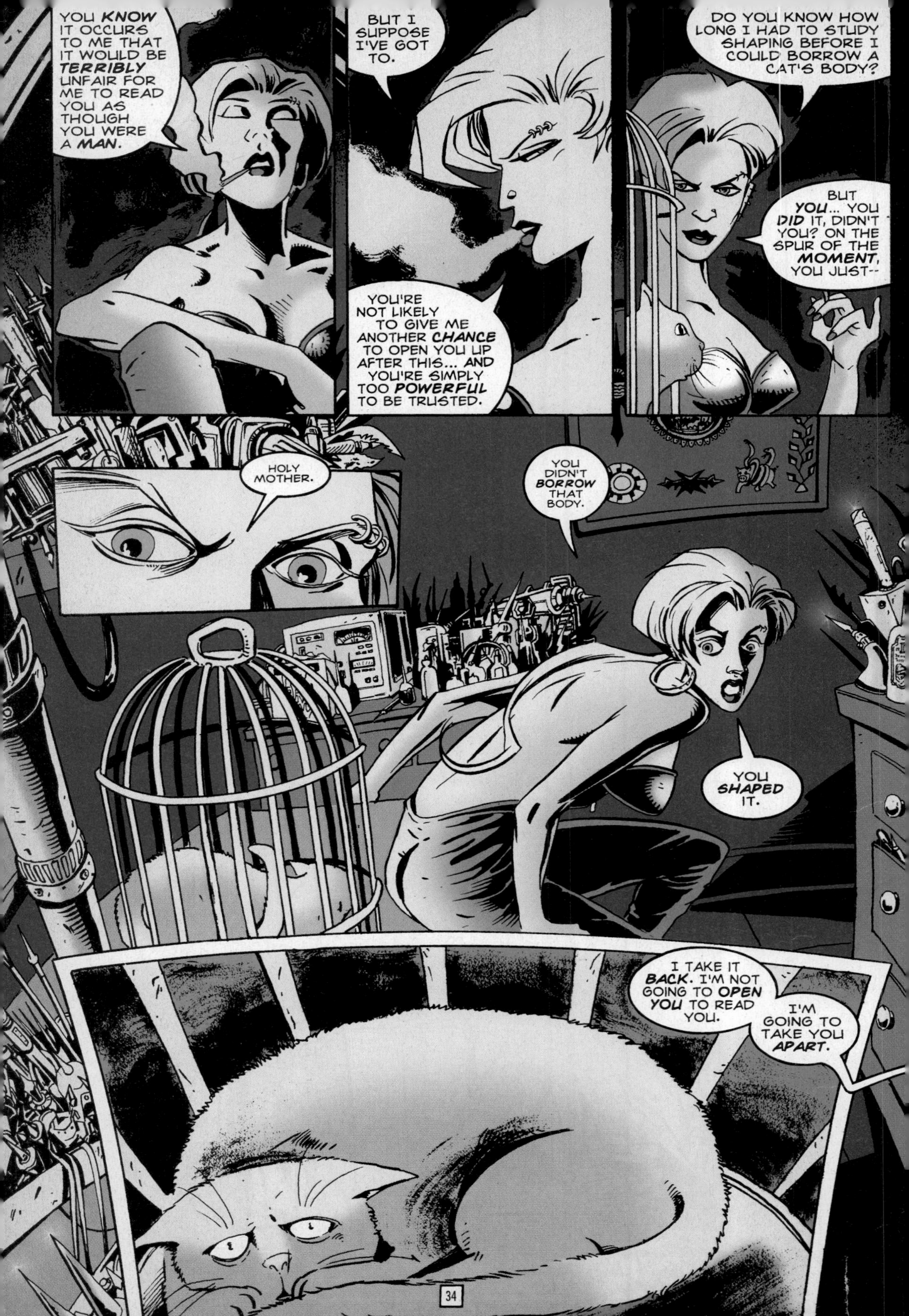
YOU KNOW IT OCCURS TO ME THAT IT WOULD BE TERRIBLY UNFAIR FOR ME TO READ YOU AS THOUGH YOU WERE A MAN.
BUT I SUPPOSE I'VE GOT TO.
YOU'RE NOT LIKELY TO GIVE ME ANOTHER CHANCE TO OPEN YOU UP AFTER THIS... AND YOU'RE SIMPLY TOO POWERFUL TO BE TRUSTED.
DO YOU KNOW HOW LONG I HAD TO STUDY SHAPING BEFORE I COULD BORROW A CAT'S BODY?
BUT YOU... YOU DID IT, DIDN'T YOU? ON THE SPUR OF THE MOMENT, YOU JUST--
HOLY MOTHER.
YOU DIDN'T BORROW THAT BODY.
YOU SHAPED IT.
I TAKE IT BACK. I'M NOT GOING TO OPEN YOU TO READ YOU.
I'M GOING TO TAKE YOU APART.

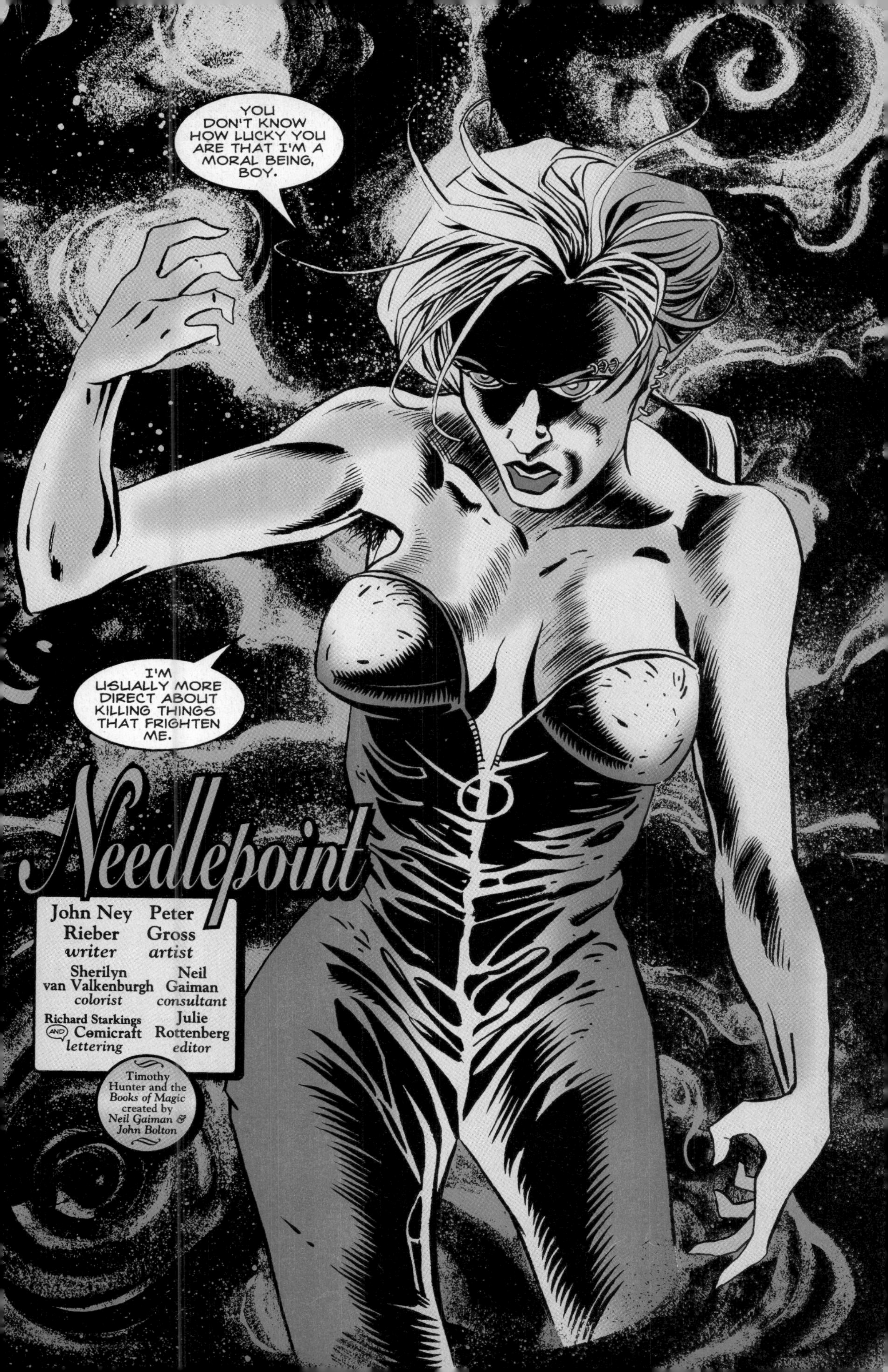
YOU DON'T KNOW HOW LUCKY YOU ARE THAT I'M A MORAL BEING, BOY.
I'M USUALLY MORE DIRECT ABOUT KILLING THINGS THAT FRIGHTEN ME.
Needlepoint
John Ney Rieber writer
Peter Gross artist
Sherilyn van Valkenburgh colorist
Neil Gaiman consultant
Richard Starkings AND Comicraft lettering
Julie Rottenberg editor
Timothy Hunter and the Books of Magic created by Neil Gaiman & John Bolton

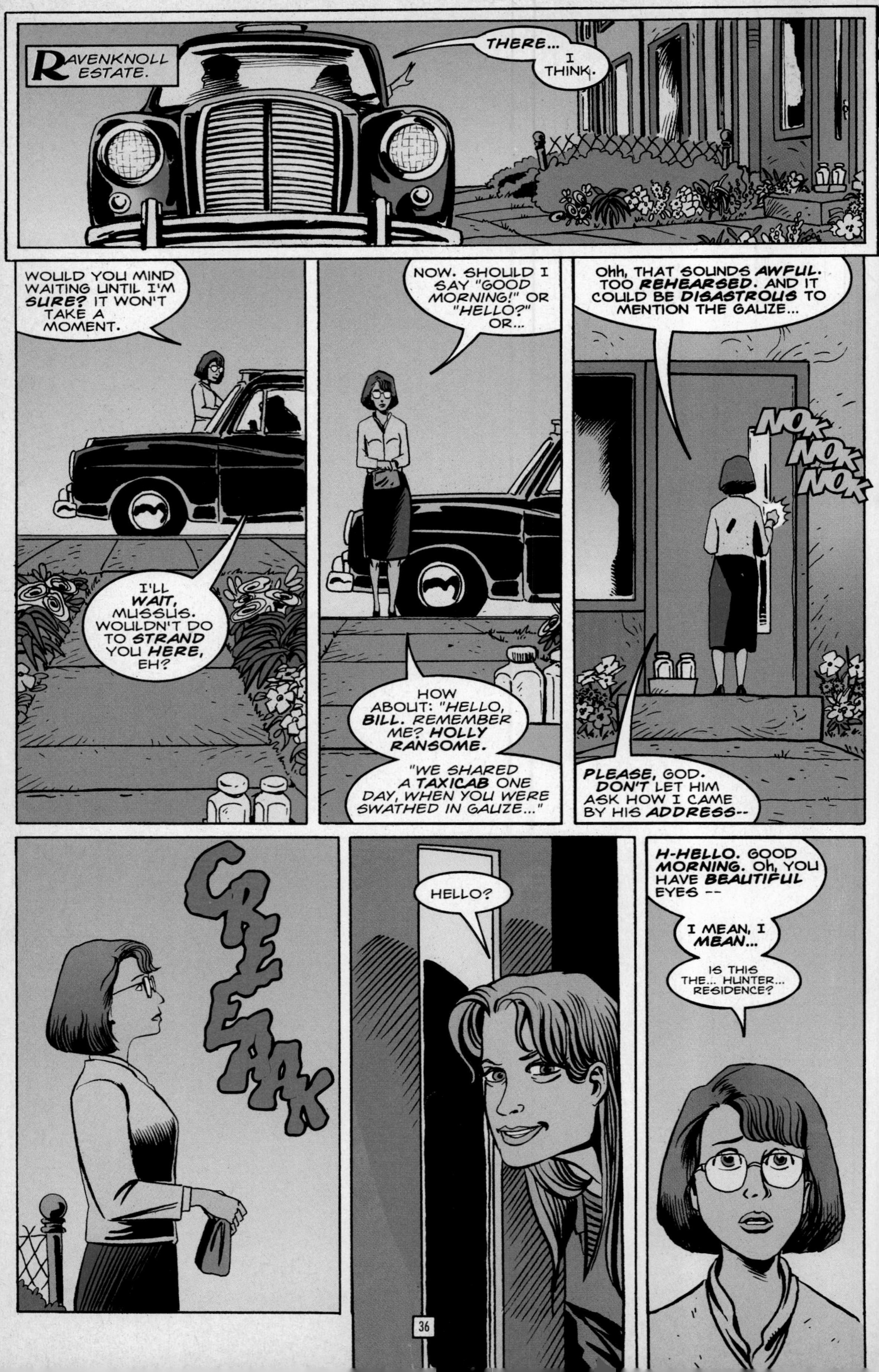
RAVENKNOLL ESTATE.
THERE... I THINK.
WOULD YOU MIND WAITING UNTIL I'M SURE? IT WON'T TAKE A MOMENT.
I'LL WAIT, MUSSUS. WOULDN'T DO TO STRAND YOU HERE, EH?
NOW. SHOULD I SAY "GOOD MORNING!" OR "HELLO?" OR...
HOW ABOUT: "HELLO, BILL. REMEMBER ME? HOLLY RANSOME.
"WE SHARED A TAXICAB ONE DAY, WHEN YOU WERE SWATHED IN GAUZE..."
Ohh, THAT SOUNDS AWFUL. TOO REHEARSED. AND IT COULD BE DISASTROUS TO MENTION THE GAUZE...
NOK NOK NOK
PLEASE, GOD. DON'T LET HIM ASK HOW I CAME BY HIS ADDRESS--
CREEAAK
HELLO?
H-HELLO. GOOD MORNING. Oh, YOU HAVE BEAUTIFUL EYES --
I MEAN, I MEAN...
IS THIS THE... HUNTER... RESIDENCE?

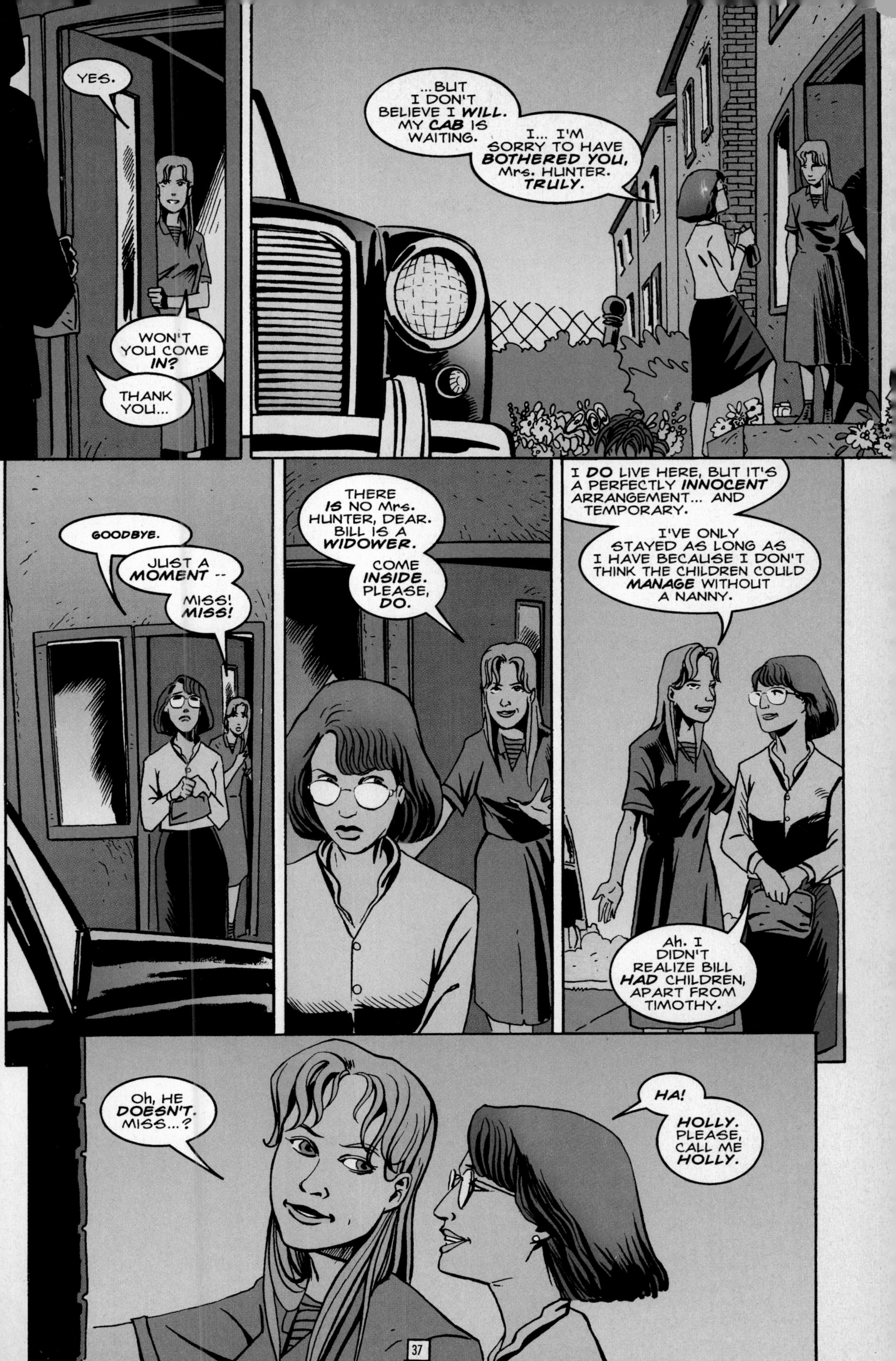

YES.
WON'T YOU COME IN?
THANK YOU...
...BUT I DON'T BELIEVE I WILL. MY CAB IS WAITING.
I... I'M SORRY TO HAVE BOTHERED YOU, Mrs. HUNTER. TRULY.
GOODBYE.
JUST A MOMENT --
MISS! MISS!
THERE IS NO Mrs. HUNTER, DEAR. BILL IS A WIDOWER.
COME INSIDE. PLEASE, DO.
I DO LIVE HERE, BUT IT'S A PERFECTLY INNOCENT ARRANGEMENT... AND TEMPORARY.
I'VE ONLY STAYED AS LONG AS I HAVE BECAUSE I DON'T THINK THE CHILDREN COULD MANAGE WITHOUT A NANNY.
Ah. I DIDN'T REALIZE BILL HAD CHILDREN, APART FROM TIMOTHY.
Oh, HE DOESN'T. MISS...?
HA!
HOLLY. PLEASE, CALL ME HOLLY.

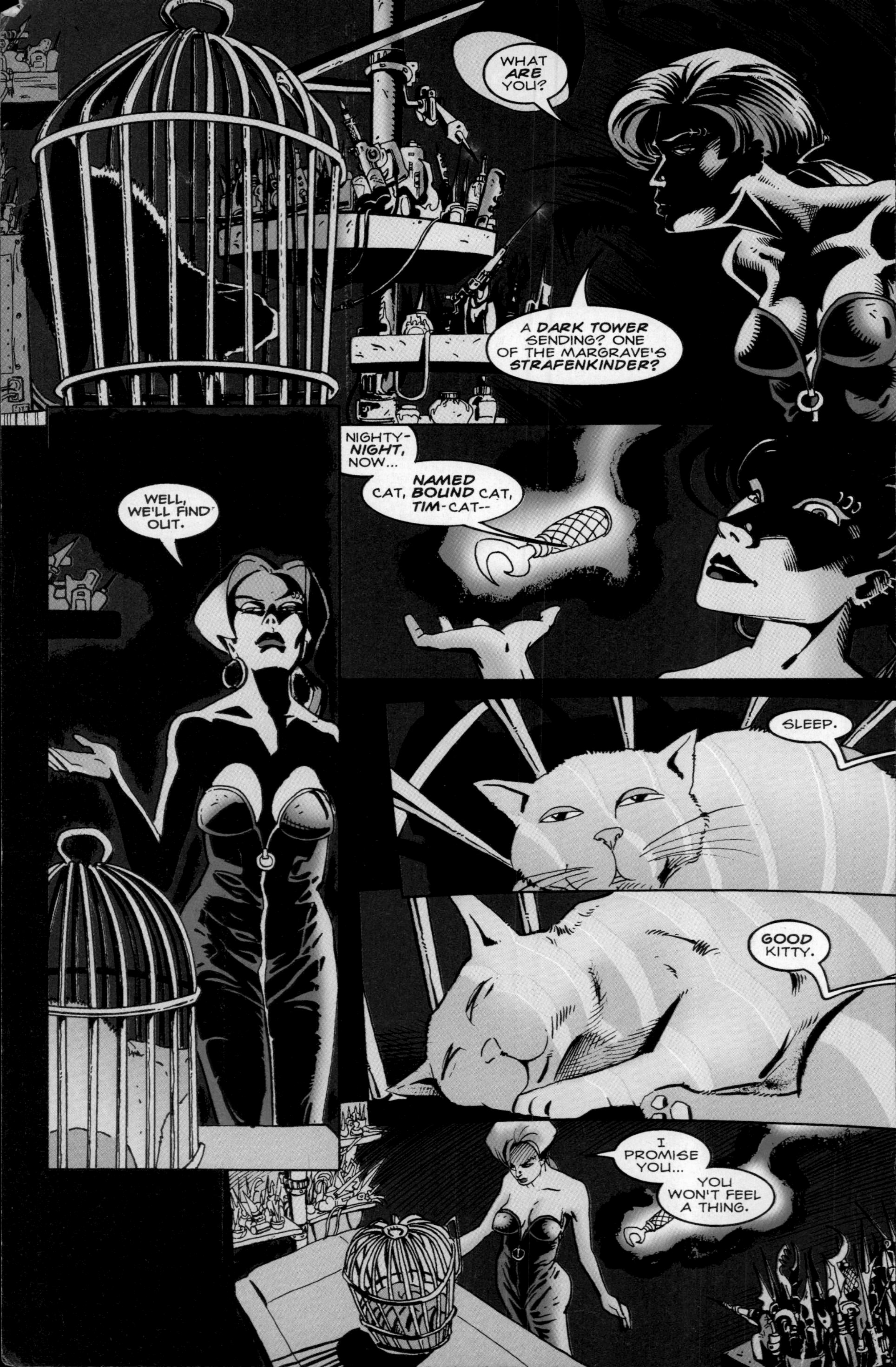
WHAT ARE YOU?
A DARK TOWER SENDING? ONE OF THE MARGRAVE'S STRAFENKINDER?
WELL, WE'LL FIND OUT.
NIGHTY-NIGHT, NOW...
NAMED CAT, BOUND CAT, TIM-CAT--
SLEEP.
GOOD KITTY.
I PROMISE YOU...
YOU WON'T FEEL A THING.

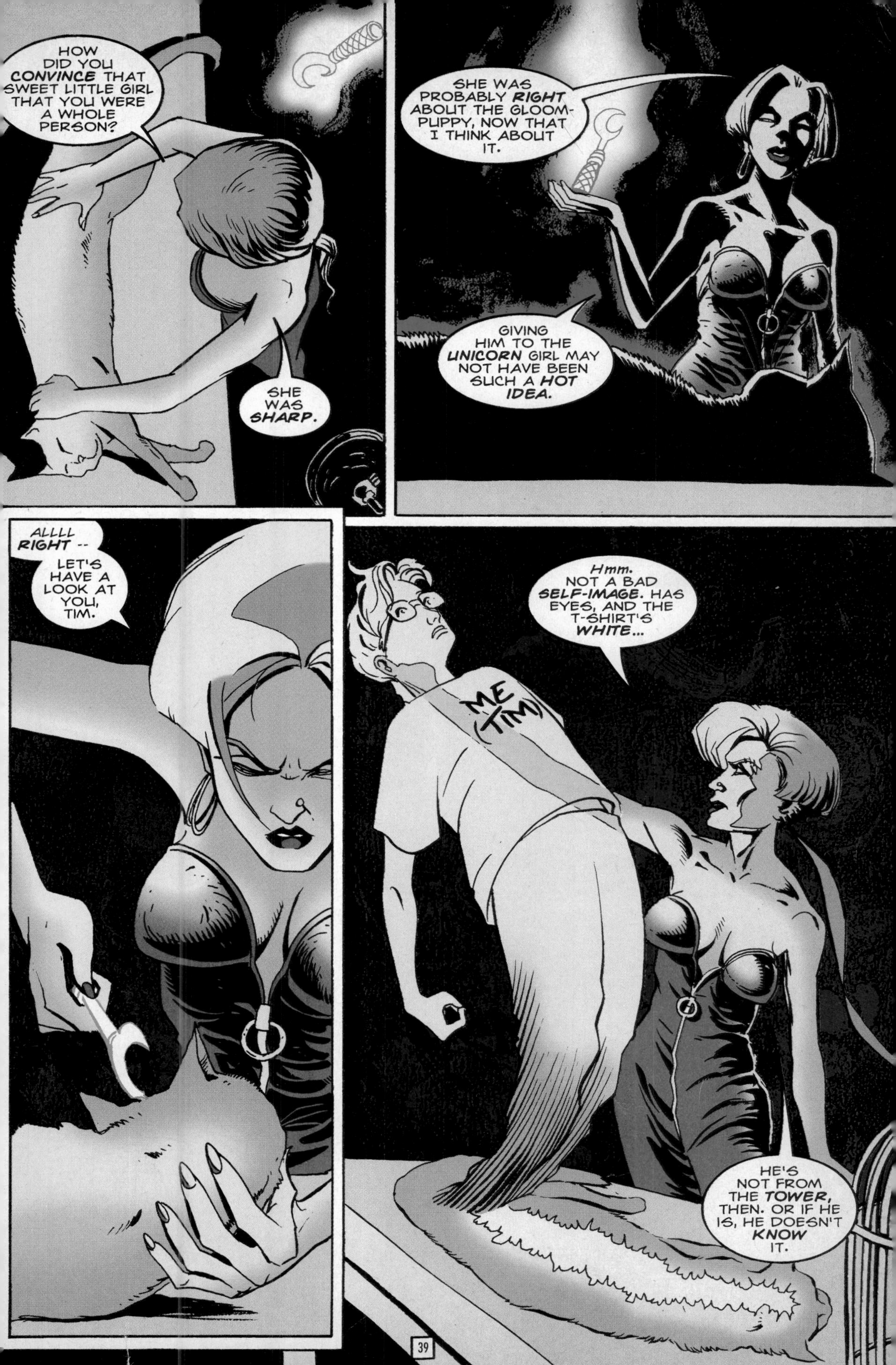
HOW DID YOU CONVINCE THAT SWEET LITTLE GIRL THAT YOU WERE A WHOLE PERSON?
SHE WAS SHARP.
SHE WAS PROBABLY RIGHT ABOUT THE GLOOM-PUPPY, NOW THAT I THINK ABOUT IT.
GIVING HIM TO THE UNICORN GIRL MAY NOT HAVE BEEN SUCH A HOT IDEA.
ALLLL RIGHT --
LET'S HAVE A LOOK AT YOU, TIM.
Hmm. NOT A BAD SELF-IMAGE. HAS EYES, AND THE T-SHIRT'S WHITE...
ME (TIM)
HE'S NOT FROM THE TOWER, THEN. OR IF HE IS, HE DOESN'T KNOW IT.

SEAMRIPPER.

ME (TIM)

NO, NO -- NOT *YOU, YOU.* WITH THE *INSULATED GRIP.*

Huh. NO *RESISTANCE.* THAT'S ODD.

DILATOR--?

SSHAAA

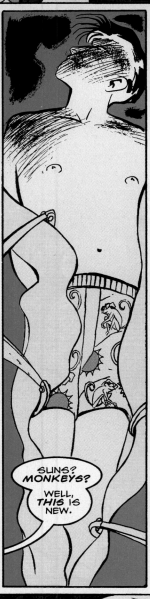

SUNS? MONKEYS?

WELL, *THIS* IS NEW.

I DON'T UNDERSTAND.

I SHOULD HAVE HIT *SOME* DARKNESS BY NOW, IF HE'S SOMEONE WHO COULD GROW UP TO BE THE *MONSTER* MOLLY TALKED ABOUT.

BUT I HAVEN'T EVEN *TOUCHED* MAGIC, YET. SOMETHING'S *WRONG.*

SOMETHING'S *MISSING* --

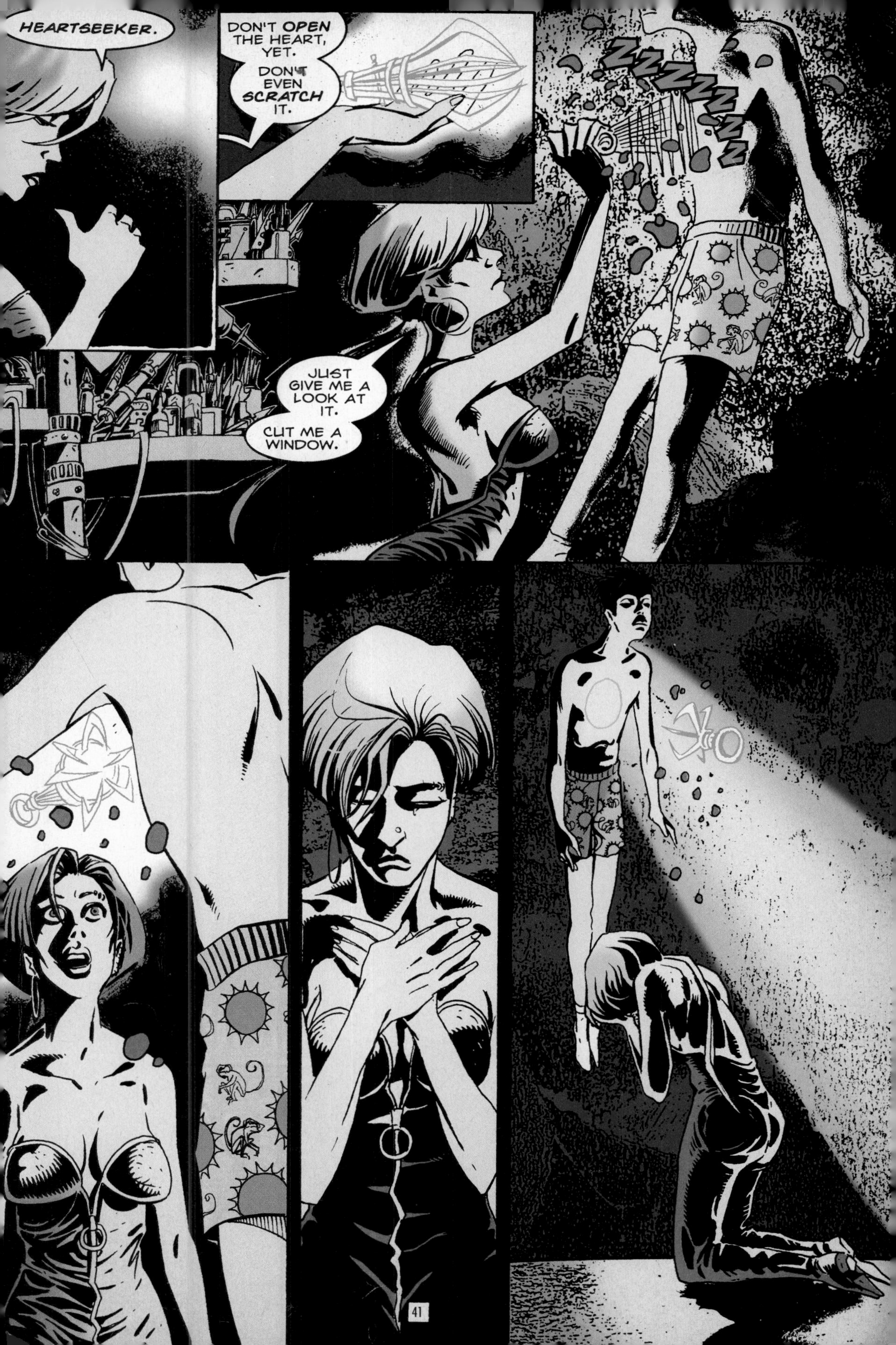
HEARTSEEKER.
DON'T OPEN THE HEART, YET.
DON'T EVEN SCRATCH IT.
ZZZZZZZZZ
JUST GIVE ME A LOOK AT IT.
CUT ME A WINDOW.

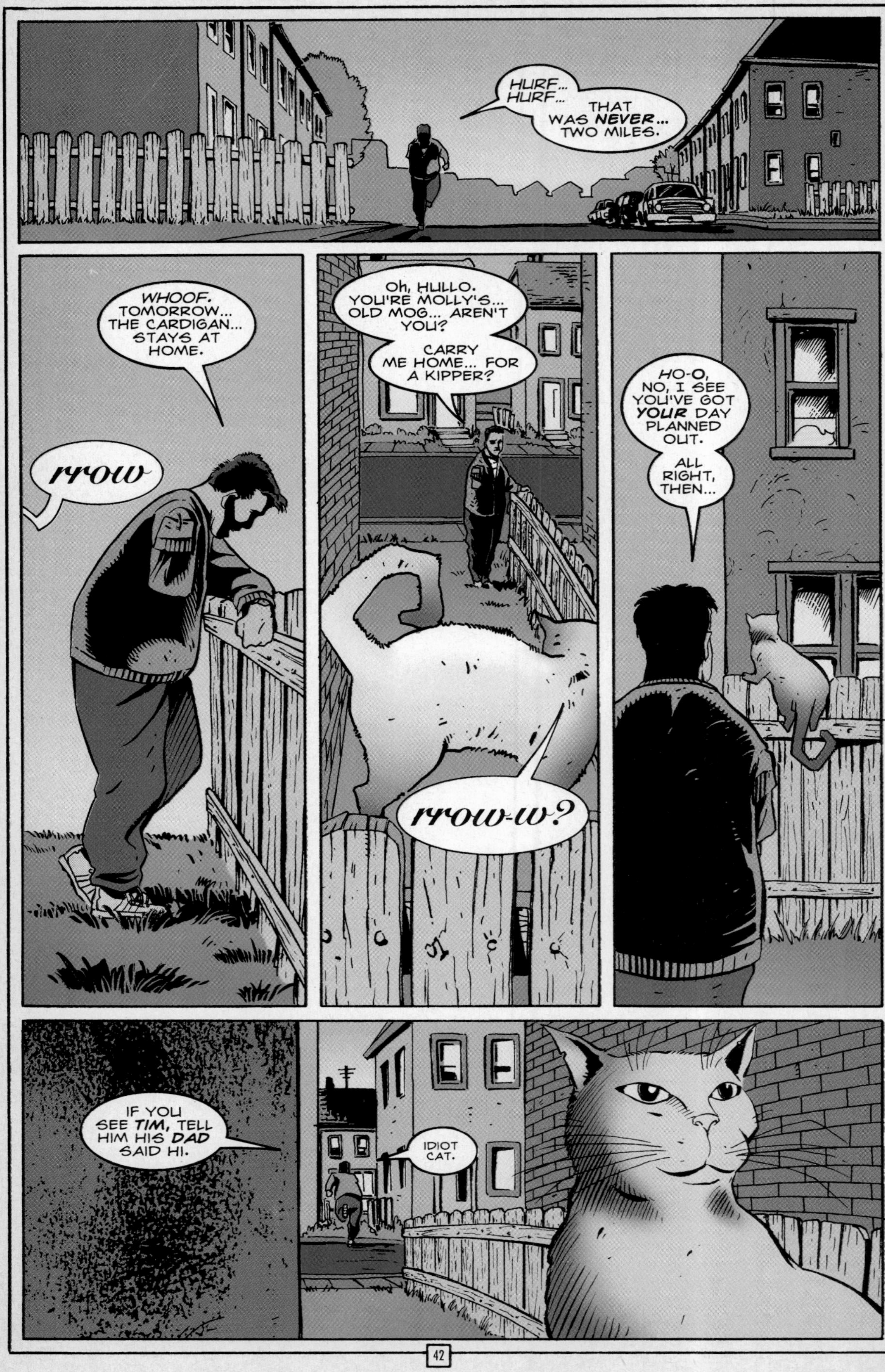
HURF... HURF...
THAT WAS NEVER... TWO MILES.
WHOOF. TOMORROW... THE CARDIGAN... STAYS AT HOME.
rrow
Oh, HULLO. YOU'RE MOLLY'S... OLD MOG... AREN'T YOU?
CARRY ME HOME... FOR A KIPPER?
rrow-w?
HO-O, NO, I SEE YOU'VE GOT YOUR DAY PLANNED OUT.
ALL RIGHT, THEN...
IF YOU SEE TIM, TELL HIM HIS DAD SAID HI.
IDIOT CAT.

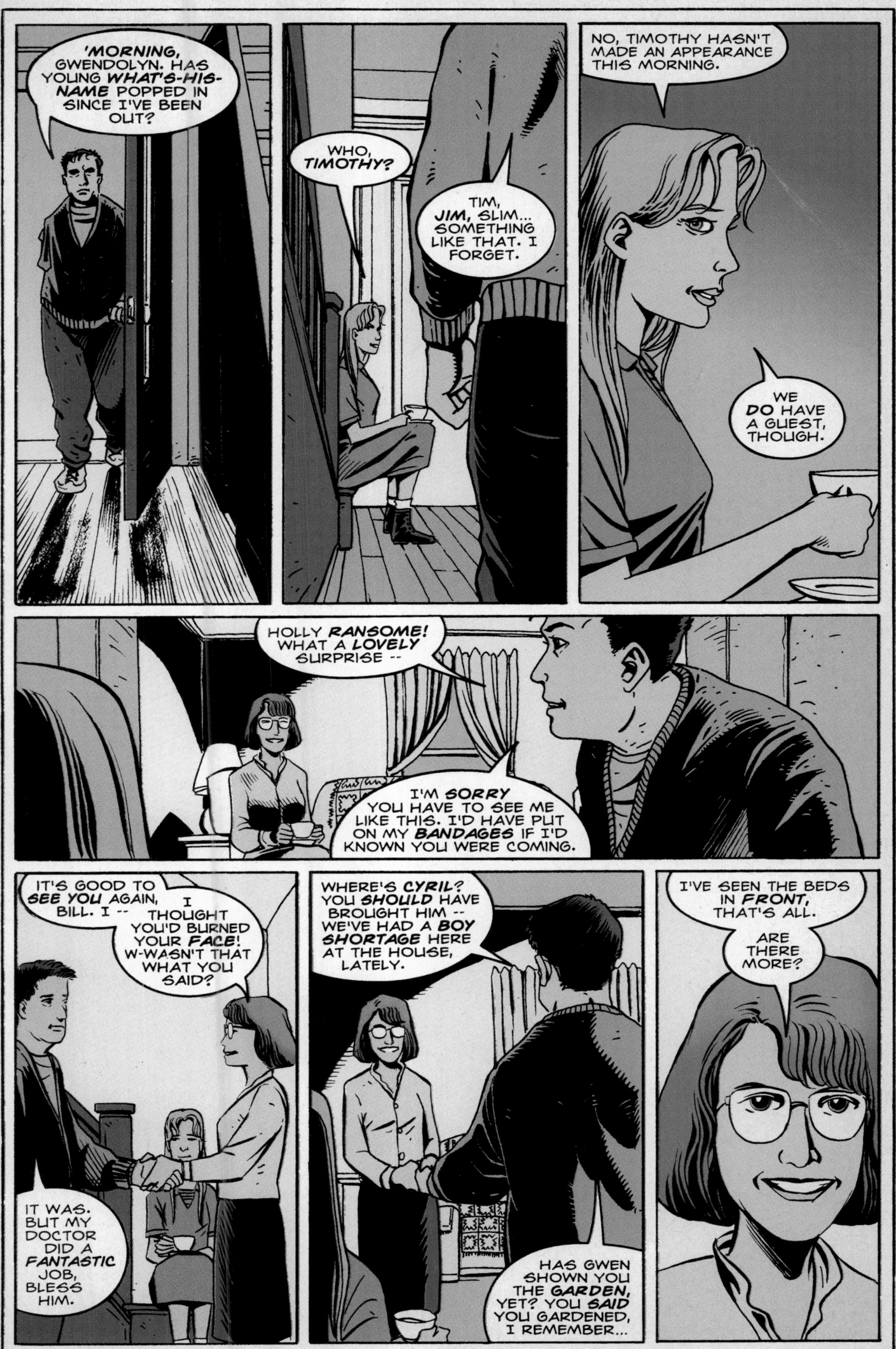
'MORNING, GWENDOLYN. HAS YOUNG WHAT'S-HIS-NAME POPPED IN SINCE I'VE BEEN OUT?
WHO, TIMOTHY?
TIM, JIM, SLIM... SOMETHING LIKE THAT. I FORGET.
NO, TIMOTHY HASN'T MADE AN APPEARANCE THIS MORNING.
WE DO HAVE A GUEST, THOUGH.
HOLLY RANSOME! WHAT A LOVELY SURPRISE --
I'M SORRY YOU HAVE TO SEE ME LIKE THIS. I'D HAVE PUT ON MY BANDAGES IF I'D KNOWN YOU WERE COMING.
IT'S GOOD TO SEE YOU AGAIN, BILL. I --
I THOUGHT YOU'D BURNED YOUR FACE! W-WASN'T THAT WHAT YOU SAID?
IT WAS. BUT MY DOCTOR DID A FANTASTIC JOB, BLESS HIM.
WHERE'S CYRIL? YOU SHOULD HAVE BROUGHT HIM -- WE'VE HAD A BOY SHORTAGE HERE AT THE HOUSE, LATELY.
HAS GWEN SHOWN YOU THE GARDEN, YET? YOU SAID YOU GARDENED, I REMEMBER...
I'VE SEEN THE BEDS IN FRONT, THAT'S ALL.
ARE THERE MORE?

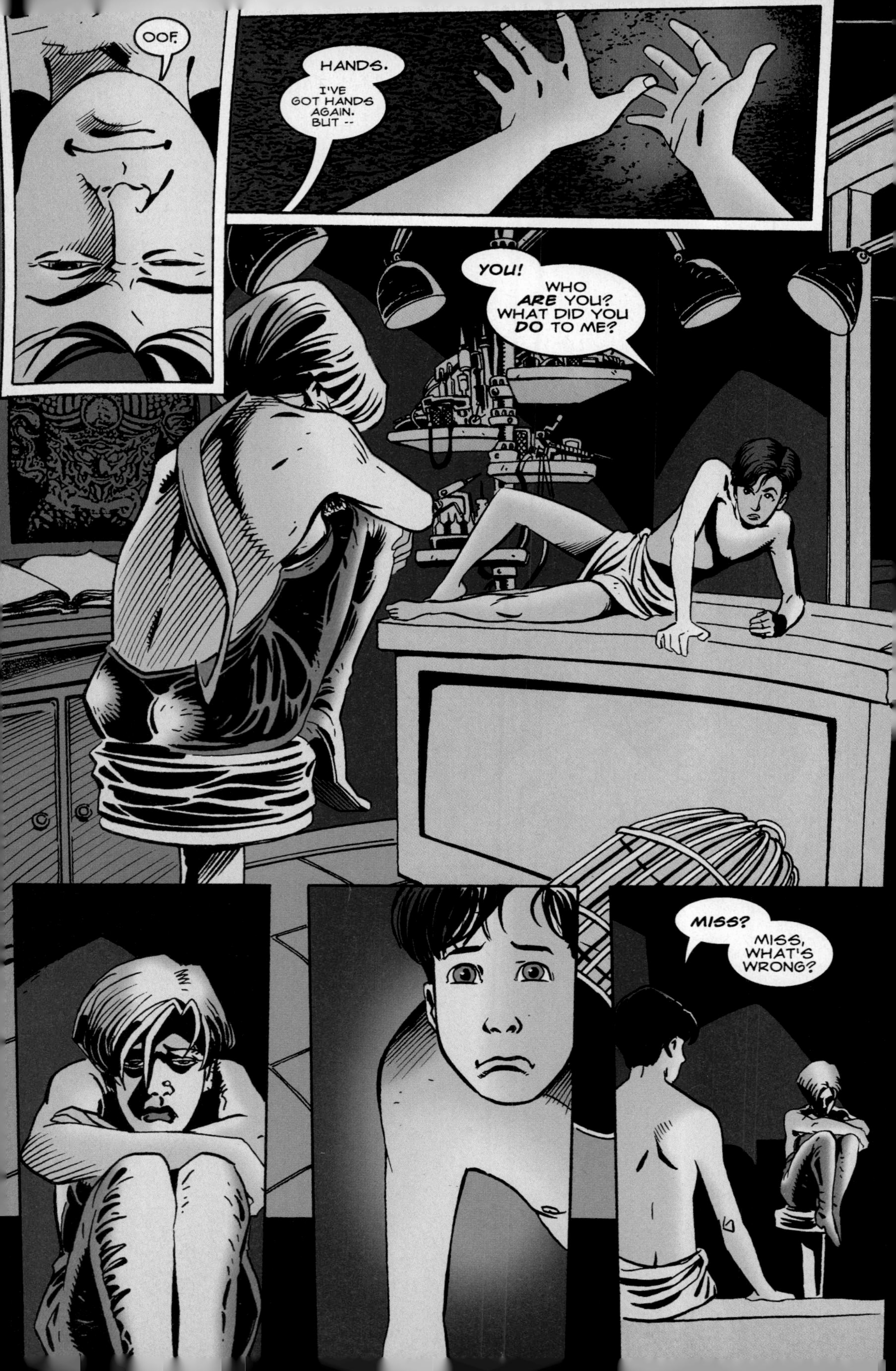
OOF.
HANDS.
I'VE GOT HANDS AGAIN. BUT --
YOU!
WHO ARE YOU? WHAT DID YOU DO TO ME?
MISS?
MISS, WHAT'S WRONG?

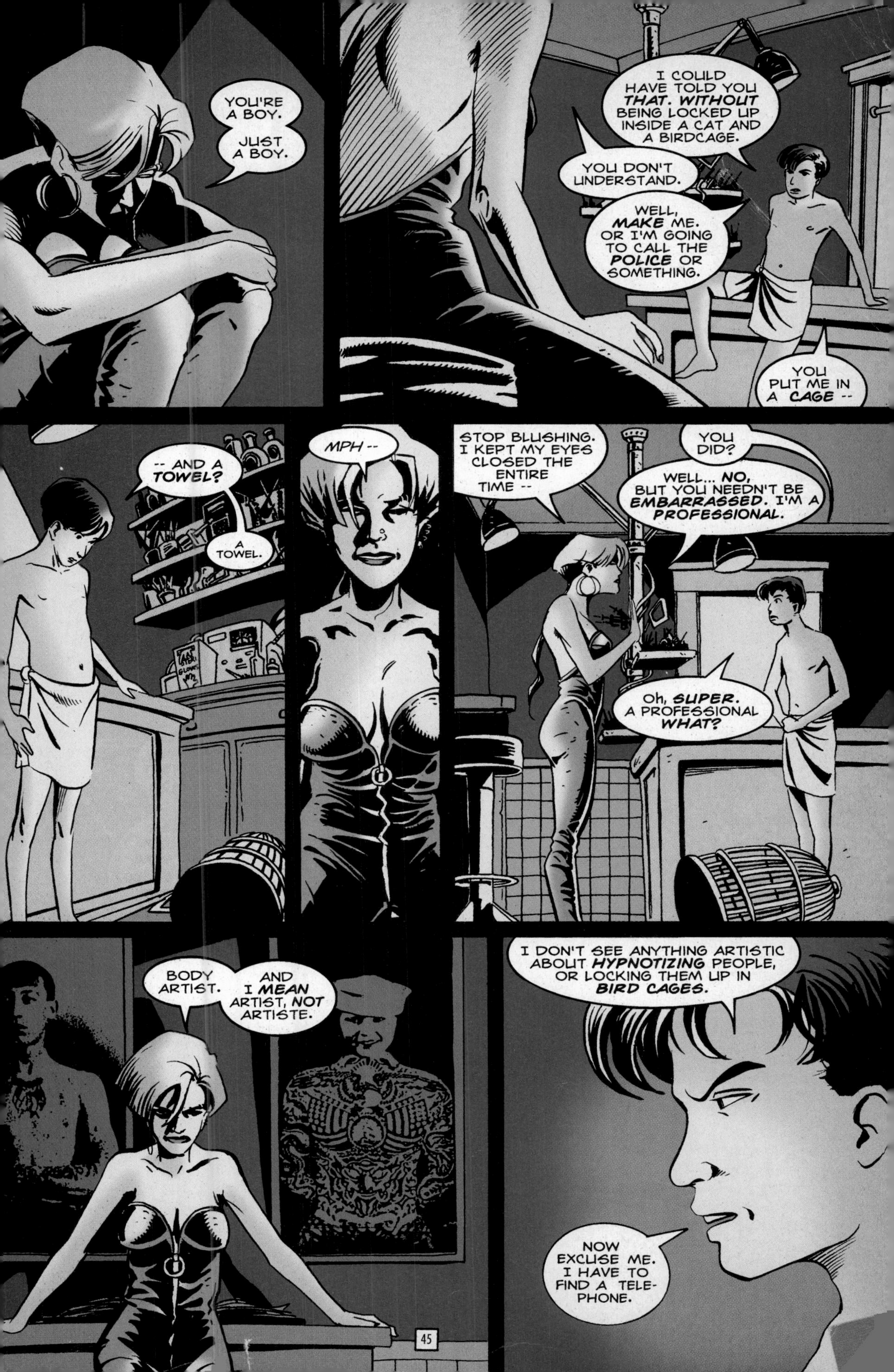
YOU'RE A BOY.
JUST A BOY.
I COULD HAVE TOLD YOU THAT. WITHOUT BEING LOCKED UP INSIDE A CAT AND A BIRDCAGE.
YOU DON'T UNDERSTAND.
WELL, MAKE ME. OR I'M GOING TO CALL THE POLICE OR SOMETHING.
YOU PUT ME IN A CAGE --
-- AND A TOWEL?
A TOWEL.
MPH --
STOP BLUSHING. I KEPT MY EYES CLOSED THE ENTIRE TIME --
YOU DID?
WELL... NO, BUT YOU NEEDN'T BE EMBARRASSED. I'M A PROFESSIONAL.
Oh, SUPER. A PROFESSIONAL WHAT?
BODY ARTIST.
AND I MEAN ARTIST, NOT ARTISTE.
I DON'T SEE ANYTHING ARTISTIC ABOUT HYPNOTIZING PEOPLE, OR LOCKING THEM UP IN BIRD CAGES.
NOW EXCUSE ME. I HAVE TO FIND A TELEPHONE.

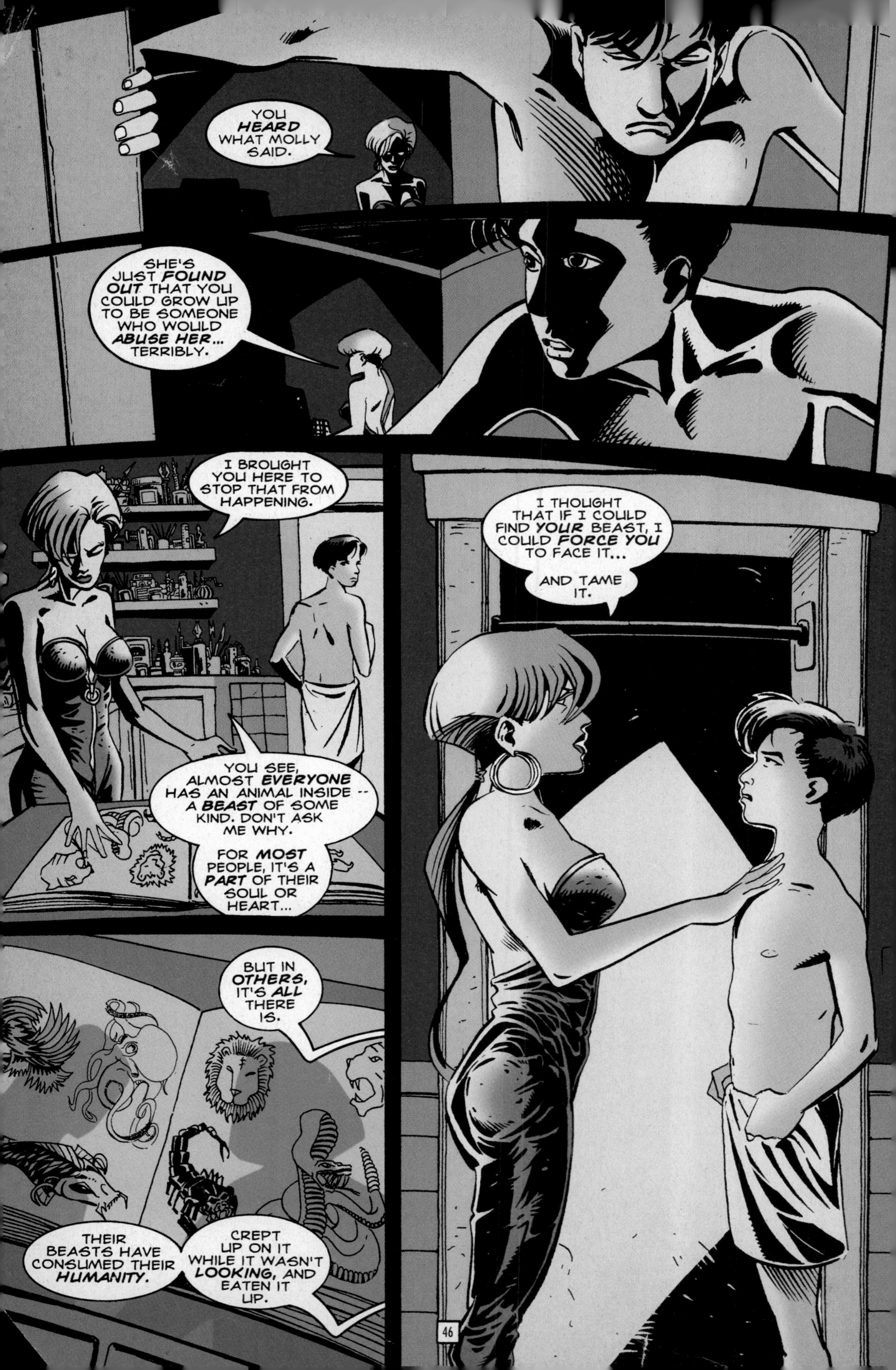
YOU HEARD WHAT MOLLY SAID.
SHE'S JUST FOUND OUT THAT YOU COULD GROW UP TO BE SOMEONE WHO WOULD ABUSE HER... TERRIBLY.
I BROUGHT YOU HERE TO STOP THAT FROM HAPPENING.
YOU SEE, ALMOST EVERYONE HAS AN ANIMAL INSIDE -- A BEAST OF SOME KIND. DON'T ASK ME WHY.
FOR MOST PEOPLE, IT'S A PART OF THEIR SOUL OR HEART...
BUT IN OTHERS, IT'S ALL THERE IS.
THEIR BEASTS HAVE CONSUMED THEIR HUMANITY.
CREPT UP ON IT WHILE IT WASN'T LOOKING, AND EATEN IT UP.
I THOUGHT THAT IF I COULD FIND YOUR BEAST, I COULD FORCE YOU TO FACE IT...
AND TAME IT.

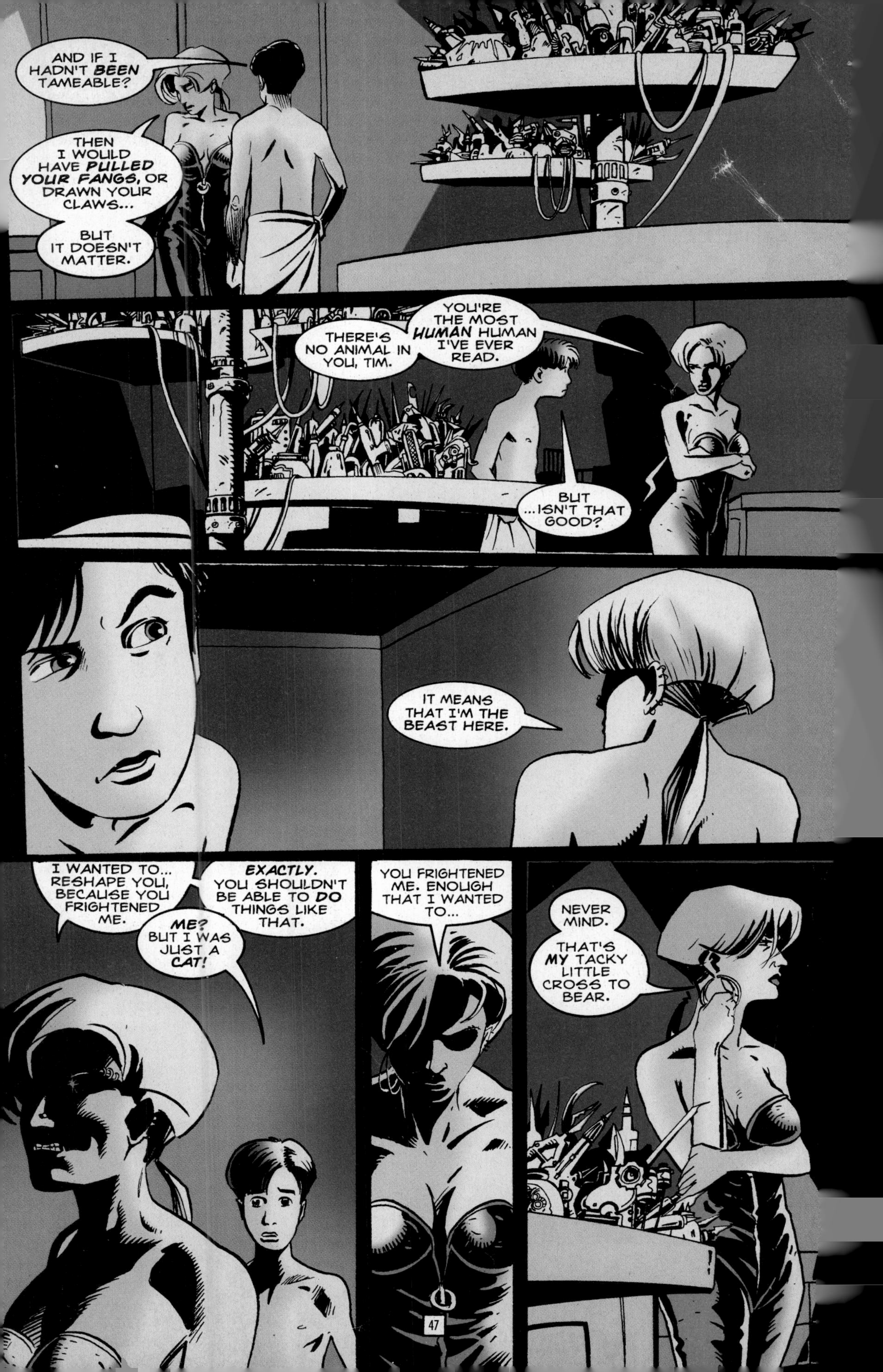
AND IF I HADN'T BEEN TAMEABLE?
THEN I WOULD HAVE PULLED YOUR FANGS, OR DRAWN YOUR CLAWS...
BUT IT DOESN'T MATTER.
THERE'S NO ANIMAL IN YOU, TIM.
YOU'RE THE MOST HUMAN HUMAN I'VE EVER READ.
BUT ...ISN'T THAT GOOD?
IT MEANS THAT I'M THE BEAST HERE.
I WANTED TO... RESHAPE YOU, BECAUSE YOU FRIGHTENED ME.
EXACTLY. YOU SHOULDN'T BE ABLE TO DO THINGS LIKE THAT.
ME? BUT I WAS JUST A CAT!
YOU FRIGHTENED ME. ENOUGH THAT I WANTED TO...
NEVER MIND.
THAT'S MY TACKY LITTLE CROSS TO BEAR.

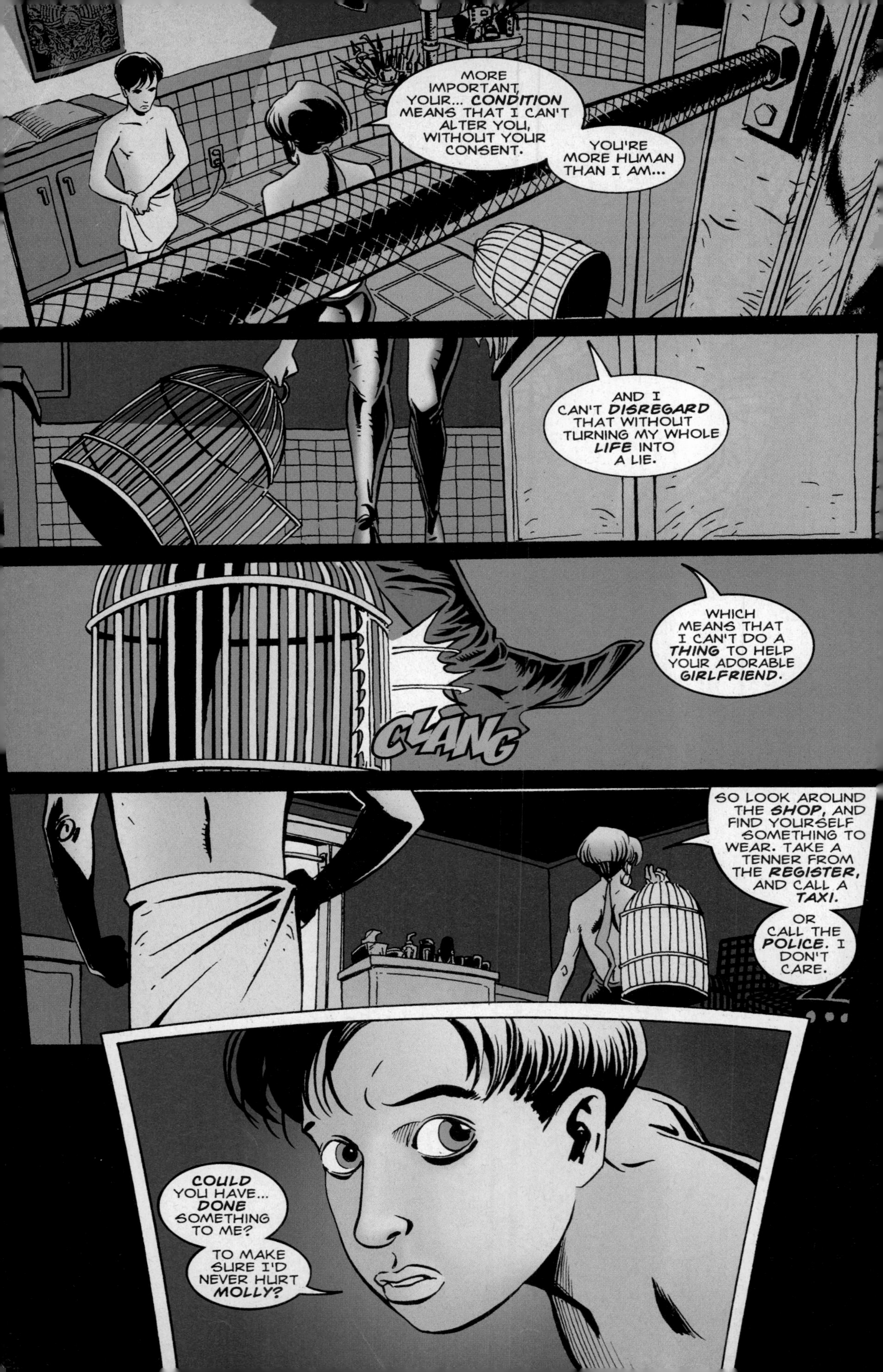
MORE IMPORTANT, YOUR... CONDITION MEANS THAT I CAN'T ALTER YOU, WITHOUT YOUR CONSENT.
YOU'RE MORE HUMAN THAN I AM...
AND I CAN'T DISREGARD THAT WITHOUT TURNING MY WHOLE LIFE INTO A LIE.
WHICH MEANS THAT I CAN'T DO A THING TO HELP YOUR ADORABLE GIRLFRIEND.
CLANG
SO LOOK AROUND THE SHOP, AND FIND YOURSELF SOMETHING TO WEAR. TAKE A TENNER FROM THE REGISTER, AND CALL A TAXI.
OR CALL THE POLICE. I DON'T CARE.
COULD YOU HAVE... DONE SOMETHING TO ME?
TO MAKE SURE I'D NEVER HURT MOLLY?

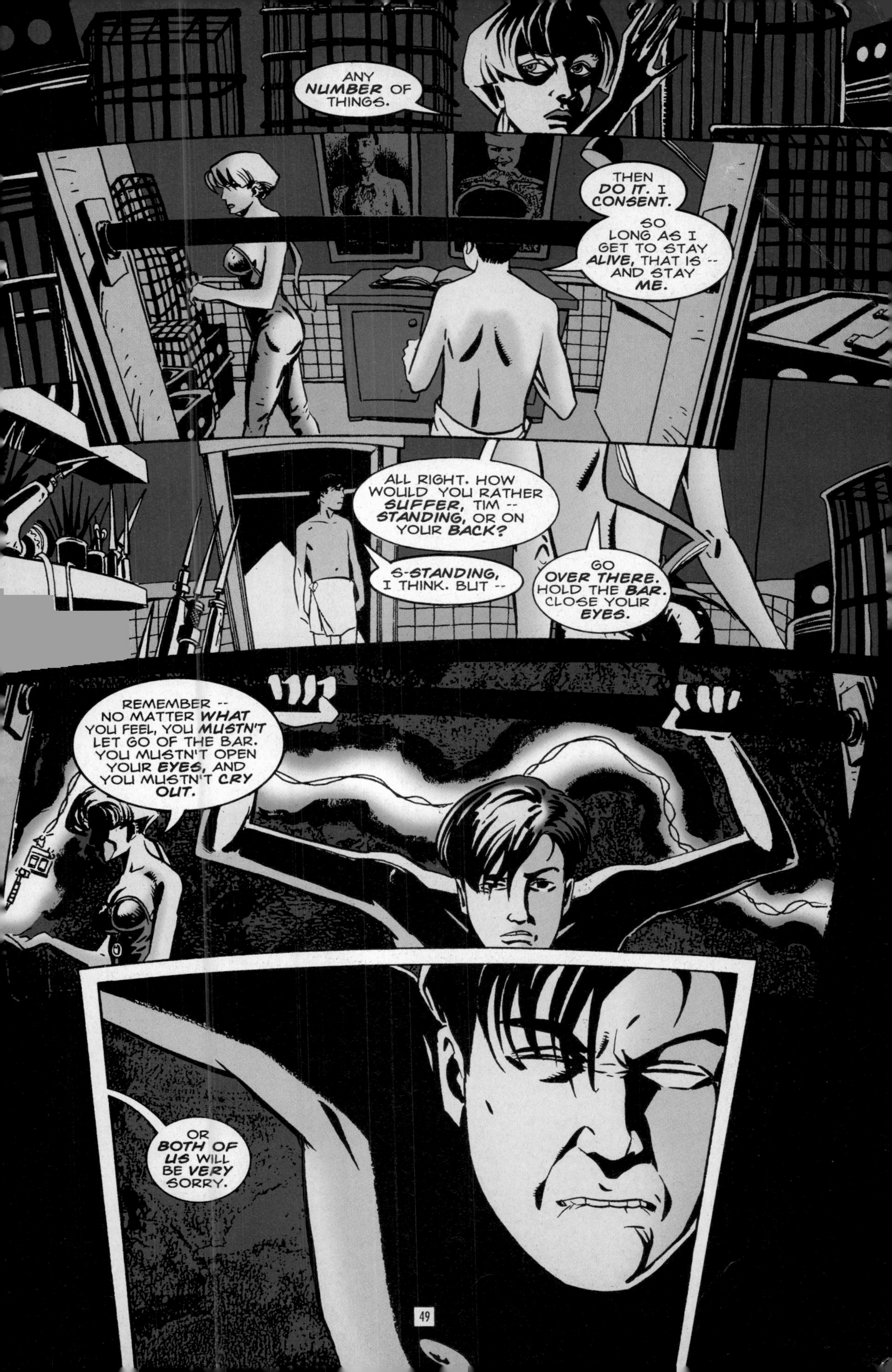
ANY NUMBER OF THINGS.
THEN DO IT. I CONSENT.
SO LONG AS I GET TO STAY ALIVE, THAT IS -- AND STAY ME.
ALL RIGHT. HOW WOULD YOU RATHER SUFFER, TIM -- STANDING, OR ON YOUR BACK?
S-STANDING, I THINK. BUT --
GO OVER THERE. HOLD THE BAR. CLOSE YOUR EYES.
REMEMBER -- NO MATTER WHAT YOU FEEL, YOU MUSTN'T LET GO OF THE BAR. YOU MUSTN'T OPEN YOUR EYES, AND YOU MUSTN'T CRY OUT.
OR BOTH OF US WILL BE VERY SORRY.

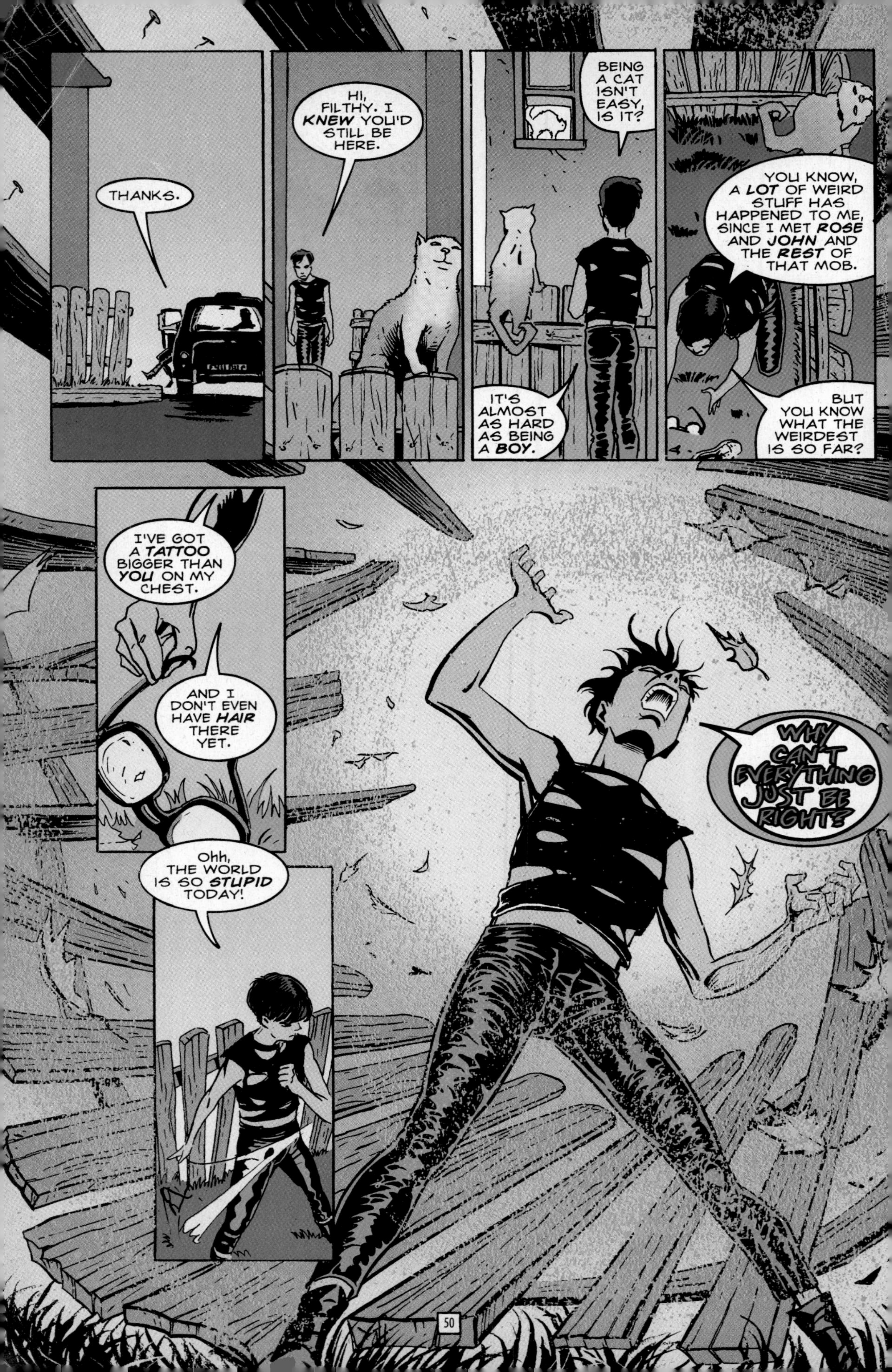
THANKS.
HI, FILTHY. I KNEW YOU'D STILL BE HERE.
BEING A CAT ISN'T EASY, IS IT?
IT'S ALMOST AS HARD AS BEING A BOY.
YOU KNOW, A LOT OF WEIRD STUFF HAS HAPPENED TO ME, SINCE I MET ROSE AND JOHN AND THE REST OF THAT MOB.
BUT YOU KNOW WHAT THE WEIRDEST IS SO FAR?
I'VE GOT A TATTOO BIGGER THAN YOU ON MY CHEST.
AND I DON'T EVEN HAVE HAIR THERE YET.
Ohh, THE WORLD IS SO STUPID TODAY!
WHY CAN'T EVERYTHING JUST BE RIGHT?

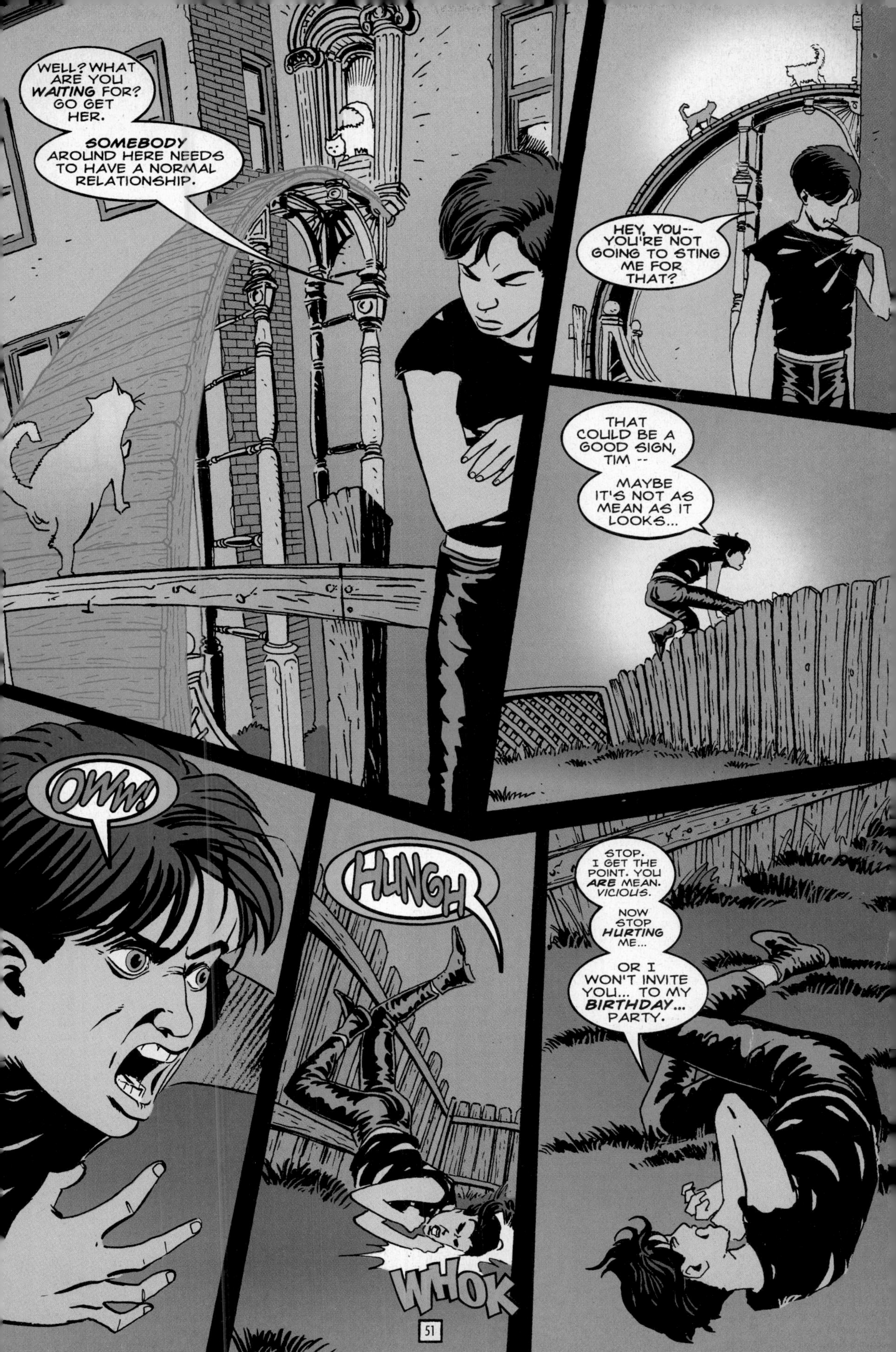
WELL? WHAT ARE YOU *WAITING* FOR? GO GET HER.
SOMEBODY AROUND HERE NEEDS TO HAVE A NORMAL RELATIONSHIP.
HEY, YOU-- YOU'RE NOT GOING TO STING ME FOR THAT?
THAT COULD BE A GOOD SIGN, TIM --
MAYBE IT'S NOT AS MEAN AS IT LOOKS...
OWW!
HUNGH
WHOK
STOP. I GET THE POINT. YOU *ARE* MEAN. *VICIOUS*.
NOW STOP *HURTING* ME...
OR I WON'T INVITE YOU... TO MY *BIRTHDAY*... PARTY.

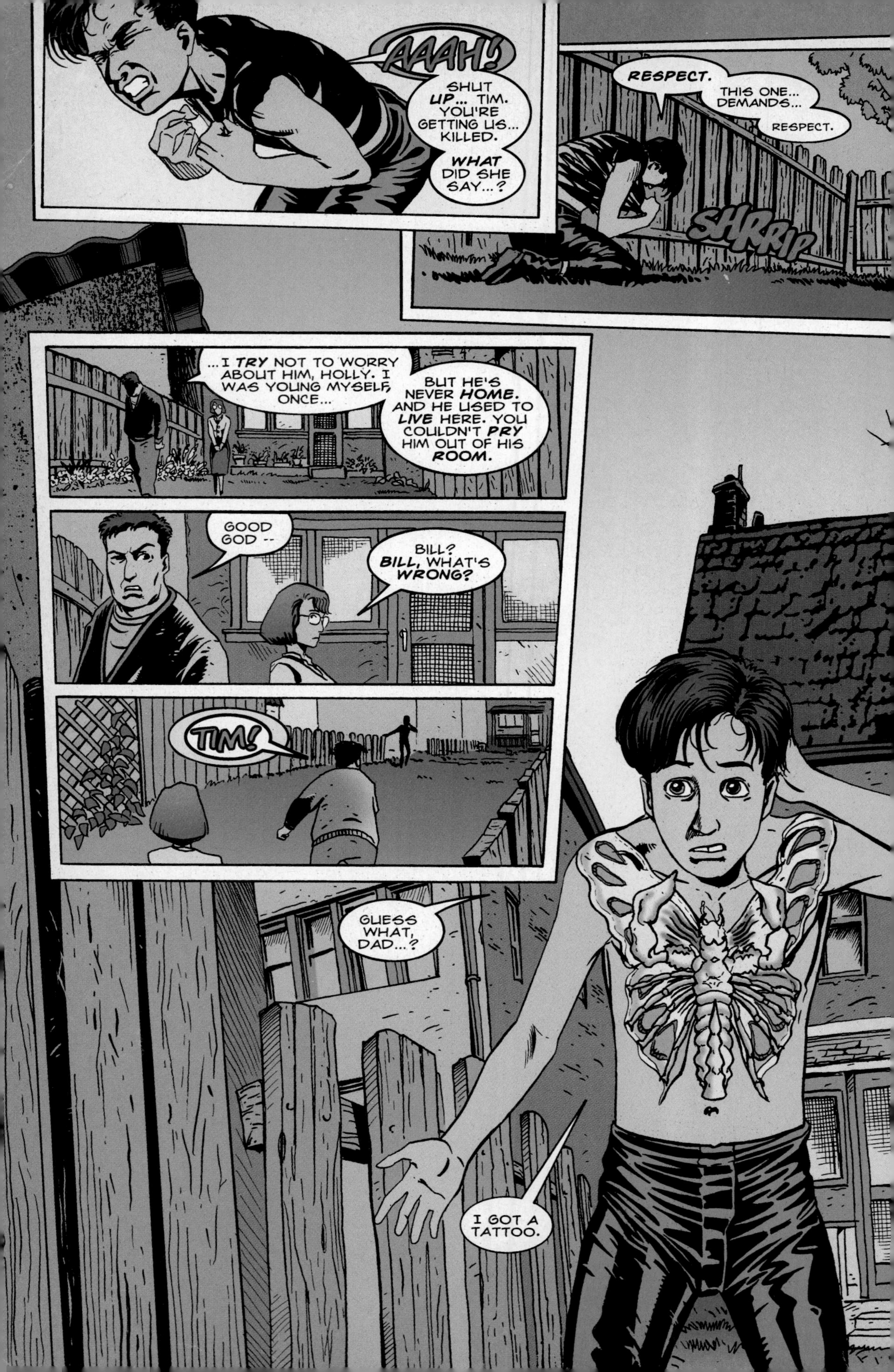
AAAH!
SHUT UP... TIM. YOU'RE GETTING US... KILLED.
WHAT DID SHE SAY...?
RESPECT.
THIS ONE... DEMANDS...
RESPECT.
SHRRIP
...I TRY NOT TO WORRY ABOUT HIM, HOLLY. I WAS YOUNG MYSELF, ONCE...
BUT HE'S NEVER HOME. AND HE USED TO LIVE HERE. YOU COULDN'T PRY HIM OUT OF HIS ROOM.
GOOD GOD --
BILL? BILL, WHAT'S WRONG?
TIM!
GUESS WHAT, DAD...?
I GOT A TATTOO.

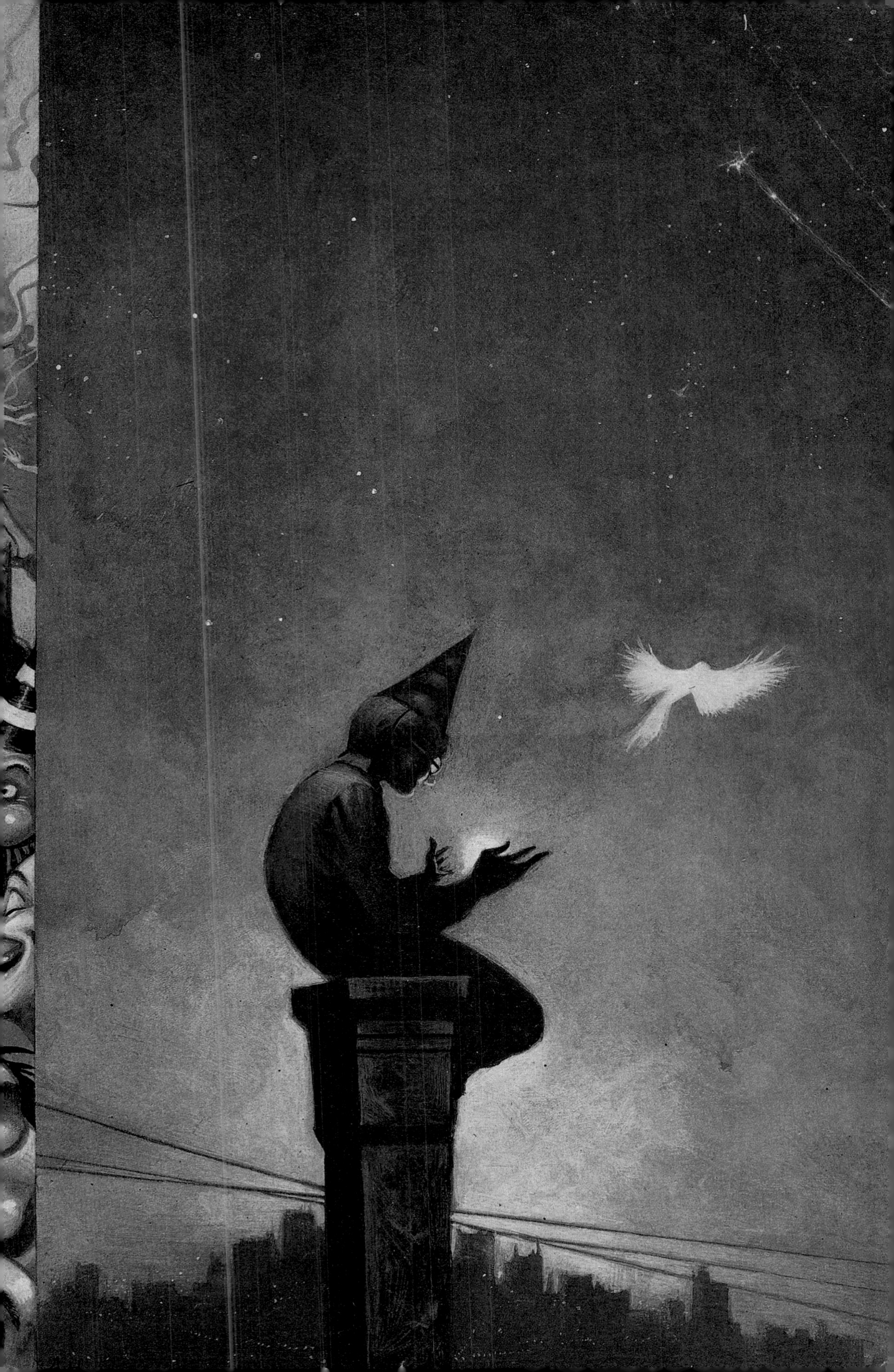

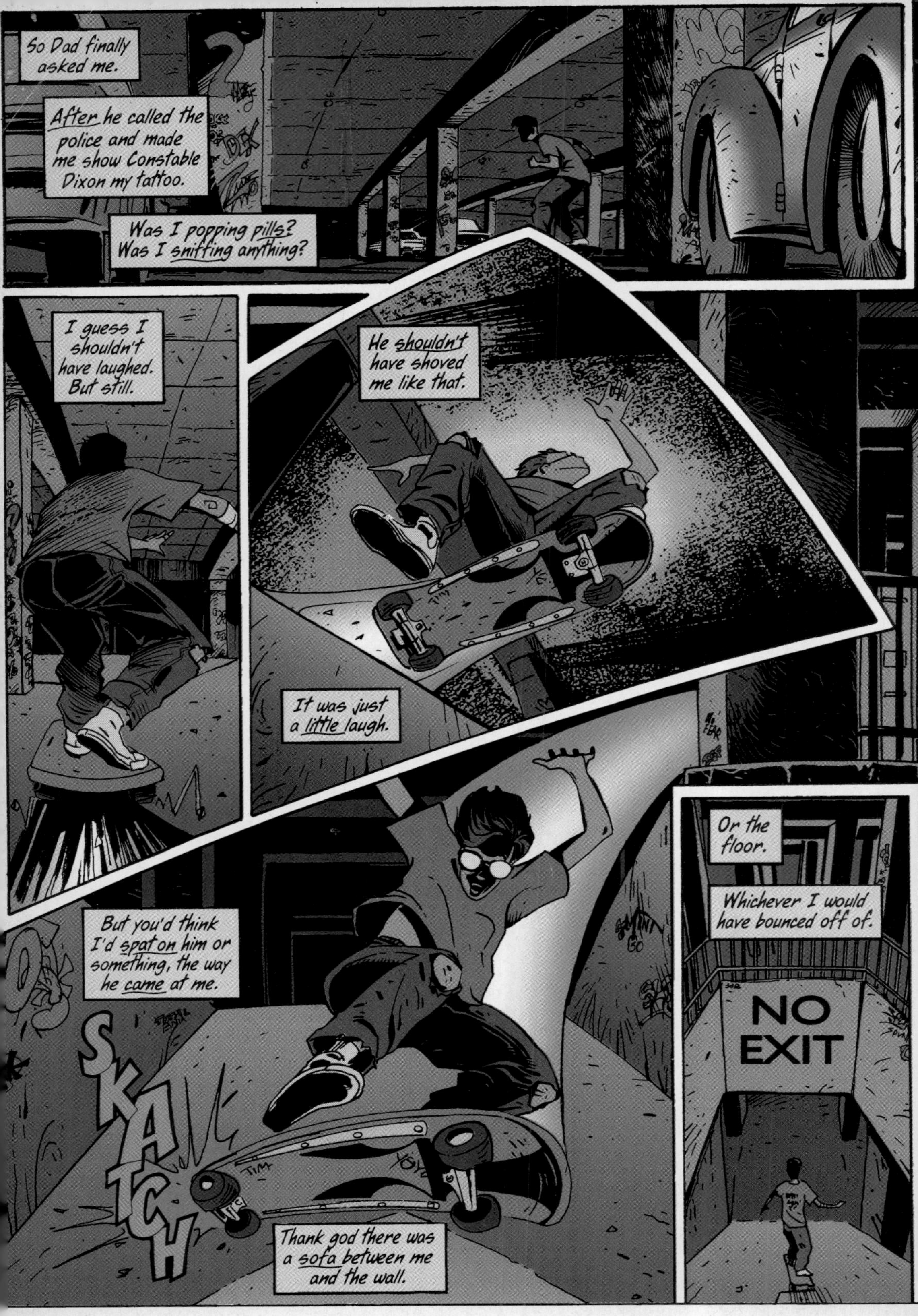
So Dad finally asked me.
After he called the police and made me show Constable Dixon my tattoo.
Was I popping pills? Was I sniffing anything?
I guess I shouldn't have laughed. But still.
He shouldn't have shoved me like that.
It was just a little laugh.
But you'd think I'd spat on him or something, the way he came at me.
SKATCH
Thank god there was a sofa between me and the wall.
Or the floor.
Whichever I would have bounced off of.
NO EXIT

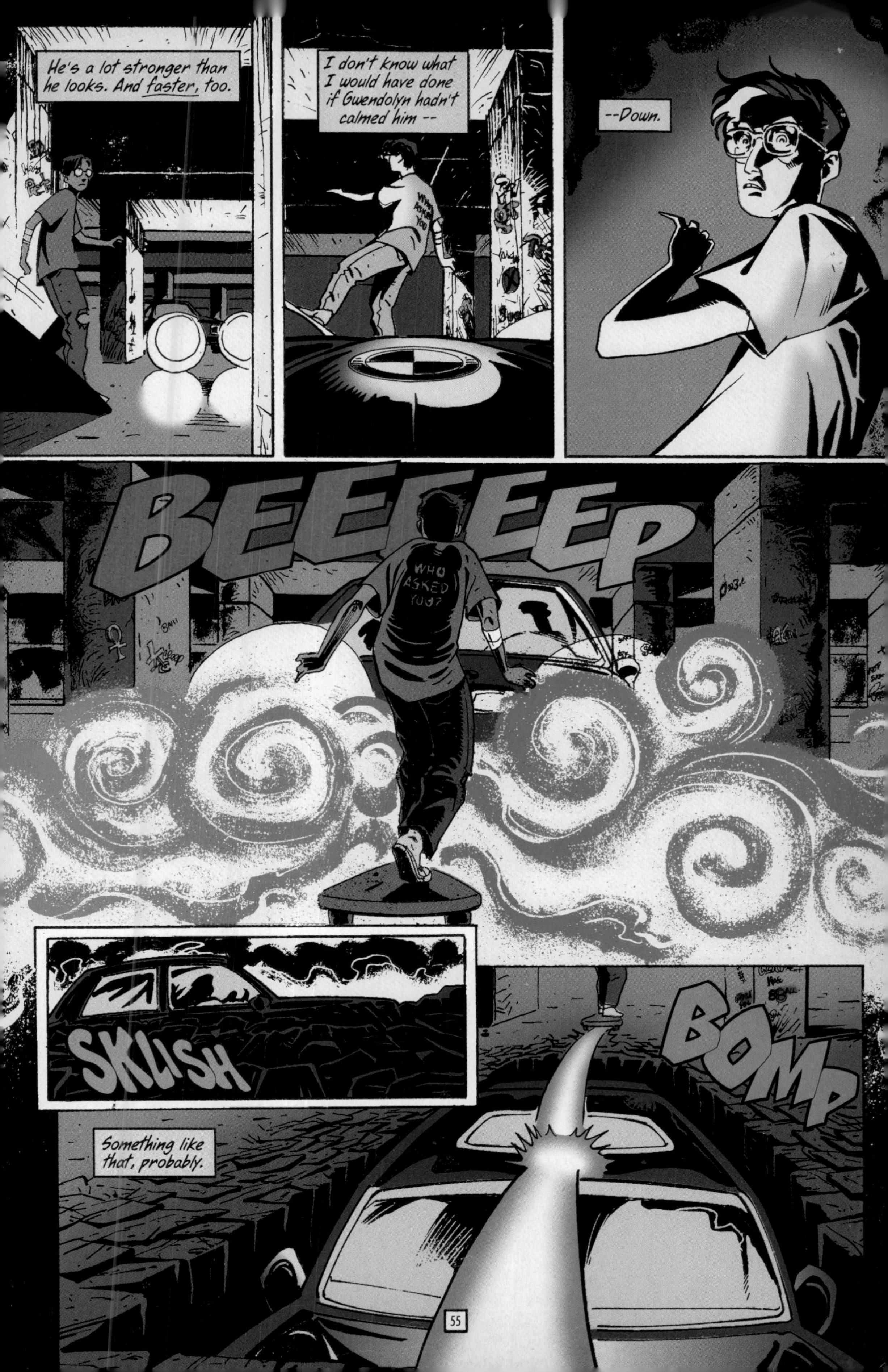

He's a lot stronger than he looks. And faster, too.
I don't know what I would have done if Gwendolyn hadn't calmed him --
--Down.
BEEEEEP
WHO ASKED YOU?
SKLISH
BOMP
Something like that, probably.

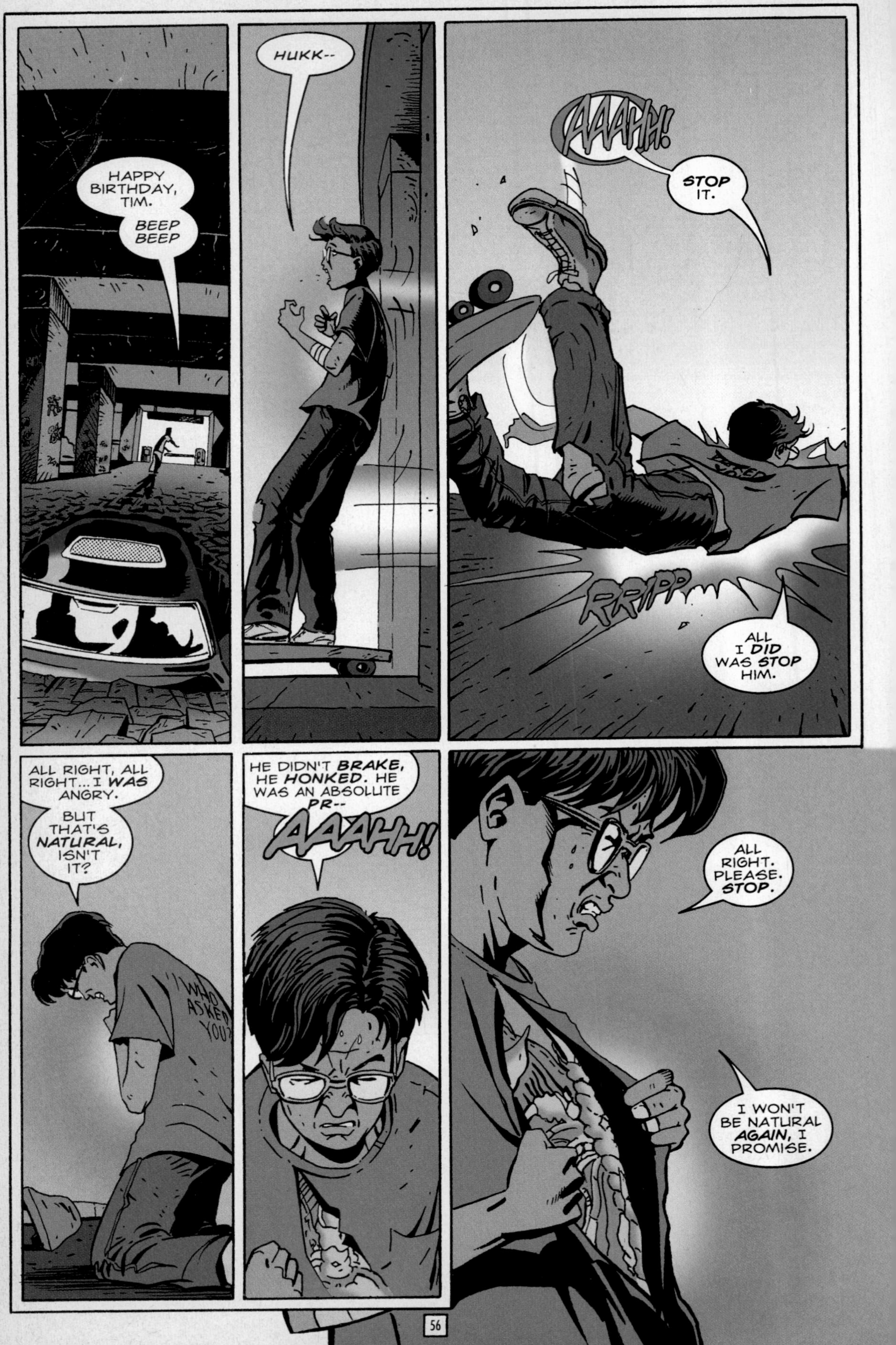
HAPPY BIRTHDAY, TIM.
BEEP BEEP
HUKK--
AAAHH!
STOP IT.
RRIPP
ALL I DID WAS STOP HIM.
ALL RIGHT, ALL RIGHT... I WAS ANGRY.
BUT THAT'S NATURAL, ISN'T IT?
WHO ASKED YOU?
HE DIDN'T BRAKE, HE HONKED. HE WAS AN ABSOLUTE PR--
AAAHH!
ALL RIGHT. PLEASE. STOP.
I WON'T BE NATURAL AGAIN, I PROMISE.

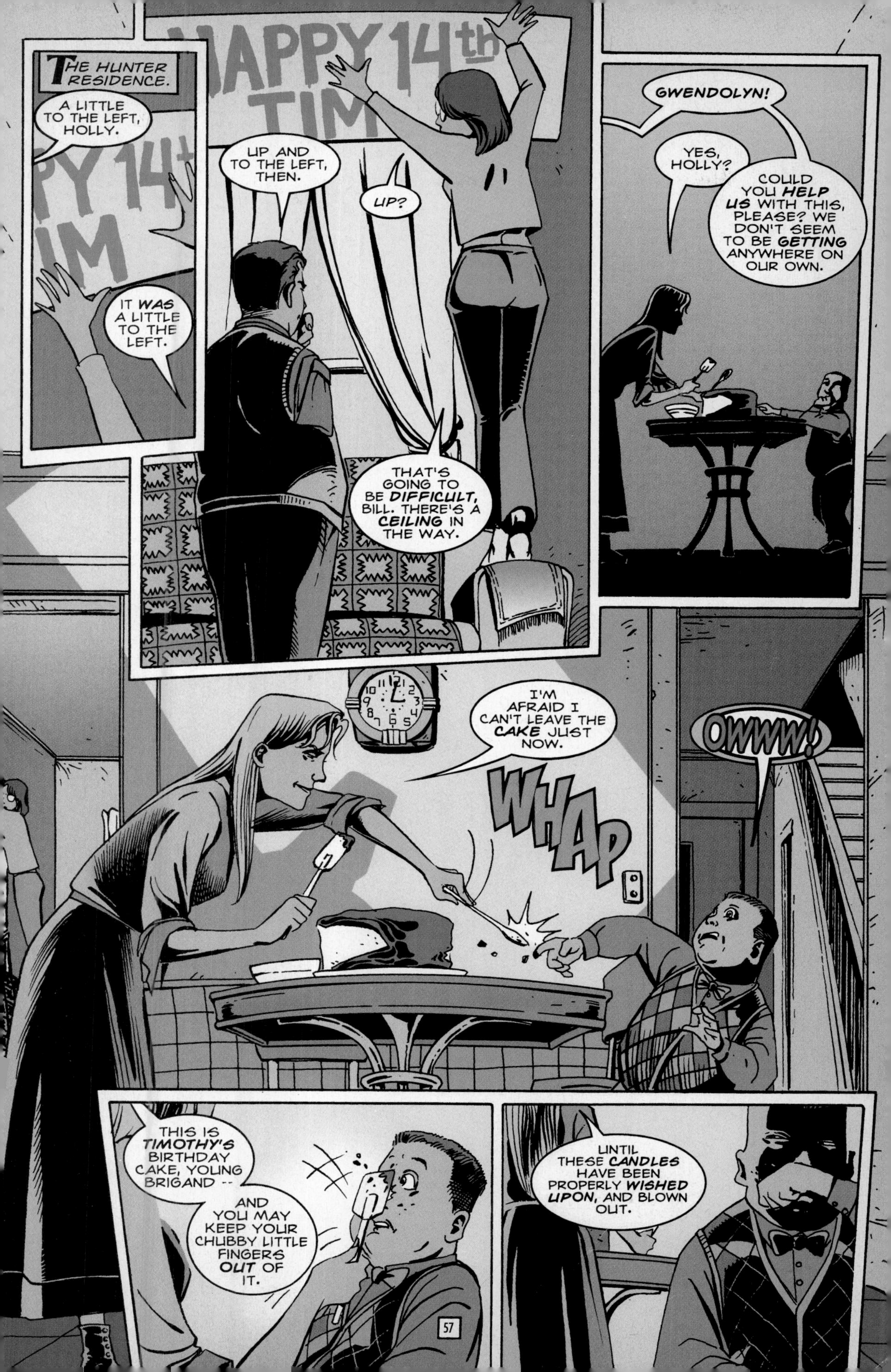
THE HUNTER RESIDENCE.
A LITTLE TO THE LEFT, HOLLY.
HAPPY 14th TIM
UP AND TO THE LEFT, THEN.
UP?
IT WAS A LITTLE TO THE LEFT.
THAT'S GOING TO BE DIFFICULT, BILL. THERE'S A CEILING IN THE WAY.
GWENDOLYN!
YES, HOLLY?
COULD YOU HELP US WITH THIS, PLEASE? WE DON'T SEEM TO BE GETTING ANYWHERE ON OUR OWN.
I'M AFRAID I CAN'T LEAVE THE CAKE JUST NOW.
WHAP
OWWW!
THIS IS TIMOTHY'S BIRTHDAY CAKE, YOUNG BRIGAND --
AND YOU MAY KEEP YOUR CHUBBY LITTLE FINGERS OUT OF IT.
UNTIL THESE CANDLES HAVE BEEN PROPERLY WISHED UPON, AND BLOWN OUT.

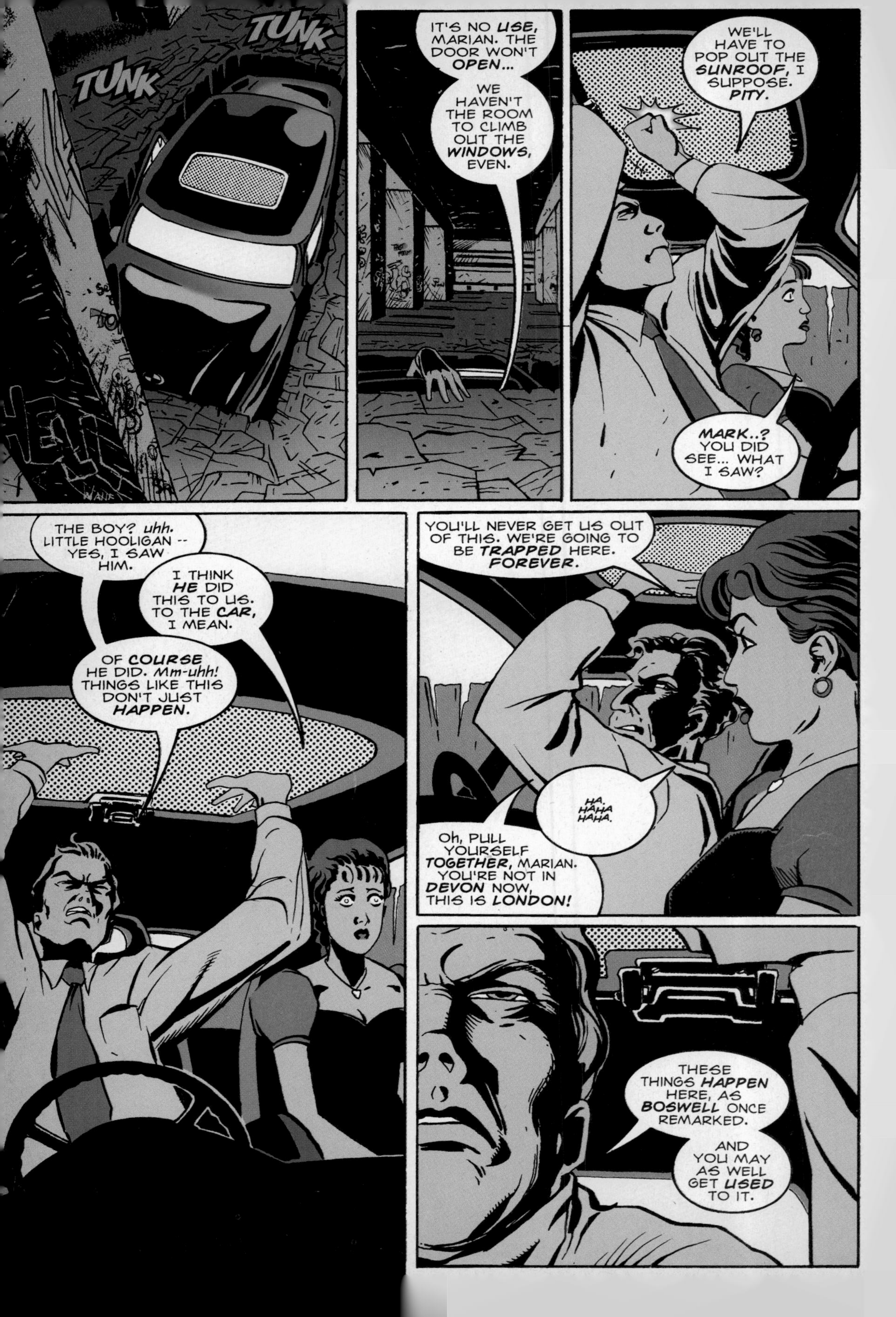
TUNK
TUNK
IT'S NO USE, MARIAN. THE DOOR WON'T OPEN...
WE HAVEN'T THE ROOM TO CLIMB OUT THE WINDOWS, EVEN.
WE'LL HAVE TO POP OUT THE SUNROOF, I SUPPOSE. PITY.
MARK..? YOU DID SEE... WHAT I SAW?
THE BOY? uhh. LITTLE HOOLIGAN -- YES, I SAW HIM.
I THINK HE DID THIS TO US. TO THE CAR, I MEAN.
OF COURSE HE DID. Mm-uhh! THINGS LIKE THIS DON'T JUST HAPPEN.
YOU'LL NEVER GET US OUT OF THIS. WE'RE GOING TO BE TRAPPED HERE. FOREVER.
HA. HAHA HAHA.
Oh, PULL YOURSELF TOGETHER, MARIAN. YOU'RE NOT IN DEVON NOW, THIS IS LONDON!
THESE THINGS HAPPEN HERE, AS BOSWELL ONCE REMARKED.
AND YOU MAY AS WELL GET USED TO IT.

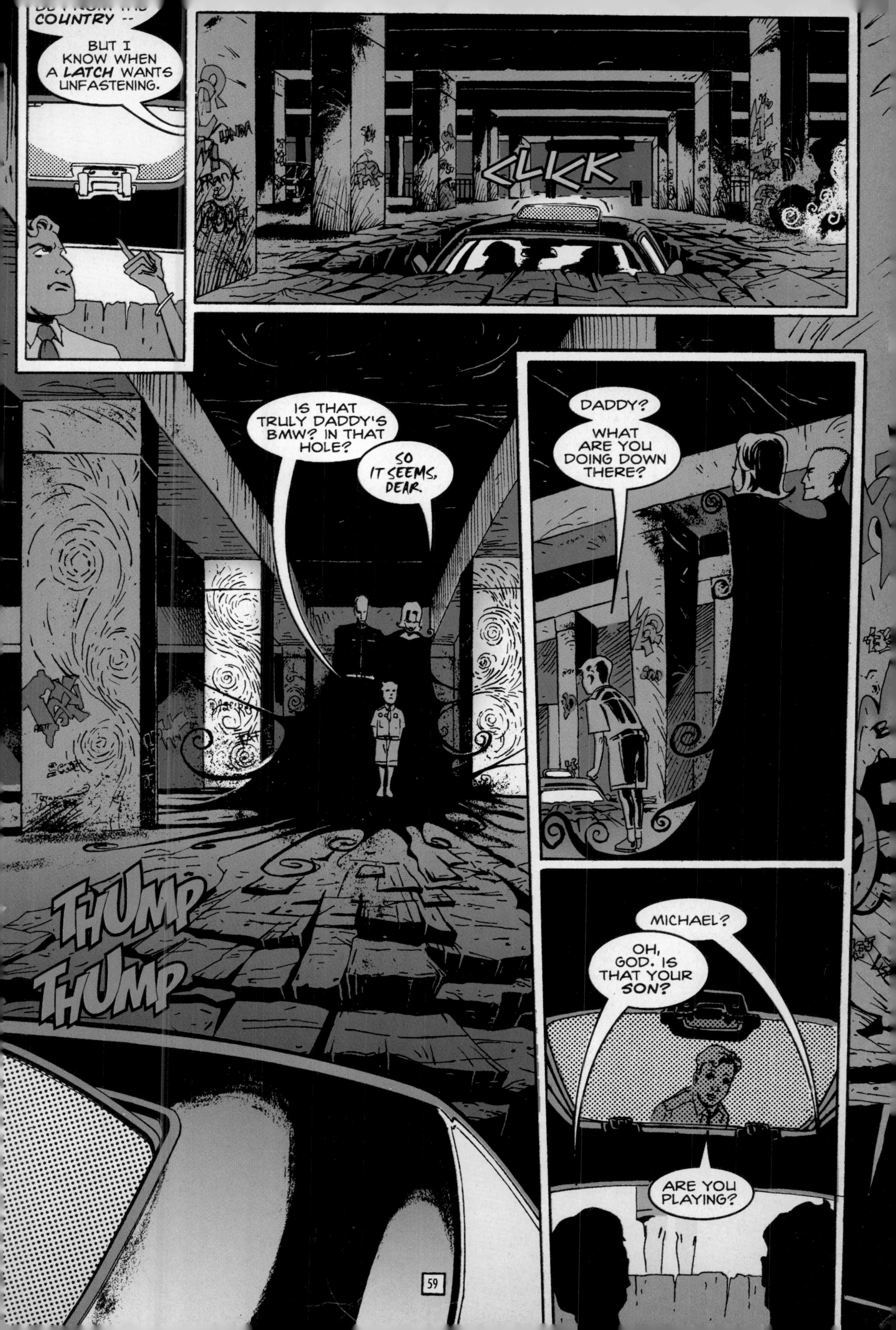
COUNTRY --
BUT I KNOW WHEN A LATCH WANTS UNFASTENING.
CLICK
IS THAT TRULY DADDY'S BMW? IN THAT HOLE?
SO IT SEEMS, DEAR.
THUMP THUMP
DADDY?
WHAT ARE YOU DOING DOWN THERE?
MICHAEL?
OH, GOD. IS THAT YOUR SON?
ARE YOU PLAYING?

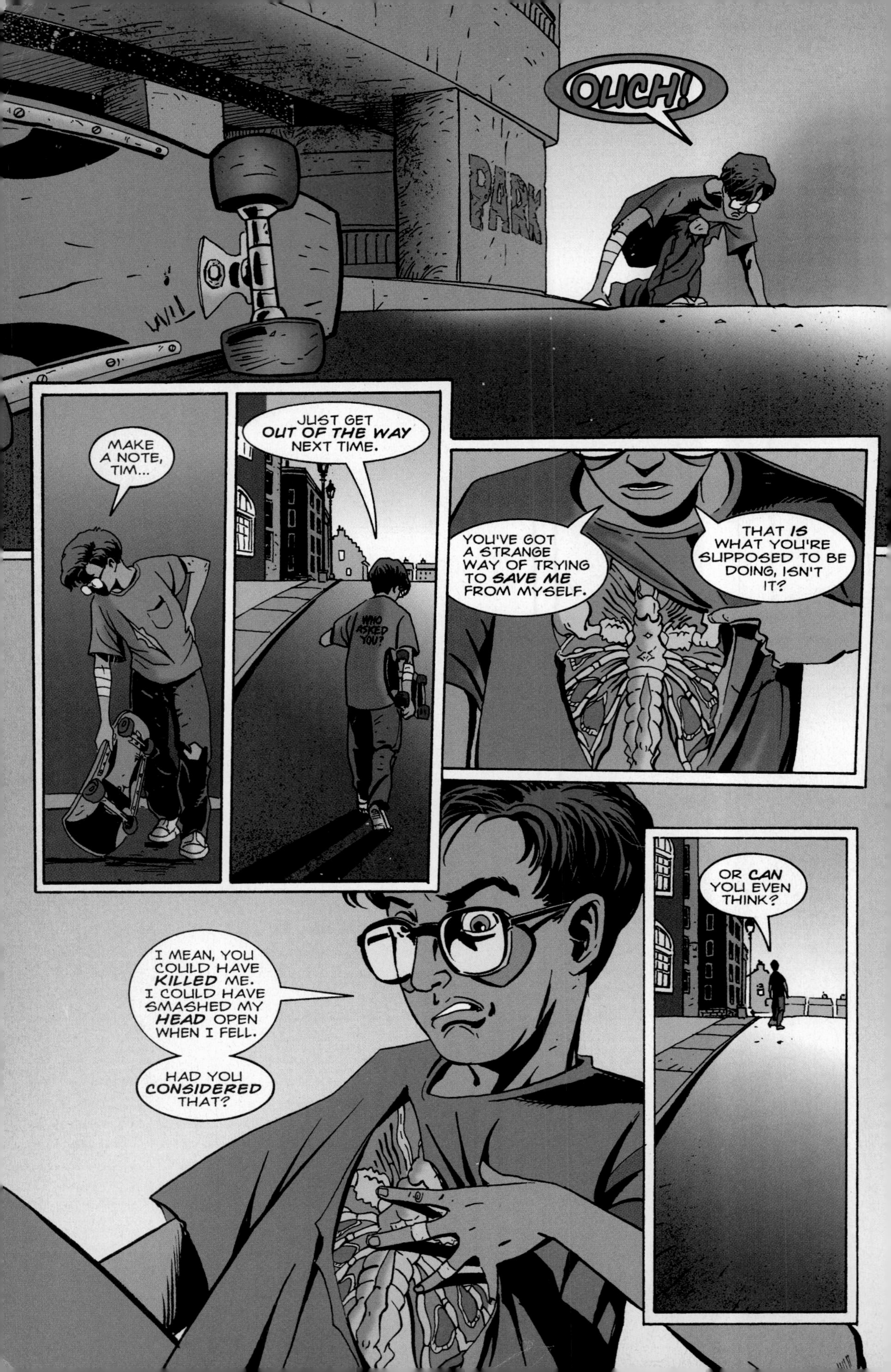
OUCH!
PARK
WILL
MAKE A NOTE, TIM...
JUST GET *OUT OF THE WAY* NEXT TIME.
WHO ASKED YOU?
YOU'VE GOT A STRANGE WAY OF TRYING TO *SAVE ME* FROM MYSELF.
THAT *IS* WHAT YOU'RE SUPPOSED TO BE DOING, ISN'T IT?
I MEAN, YOU COULD HAVE *KILLED* ME. I COULD HAVE SMASHED MY *HEAD* OPEN WHEN I FELL.
HAD YOU *CONSIDERED* THAT?
OR *CAN* YOU EVEN THINK?

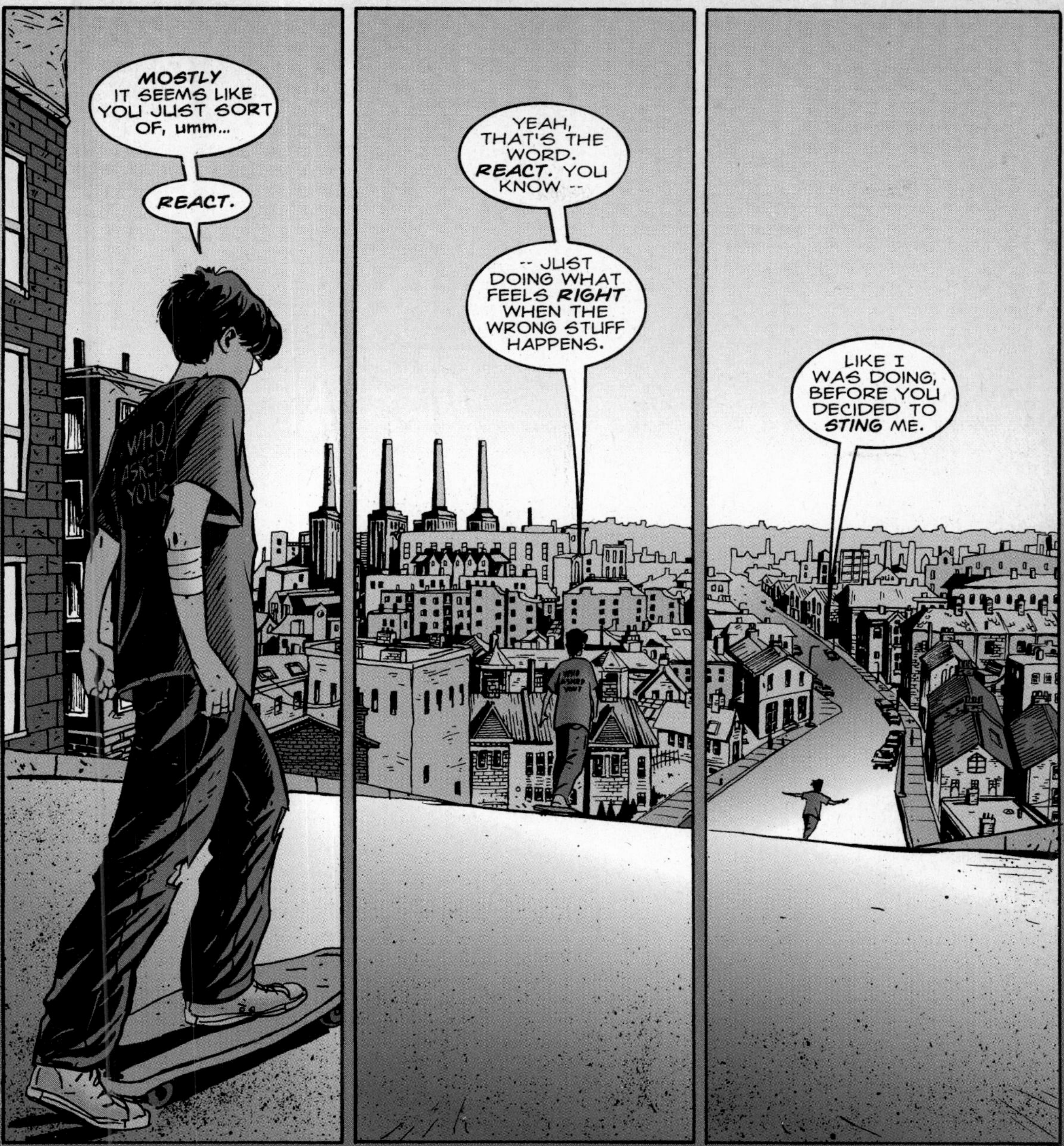

MOSTLY IT SEEMS LIKE YOU JUST SORT OF, umm...
REACT.
YEAH, THAT'S THE WORD. REACT. YOU KNOW --
-- JUST DOING WHAT FEELS RIGHT WHEN THE WRONG STUFF HAPPENS.
LIKE I WAS DOING, BEFORE YOU DECIDED TO STING ME.

Red Rover, Red Rover.

John Ney Rieber *writer*

Peter Gross *artist*

Neil Gaiman *consultant*

Sherilyn van Valkenburgh *colorist*

Richard Starkings and Comicraft *lettering*

Julie Rottenberg *editor*

Timothy Hunter and the *Books of Magic* created by *Neil Gaiman & John Bolton*

I THOUGHT YOU WERE CALLED OUT OF TOWN ON BUSINESS, DADDY. MUMMY SAID YOU WERE.

MICHAEL -- DADDY'S STUCK IN THE CAR, SON, AND HE CAN'T GET OUT.

RUN TO THE BOOTH AND FETCH THE ATTENDANT FOR HIM, WOULD YOU?

HULLO. ARE YOU MY DADDY'S SECRETARY?

YOU'RE VERY PRETTY. I WISH MUMMY WERE PRETTY AS YOU.

MICHAEL! I DON'T KNOW WHAT YOU'RE DOING HERE.

BUT YOU'D BETTER FETCH THE ATTENDANT, YOUNG MAN, AND YOU'D BEST BE QUICK ABOUT IT.

OH, I'LL GET YOU OUT, DADDY. IN JUST A MOMENT. BUT THE MARGRAVES SAID I WAS TO SHOW YOU MY ORDEN FIRST.

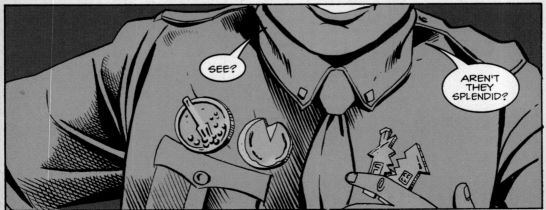

SEE?

AREN'T THEY SPLENDID?

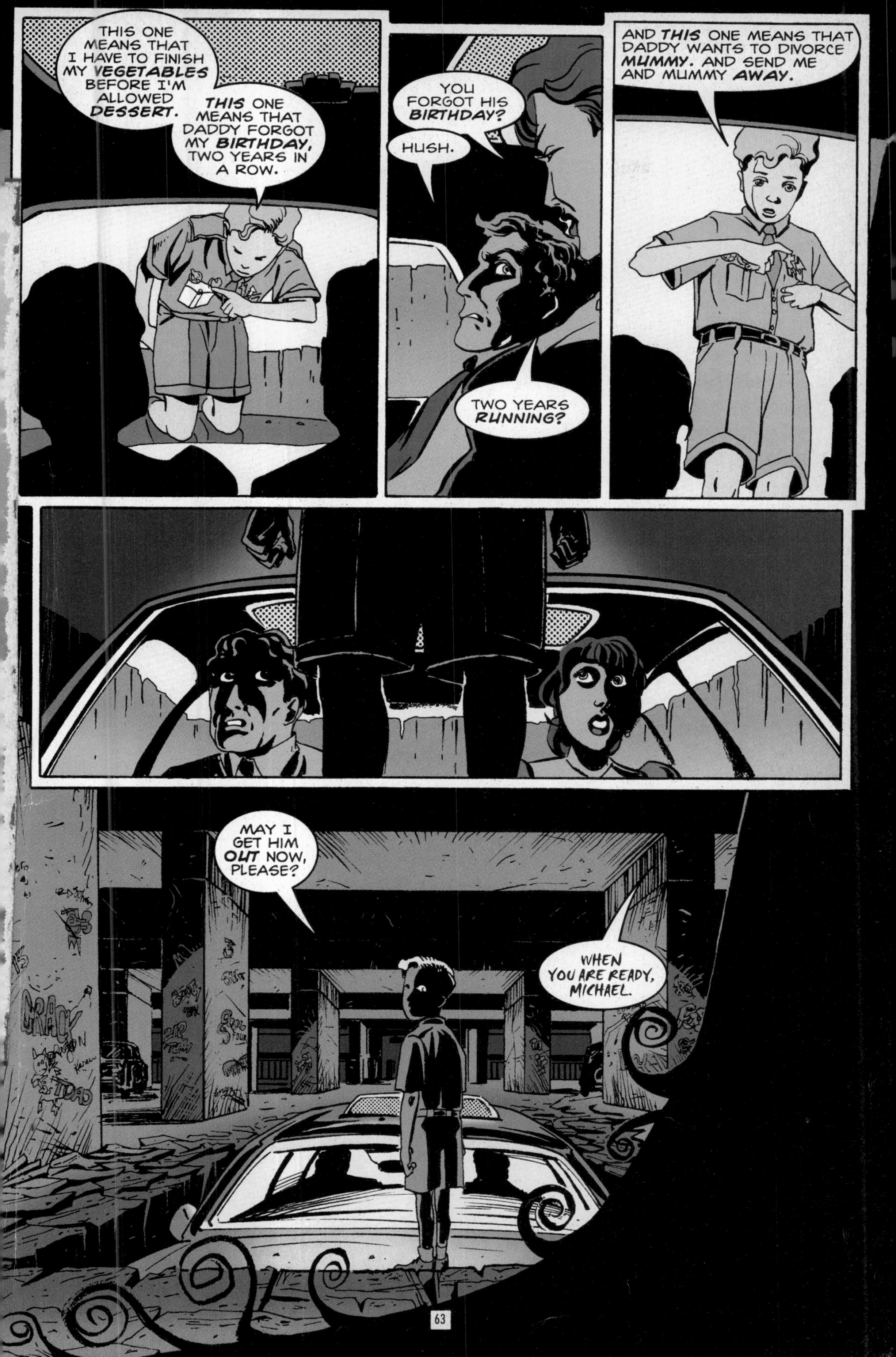
THIS ONE MEANS THAT I HAVE TO FINISH MY VEGETABLES BEFORE I'M ALLOWED DESSERT.
THIS ONE MEANS THAT DADDY FORGOT MY BIRTHDAY, TWO YEARS IN A ROW.
YOU FORGOT HIS BIRTHDAY?
HUSH.
TWO YEARS RUNNING?
AND THIS ONE MEANS THAT DADDY WANTS TO DIVORCE MUMMY. AND SEND ME AND MUMMY AWAY.
MAY I GET HIM OUT NOW, PLEASE?
WHEN YOU ARE READY, MICHAEL.

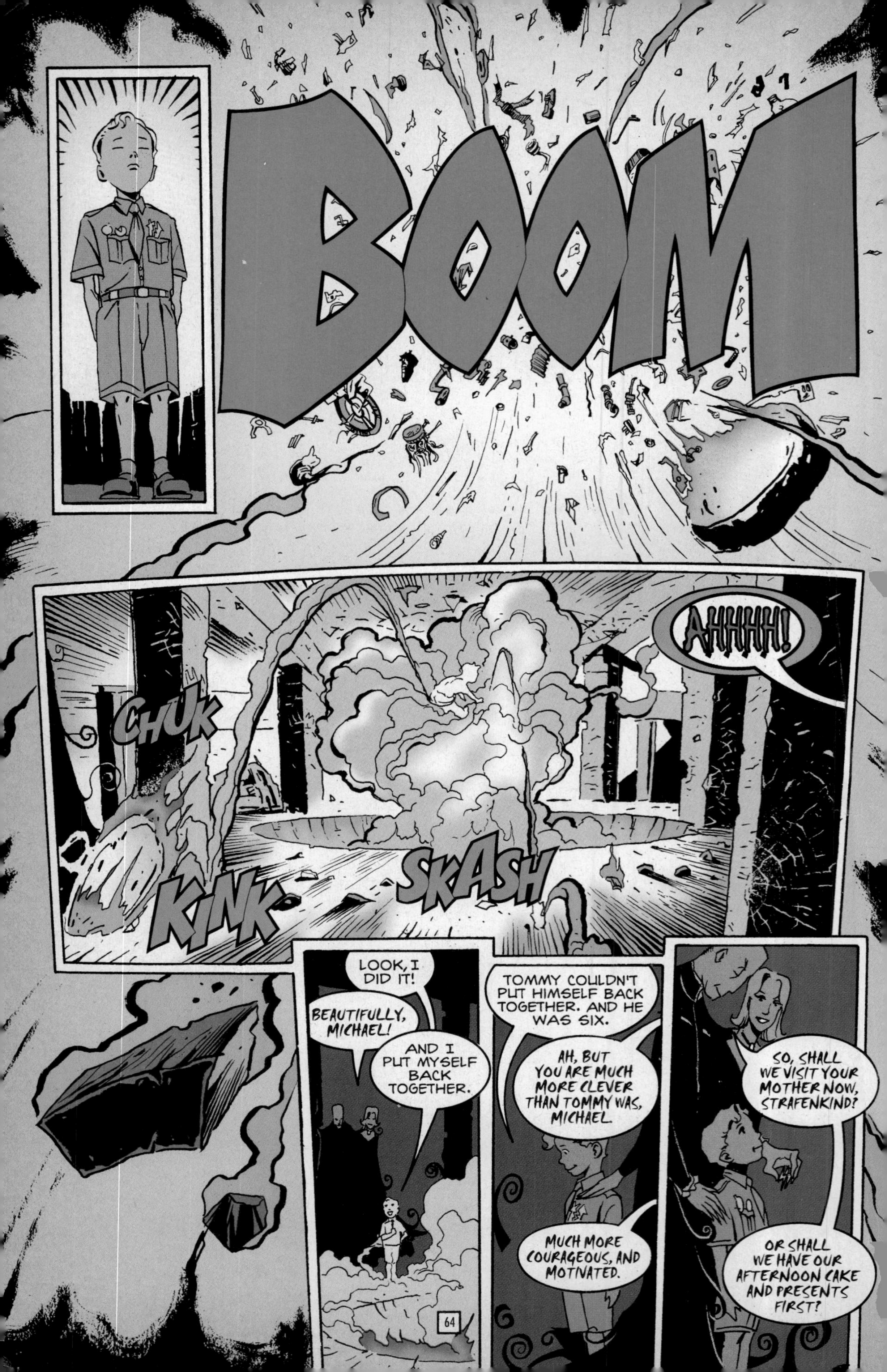
BOOM
AHHHH!
CHUK
KINK
SKASH
LOOK, I DID IT!
BEAUTIFULLY, MICHAEL!
AND I PUT MYSELF BACK TOGETHER.
TOMMY COULDN'T PUT HIMSELF BACK TOGETHER. AND HE WAS SIX.
AH, BUT YOU ARE MUCH MORE CLEVER THAN TOMMY WAS, MICHAEL.
MUCH MORE COURAGEOUS, AND MOTIVATED.
SO, SHALL WE VISIT YOUR MOTHER NOW, STRAFENKIND?
OR SHALL WE HAVE OUR AFTERNOON CAKE AND PRESENTS FIRST?

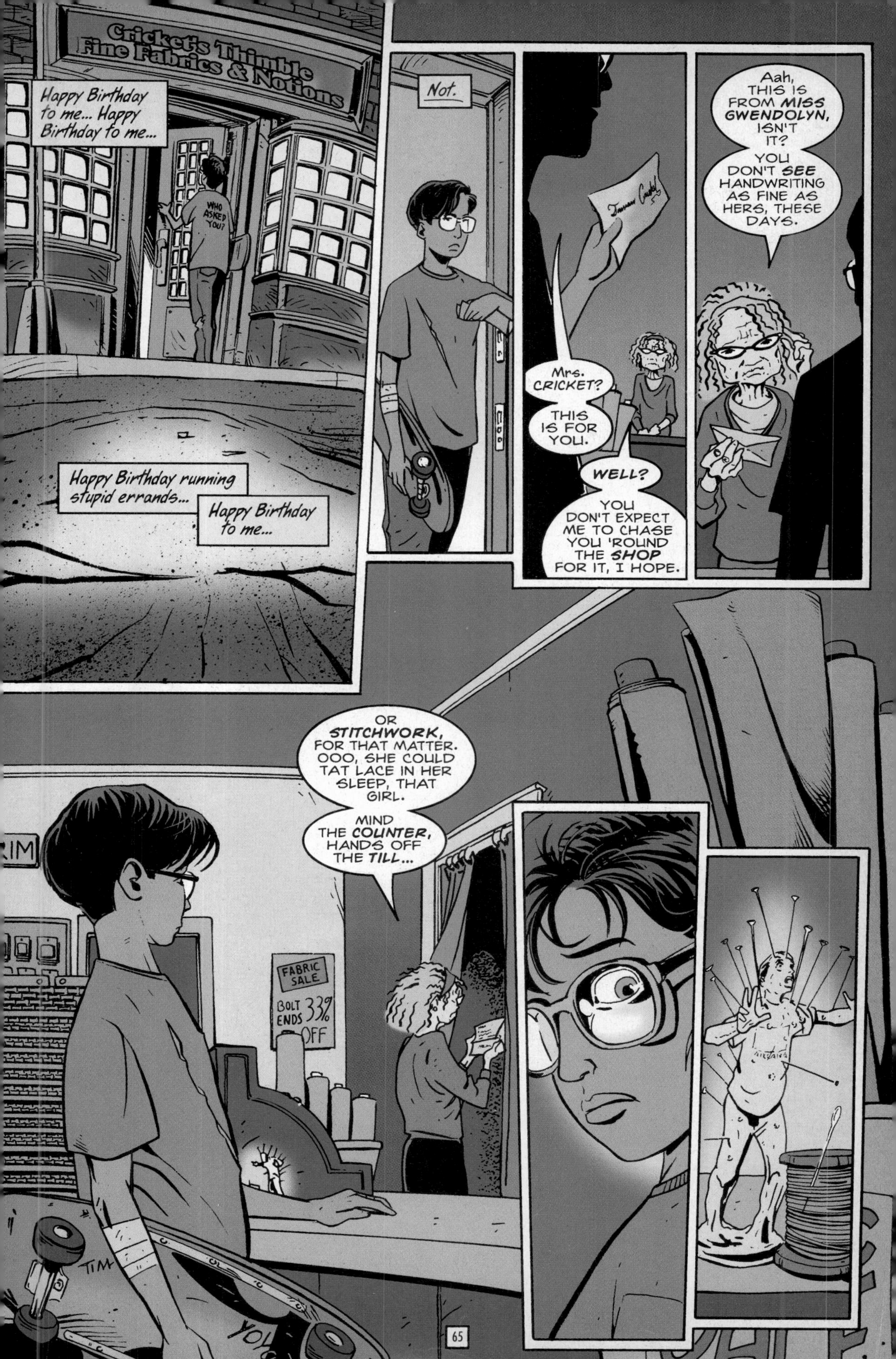

Cricket's Thimble Fine Fabrics & Notions
Happy Birthday to me... Happy Birthday to me...
WHO ASKED YOU?
Happy Birthday running stupid errands...
Happy Birthday to me...
Not.
Mrs. CRICKET?
THIS IS FOR YOU.
WELL?
YOU DON'T EXPECT ME TO CHASE YOU 'ROUND THE SHOP FOR IT, I HOPE.
Aah, THIS IS FROM MISS GWENDOLYN, ISN'T IT?
YOU DON'T SEE HANDWRITING AS FINE AS HERS, THESE DAYS.
OR STITCHWORK, FOR THAT MATTER. OOO, SHE COULD TAT LACE IN HER SLEEP, THAT GIRL.
MIND THE COUNTER, HANDS OFF THE TILL...
FABRIC SALE
BOLT ENDS 33⅓% OFF

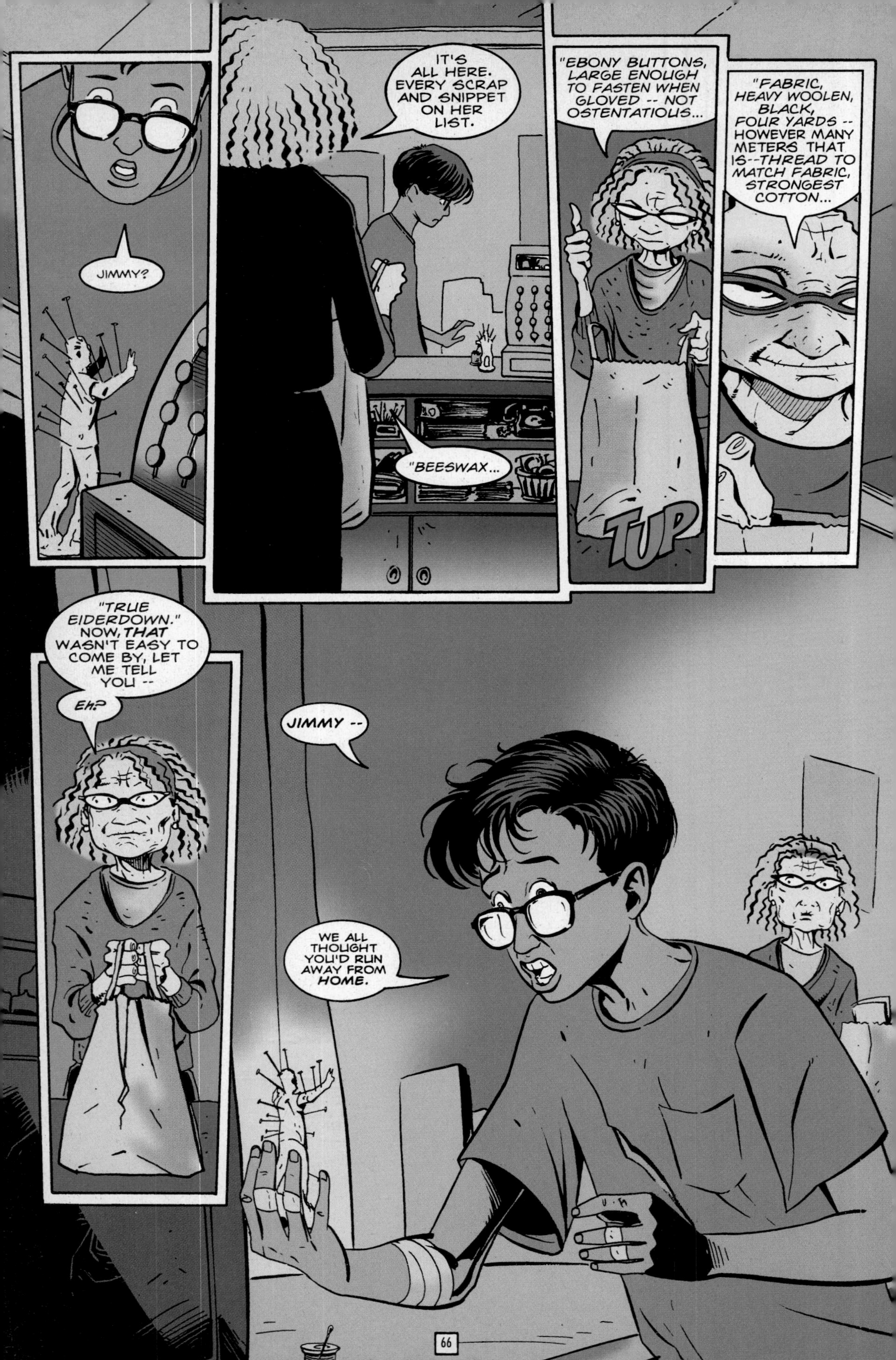
JIMMY?
IT'S ALL HERE. EVERY SCRAP AND SNIPPET ON HER LIST.
"BEESWAX...
"EBONY BUTTONS, LARGE ENOUGH TO FASTEN WHEN GLOVED -- NOT OSTENTATIOUS...
TUP
"FABRIC, HEAVY WOOLEN, BLACK, FOUR YARDS -- HOWEVER MANY METERS THAT IS--THREAD TO MATCH FABRIC, STRONGEST COTTON...
"TRUE EIDERDOWN." NOW, THAT WASN'T EASY TO COME BY, LET ME TELL YOU --
Eh?
JIMMY --
WE ALL THOUGHT YOU'D RUN AWAY FROM HOME.

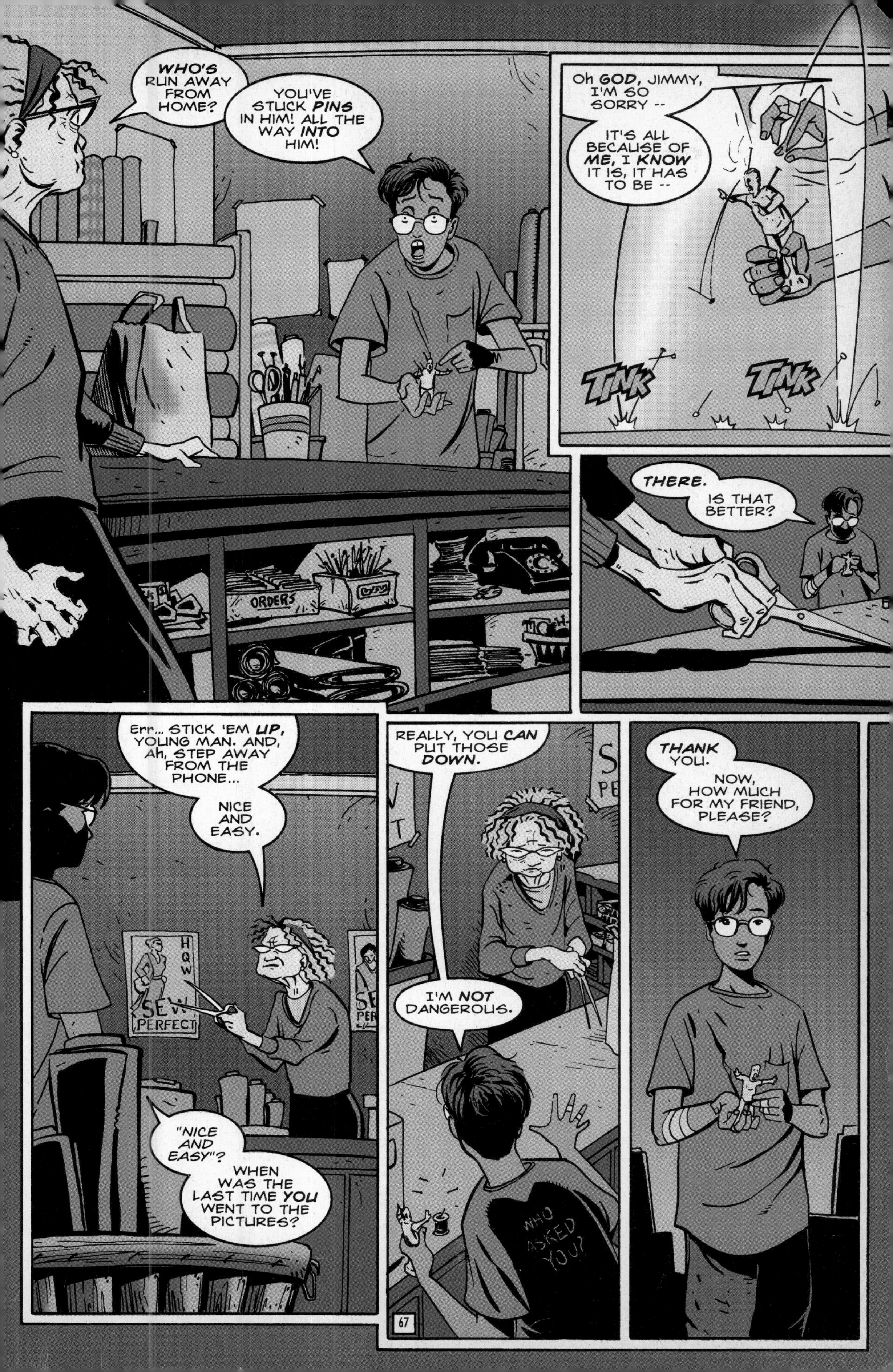
WHO'S RUN AWAY FROM HOME?
YOU'VE STUCK PINS IN HIM! ALL THE WAY INTO HIM!
Oh GOD, JIMMY, I'M SO SORRY --
IT'S ALL BECAUSE OF ME, I KNOW IT IS, IT HAS TO BE --
TINK
TINK
ORDERS
THERE.
IS THAT BETTER?
Err... STICK 'EM UP, YOUNG MAN. AND, Ah, STEP AWAY FROM THE PHONE...
NICE AND EASY.
HQW
SEW PERFECT
"NICE AND EASY"?
WHEN WAS THE LAST TIME YOU WENT TO THE PICTURES?
REALLY, YOU CAN PUT THOSE DOWN.
I'M NOT DANGEROUS.
WHO ASKED YOU?
THANK YOU.
NOW, HOW MUCH FOR MY FRIEND, PLEASE?

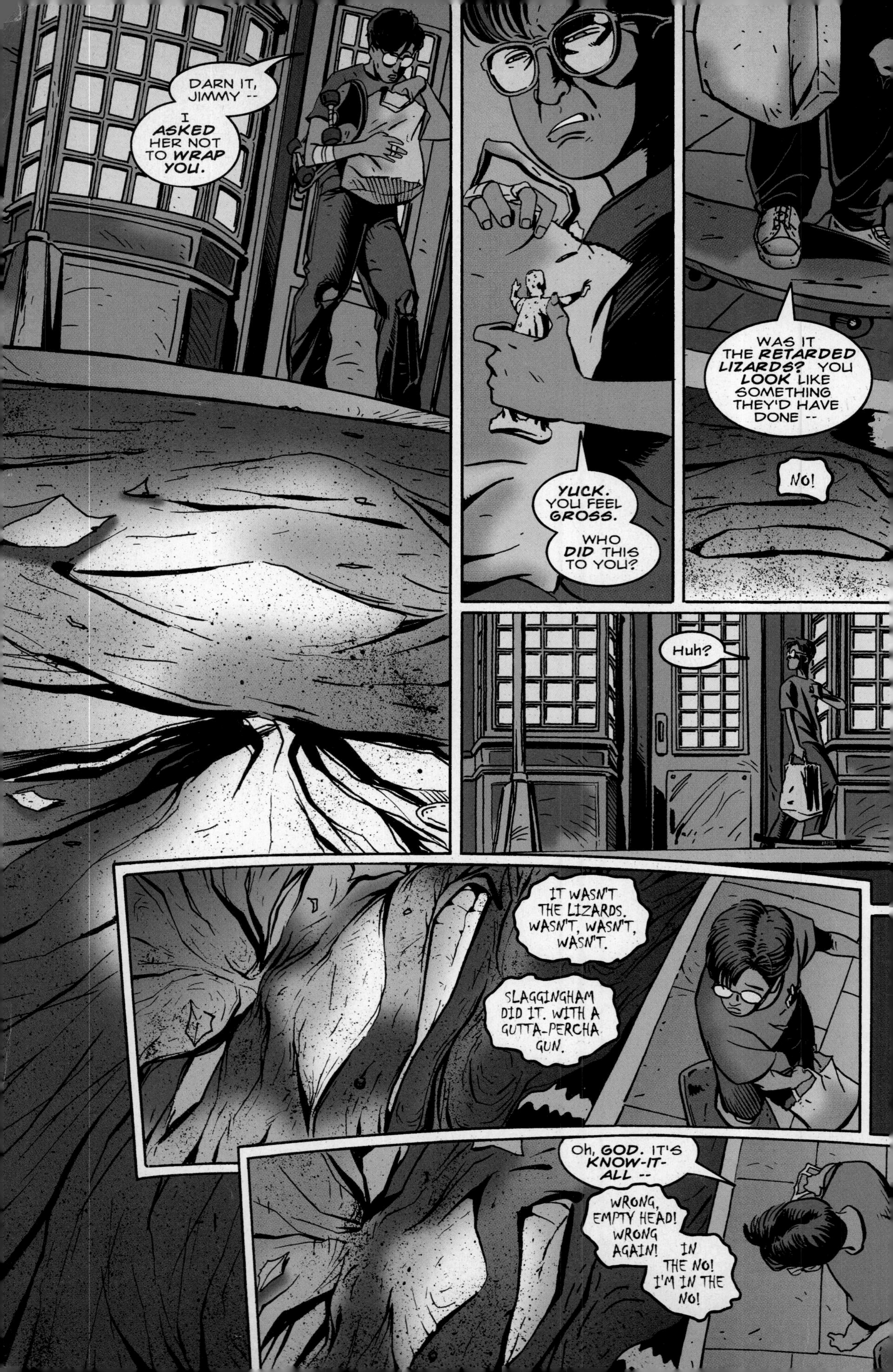
DARN IT, JIMMY --
I ASKED HER NOT TO WRAP YOU.
YUCK. YOU FEEL GROSS.
WHO DID THIS TO YOU?
WAS IT THE RETARDED LIZARDS? YOU LOOK LIKE SOMETHING THEY'D HAVE DONE --
NO!
Huh?
IT WASN'T THE LIZARDS. WASN'T, WASN'T, WASN'T.
SLAGGINGHAM DID IT. WITH A GUTTA-PERCHA GUN.
Oh, GOD. IT'S KNOW-IT-ALL --
WRONG, EMPTY HEAD! WRONG AGAIN!
IN THE NO! I'M IN THE NO!

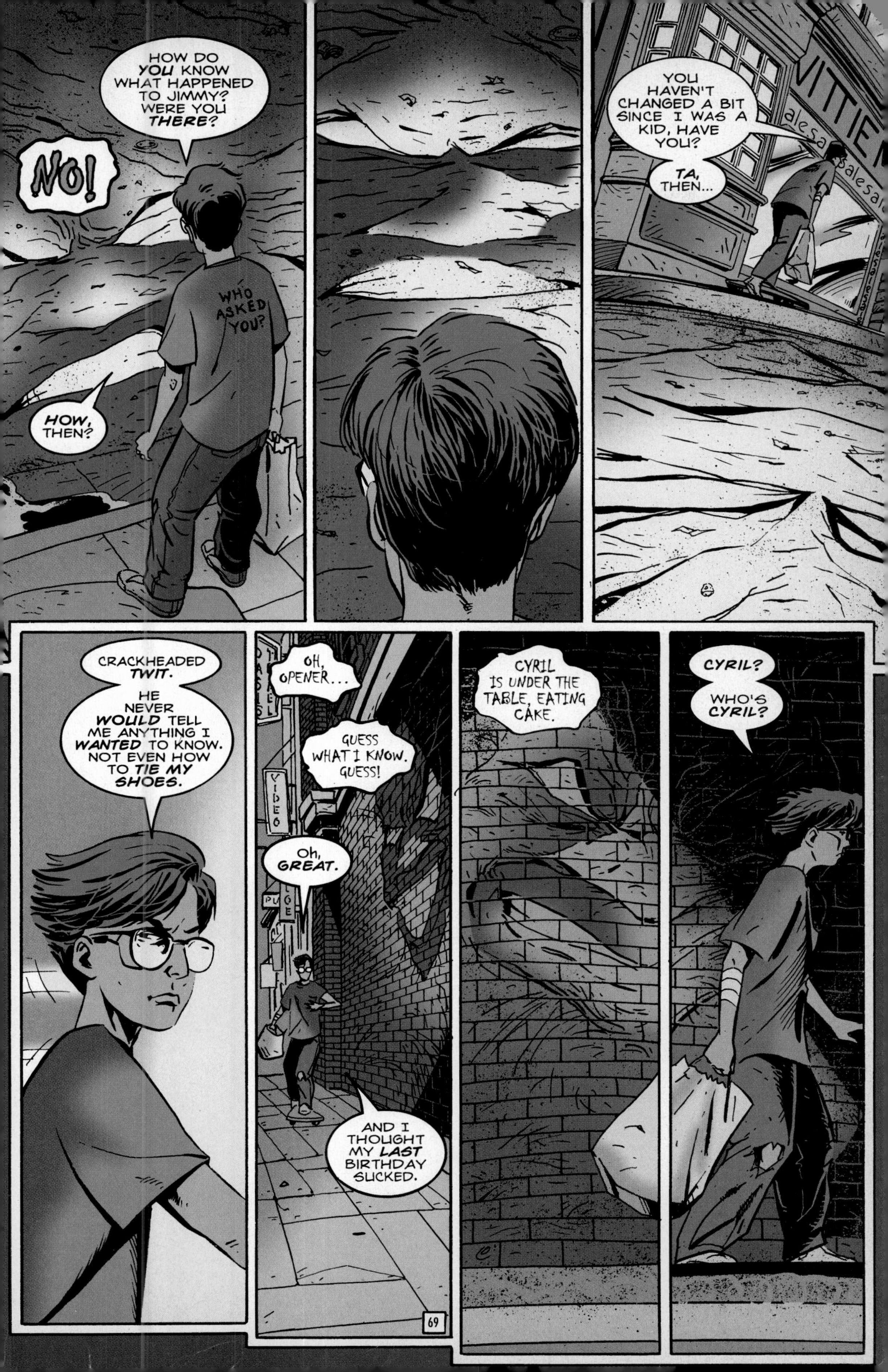
HOW DO YOU KNOW WHAT HAPPENED TO JIMMY? WERE YOU THERE?
NO!
WHO ASKED YOU?
HOW, THEN?
YOU HAVEN'T CHANGED A BIT SINCE I WAS A KID, HAVE YOU?
TA, THEN...
CRACKHEADED TWIT.
HE NEVER WOULD TELL ME ANYTHING I WANTED TO KNOW. NOT EVEN HOW TO TIE MY SHOES.
OH, OPENER...
GUESS WHAT I KNOW. GUESS!
VIDEO
Oh, GREAT.
AND I THOUGHT MY LAST BIRTHDAY SUCKED.
CYRIL IS UNDER THE TABLE, EATING CAKE.
CYRIL?
WHO'S CYRIL?

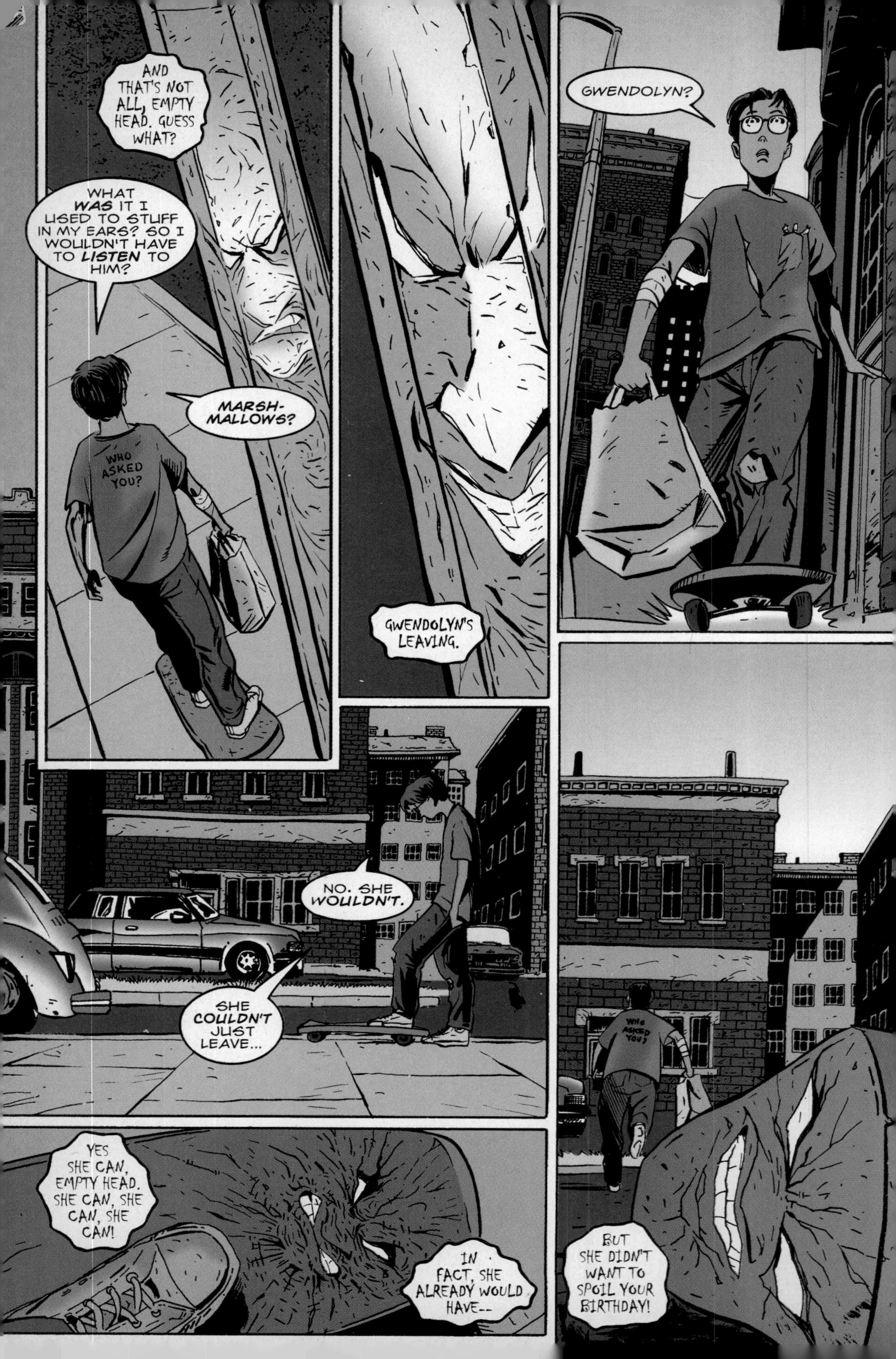
AND THAT'S NOT ALL, EMPTY HEAD. GUESS WHAT?
WHAT WAS IT I USED TO STUFF IN MY EARS? SO I WOULDN'T HAVE TO LISTEN TO HIM?
MARSH-MALLOWS?
WHO ASKED YOU?
GWENDOLYN'S LEAVING.
GWENDOLYN?
NO. SHE WOULDN'T.
SHE COULDN'T JUST LEAVE...
YES SHE CAN, EMPTY HEAD. SHE CAN, SHE CAN, SHE CAN!
IN FACT, SHE ALREADY WOULD HAVE--
BUT SHE DIDN'T WANT TO SPOIL YOUR BIRTHDAY!

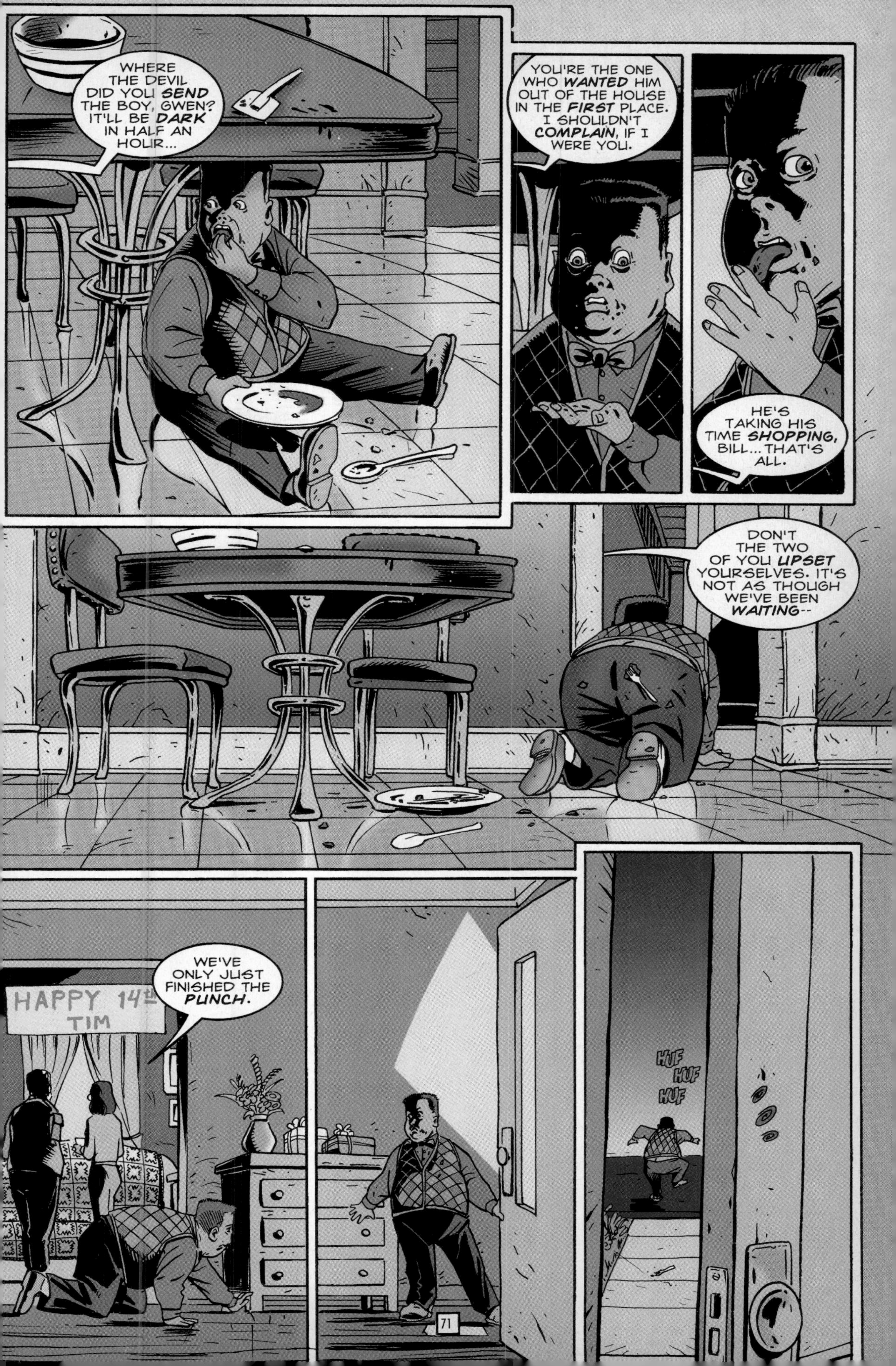

WHERE THE DEVIL DID YOU SEND THE BOY, GWEN? IT'LL BE DARK IN HALF AN HOUR...
YOU'RE THE ONE WHO WANTED HIM OUT OF THE HOUSE IN THE FIRST PLACE. I SHOULDN'T COMPLAIN, IF I WERE YOU.
HE'S TAKING HIS TIME SHOPPING, BILL... THAT'S ALL.
DON'T THE TWO OF YOU UPSET YOURSELVES. IT'S NOT AS THOUGH WE'VE BEEN WAITING--
HAPPY 14th TIM
WE'VE ONLY JUST FINISHED THE PUNCH.
HUF
HUF
HUF

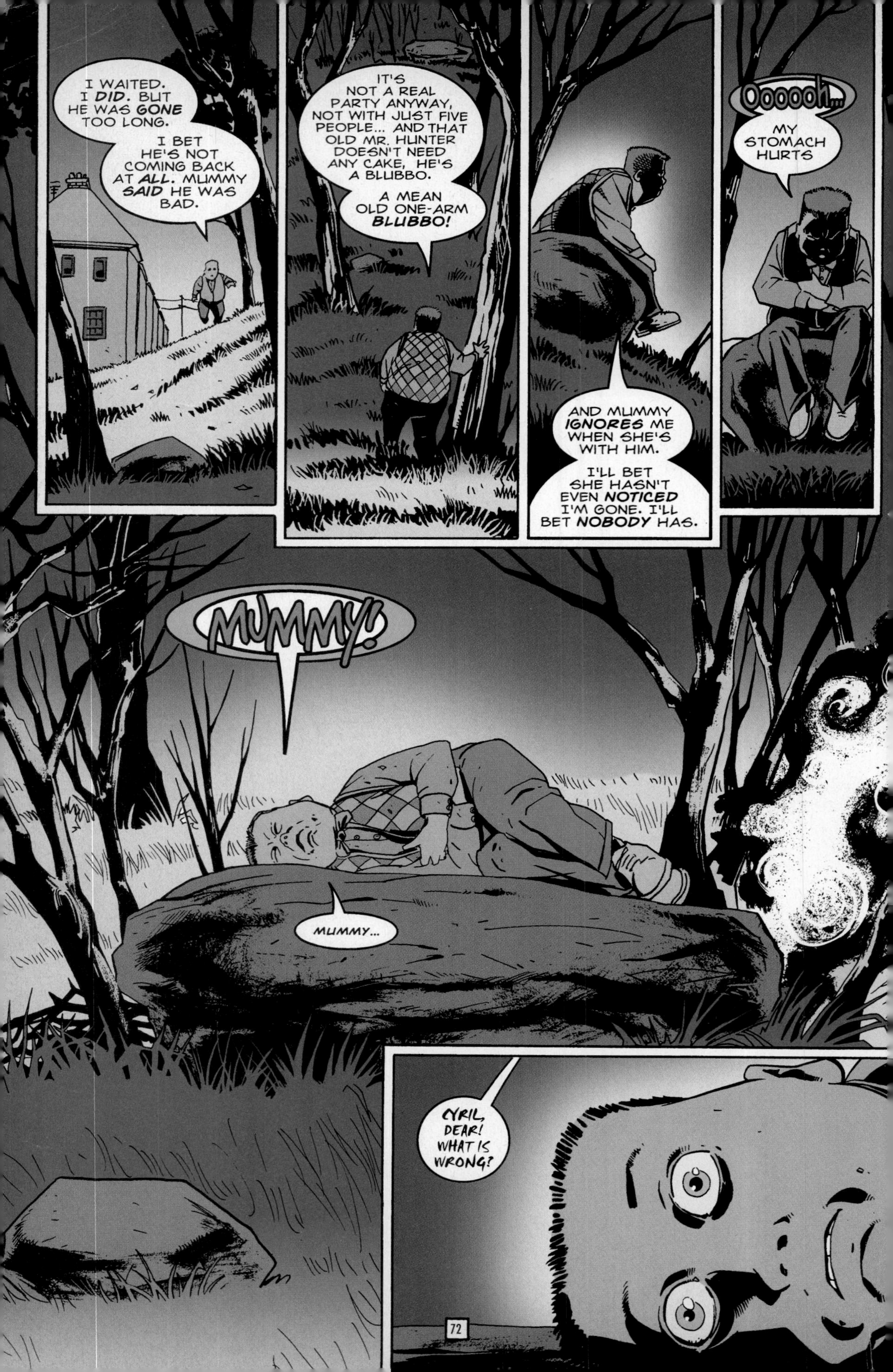
I WAITED. I DID. BUT HE WAS GONE TOO LONG.
I BET HE'S NOT COMING BACK AT ALL. MUMMY SAID HE WAS BAD.
IT'S NOT A REAL PARTY ANYWAY, NOT WITH JUST FIVE PEOPLE... AND THAT OLD MR. HUNTER DOESN'T NEED ANY CAKE, HE'S A BLUBBO.
A MEAN OLD ONE-ARM BLUBBO!
AND MUMMY IGNORES ME WHEN SHE'S WITH HIM.
I'LL BET SHE HASN'T EVEN NOTICED I'M GONE. I'LL BET NOBODY HAS.
Oooooh...
MY STOMACH HURTS
MUMMY!
MUMMY...
CYRIL, DEAR! WHAT IS WRONG?

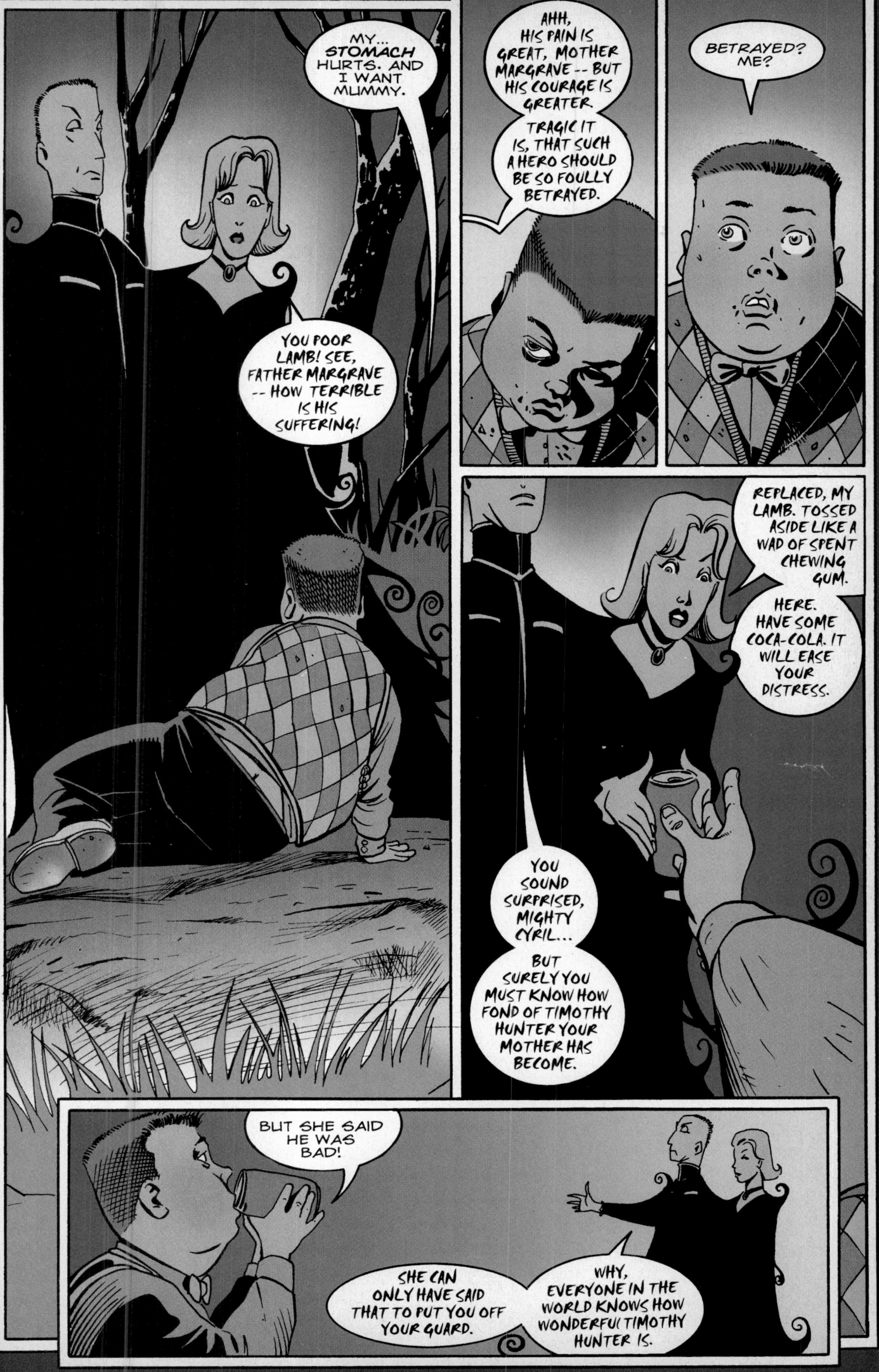
MY... STOMACH HURTS. AND I WANT MUMMY.
YOU POOR LAMB! SEE, FATHER MARGRAVE -- HOW TERRIBLE IS HIS SUFFERING!
AHH, HIS PAIN IS GREAT, MOTHER MARGRAVE -- BUT HIS COURAGE IS GREATER.
TRAGIC IT IS, THAT SUCH A HERO SHOULD BE SO FOULLY BETRAYED.
BETRAYED? ME?
YOU SOUND SURPRISED, MIGHTY CYRIL...
BUT SURELY YOU MUST KNOW HOW FOND OF TIMOTHY HUNTER YOUR MOTHER HAS BECOME.
REPLACED, MY LAMB. TOSSED ASIDE LIKE A WAD OF SPENT CHEWING GUM.
HERE. HAVE SOME COCA-COLA. IT WILL EASE YOUR DISTRESS.
BUT SHE SAID HE WAS BAD!
SHE CAN ONLY HAVE SAID THAT TO PUT YOU OFF YOUR GUARD.
WHY, EVERYONE IN THE WORLD KNOWS HOW WONDERFUL TIMOTHY HUNTER IS.

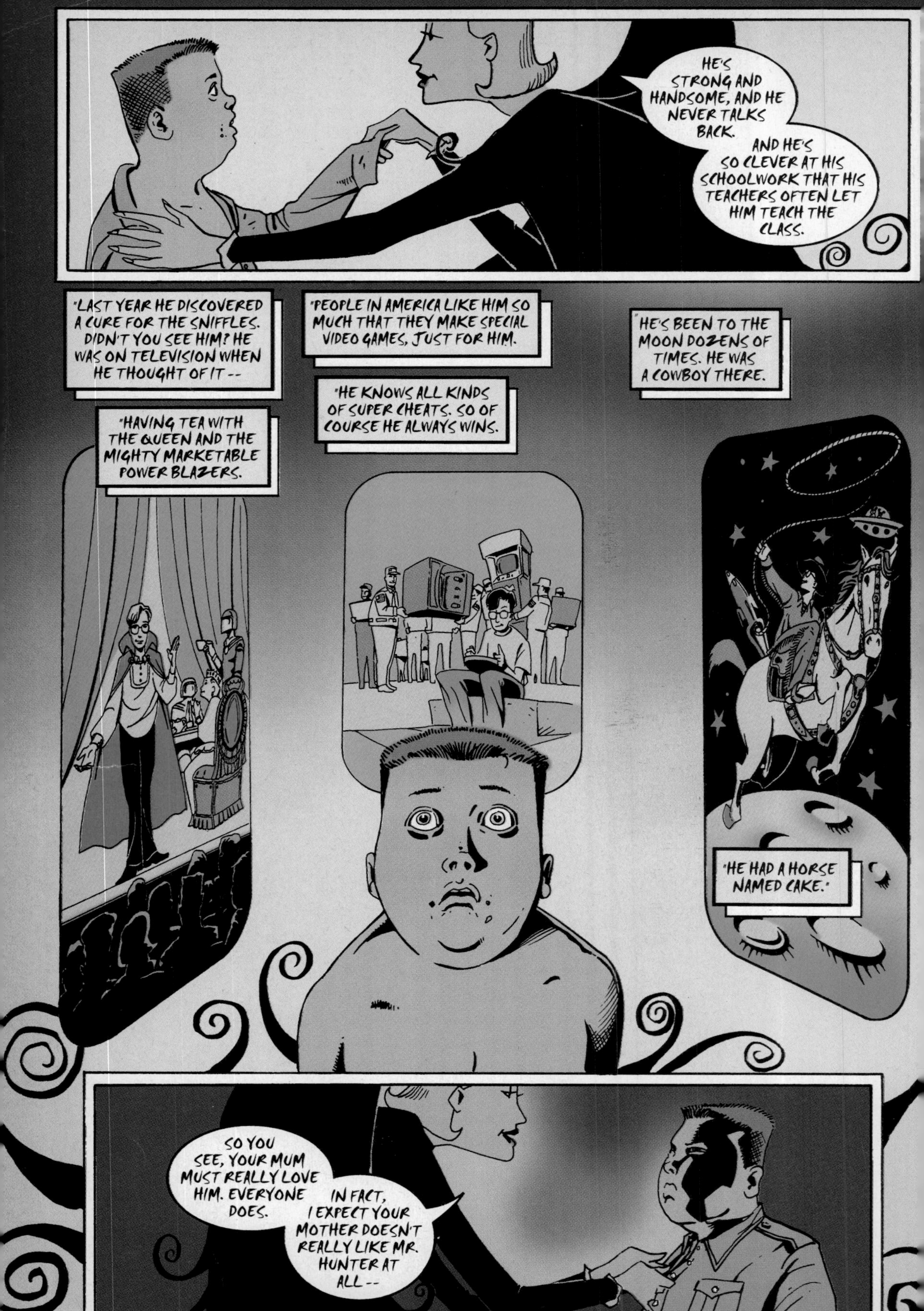
HE'S STRONG AND HANDSOME, AND HE NEVER TALKS BACK.
AND HE'S SO CLEVER AT HIS SCHOOLWORK THAT HIS TEACHERS OFTEN LET HIM TEACH THE CLASS.
"LAST YEAR HE DISCOVERED A CURE FOR THE SNIFFLES. DIDN'T YOU SEE HIM? HE WAS ON TELEVISION WHEN HE THOUGHT OF IT --
"HAVING TEA WITH THE QUEEN AND THE MIGHTY MARKETABLE POWER BLAZERS.
"PEOPLE IN AMERICA LIKE HIM SO MUCH THAT THEY MAKE SPECIAL VIDEO GAMES, JUST FOR HIM.
"HE KNOWS ALL KINDS OF SUPER CHEATS. SO OF COURSE HE ALWAYS WINS.
"HE'S BEEN TO THE MOON DOZENS OF TIMES. HE WAS A COWBOY THERE.
"HE HAD A HORSE NAMED CAKE."
SO YOU SEE, YOUR MUM MUST REALLY LOVE HIM. EVERYONE DOES.
IN FACT, I EXPECT YOUR MOTHER DOESN'T REALLY LIKE MR. HUNTER AT ALL --

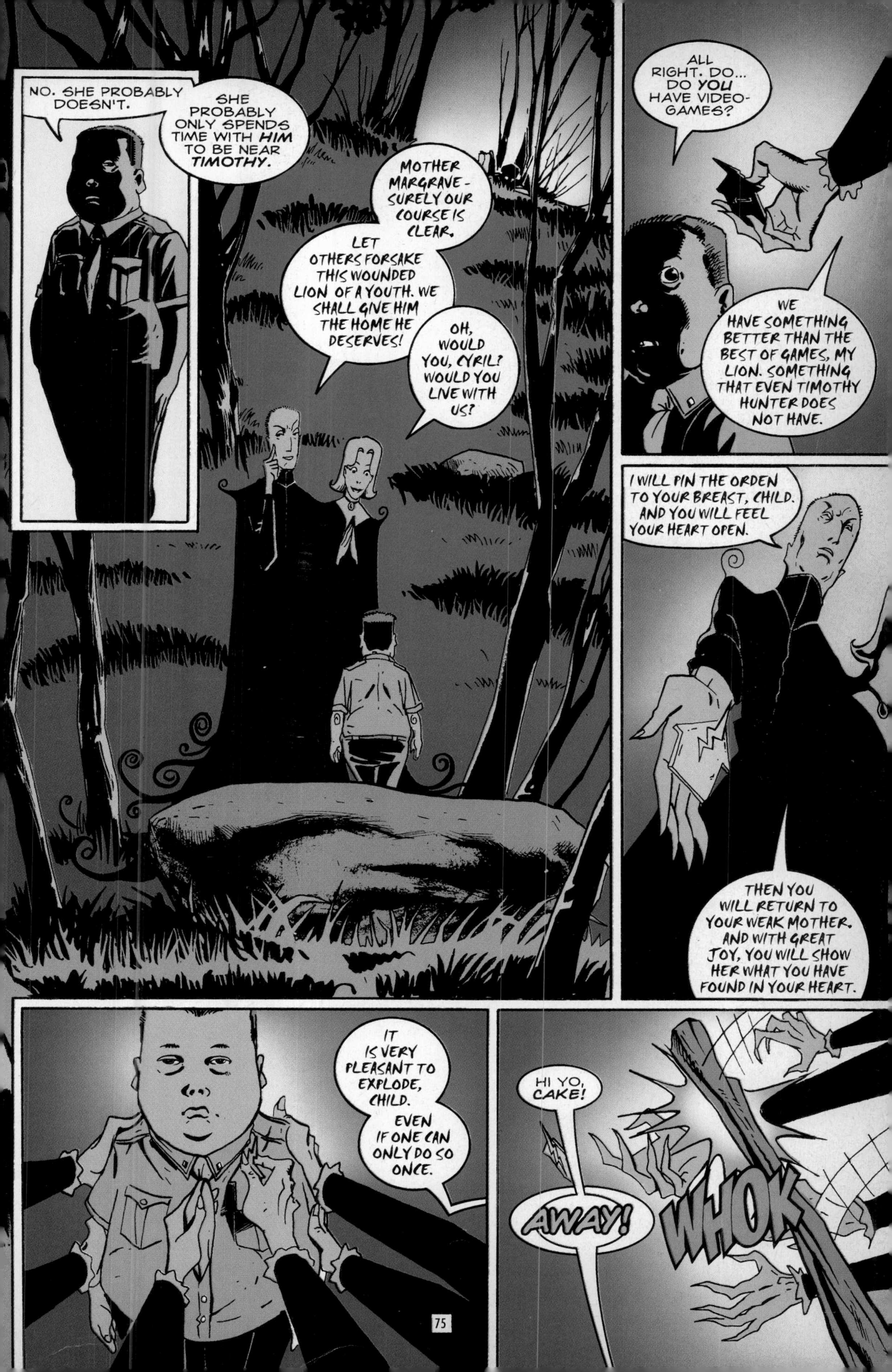
NO. SHE PROBABLY DOESN'T.
SHE PROBABLY ONLY SPENDS TIME WITH HIM TO BE NEAR TIMOTHY.
MOTHER MARGRAVE - SURELY OUR COURSE IS CLEAR.
LET OTHERS FORSAKE THIS WOUNDED LION OF A YOUTH. WE SHALL GIVE HIM THE HOME HE DESERVES!
OH, WOULD YOU, CYRIL? WOULD YOU LIVE WITH US?
ALL RIGHT. DO... DO YOU HAVE VIDEO-GAMES?
WE HAVE SOMETHING BETTER THAN THE BEST OF GAMES, MY LION. SOMETHING THAT EVEN TIMOTHY HUNTER DOES NOT HAVE.
I WILL PIN THE ORDEN TO YOUR BREAST, CHILD. AND YOU WILL FEEL YOUR HEART OPEN.
THEN YOU WILL RETURN TO YOUR WEAK MOTHER. AND WITH GREAT JOY, YOU WILL SHOW HER WHAT YOU HAVE FOUND IN YOUR HEART.
IT IS VERY PLEASANT TO EXPLODE, CHILD.
EVEN IF ONE CAN ONLY DO SO ONCE.
HI YO, CAKE!
AWAY!
WHOK

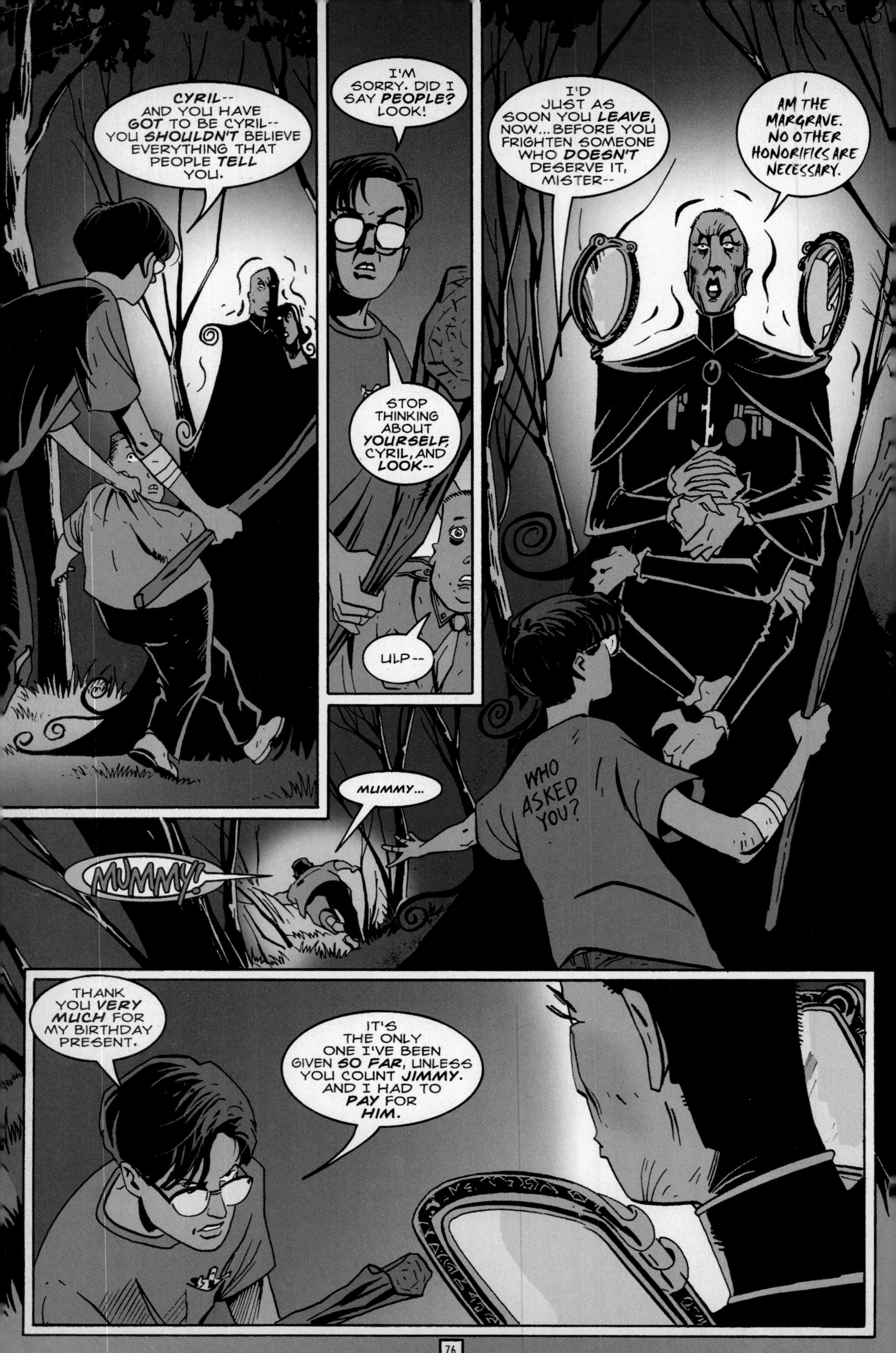
CYRIL-- AND YOU HAVE GOT TO BE CYRIL-- YOU SHOULDN'T BELIEVE EVERYTHING THAT PEOPLE TELL YOU.
I'M SORRY. DID I SAY PEOPLE? LOOK!
STOP THINKING ABOUT YOURSELF, CYRIL, AND LOOK--
ULP--
I'D JUST AS SOON YOU LEAVE, NOW... BEFORE YOU FRIGHTEN SOMEONE WHO DOESN'T DESERVE IT, MISTER--
I AM THE MARGRAVE. NO OTHER HONORIFICS ARE NECESSARY.
WHO ASKED YOU?
MUMMY...
MUMMY!
THANK YOU VERY MUCH FOR MY BIRTHDAY PRESENT.
IT'S THE ONLY ONE I'VE BEEN GIVEN SO FAR, UNLESS YOU COUNT JIMMY. AND I HAD TO PAY FOR HIM.

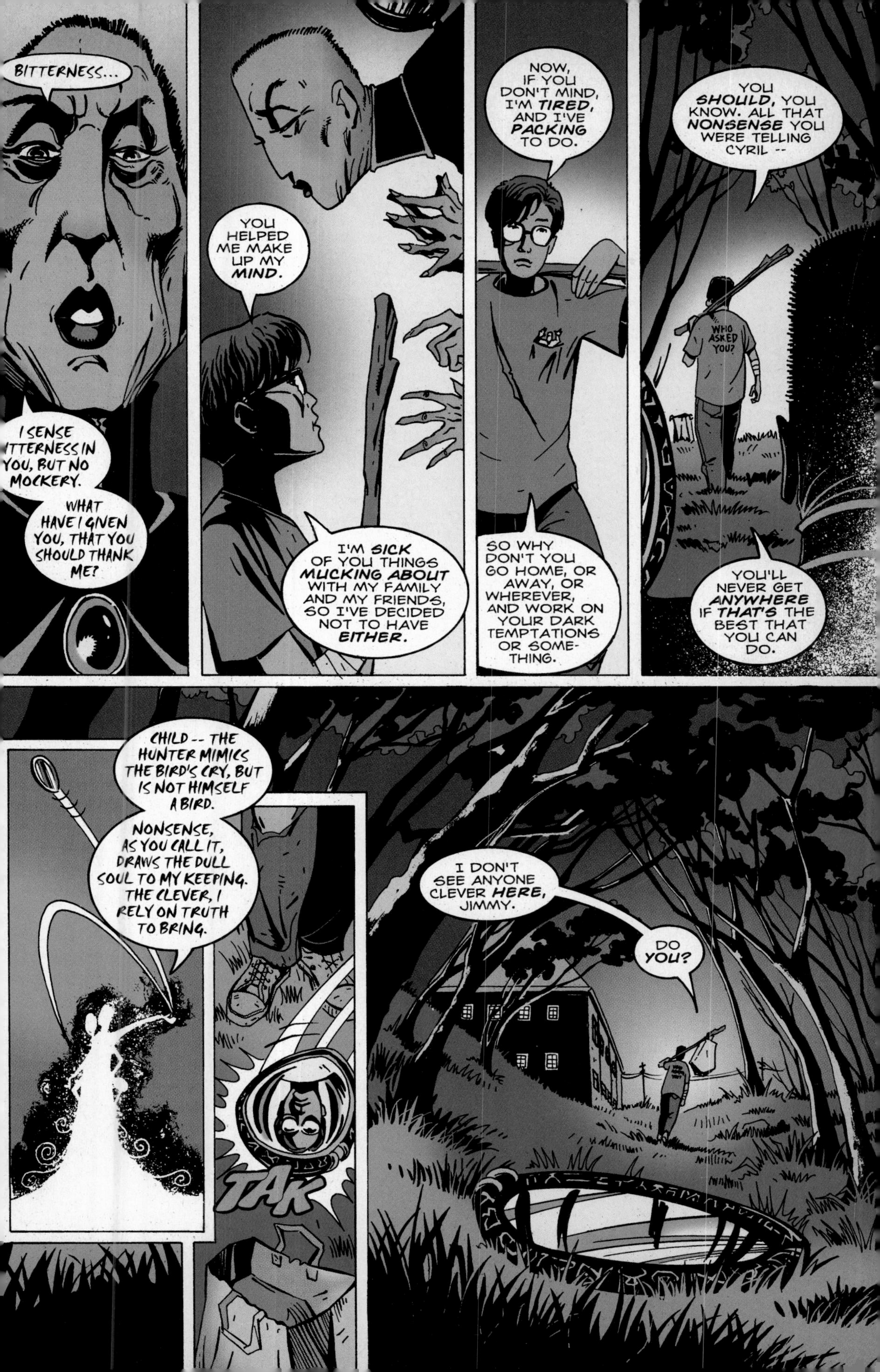
BITTERNESS...
I SENSE ITTERNESS IN YOU, BUT NO MOCKERY.
WHAT HAVE I GIVEN YOU, THAT YOU SHOULD THANK ME?
YOU HELPED ME MAKE UP MY MIND.
I'M SICK OF YOU THINGS MUCKING ABOUT WITH MY FAMILY AND MY FRIENDS, SO I'VE DECIDED NOT TO HAVE EITHER.
NOW, IF YOU DON'T MIND, I'M TIRED, AND I'VE PACKING TO DO.
SO WHY DON'T YOU GO HOME, OR AWAY, OR WHEREVER, AND WORK ON YOUR DARK TEMPTATIONS OR SOME-THING.
YOU SHOULD, YOU KNOW. ALL THAT NONSENSE YOU WERE TELLING CYRIL --
WHO ASKED YOU?
YOU'LL NEVER GET ANYWHERE IF THAT'S THE BEST THAT YOU CAN DO.
CHILD -- THE HUNTER MIMICS THE BIRD'S CRY, BUT IS NOT HIMSELF A BIRD.
NONSENSE, AS YOU CALL IT, DRAWS THE DULL SOUL TO MY KEEPING. THE CLEVER, I RELY ON TRUTH TO BRING.
TAK
I DON'T SEE ANYONE CLEVER HERE, JIMMY.
DO YOU?

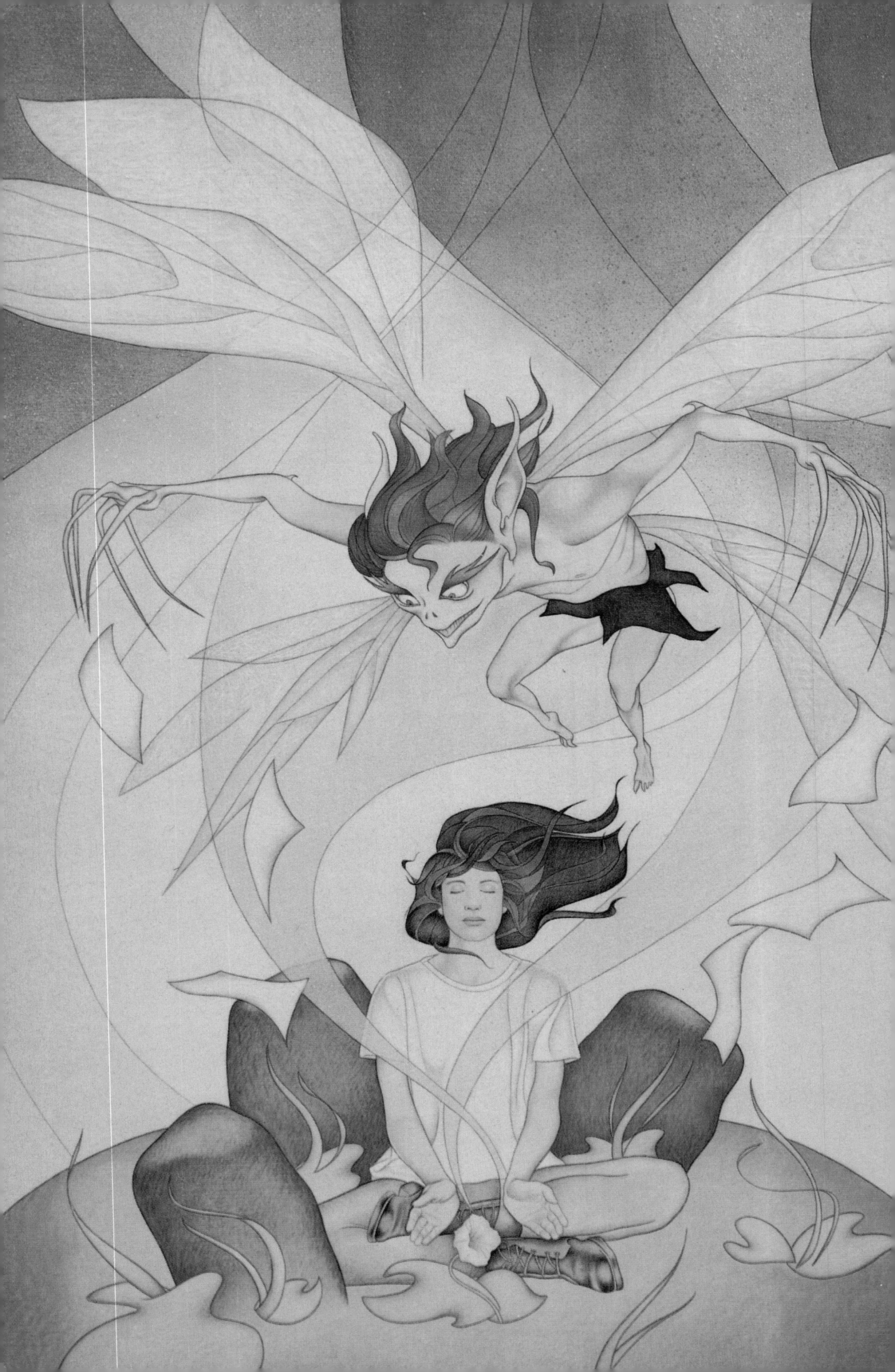

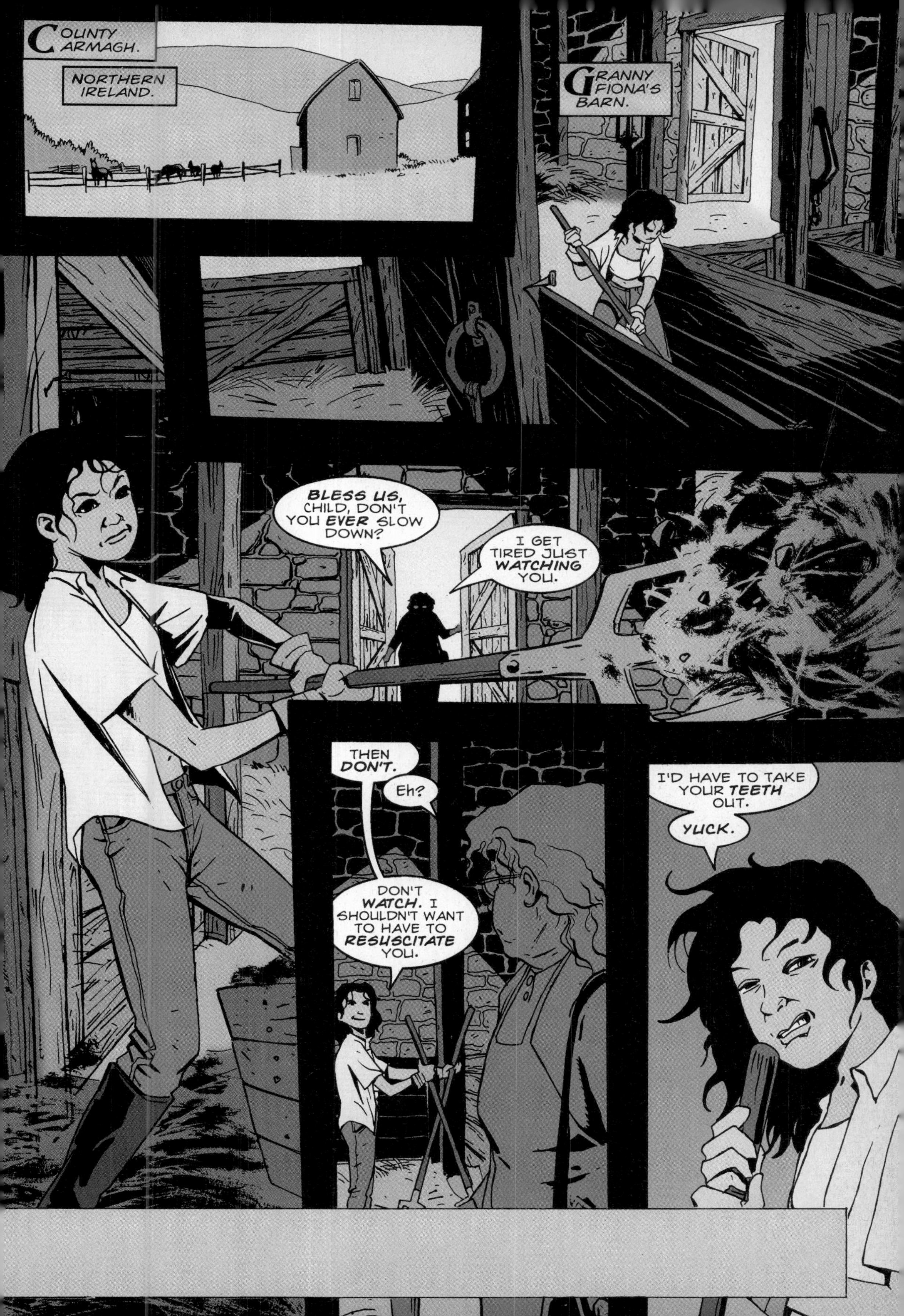
COUNTY ARMAGH.
NORTHERN IRELAND.
GRANNY FIONA'S BARN.
BLESS US, CHILD, DON'T YOU EVER SLOW DOWN?
I GET TIRED JUST WATCHING YOU.
THEN DON'T.
Eh?
DON'T WATCH. I SHOULDN'T WANT TO HAVE TO RESUSCITATE YOU.
I'D HAVE TO TAKE YOUR TEETH OUT.
YUCK.

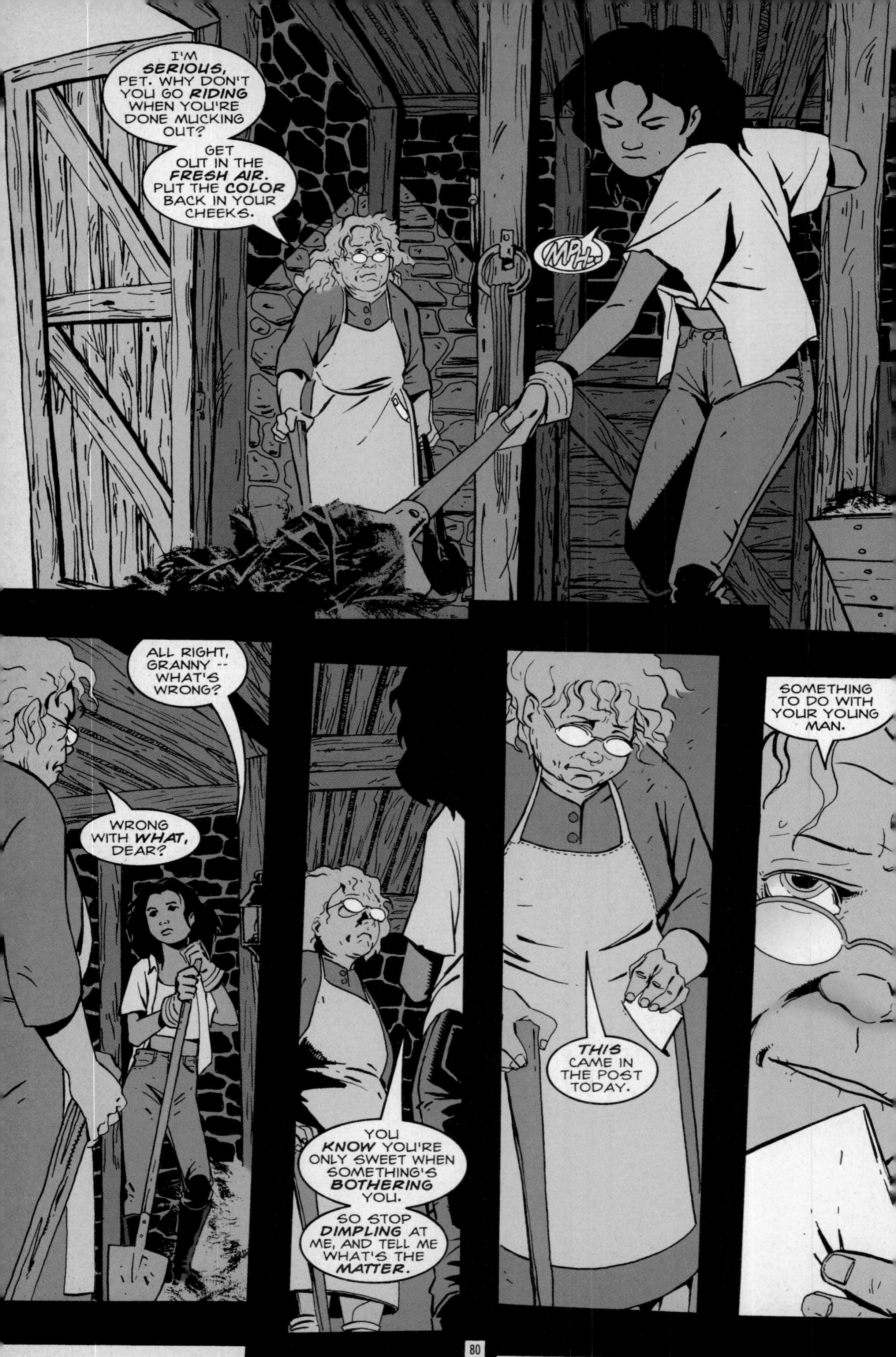

I'M SERIOUS, PET. WHY DON'T YOU GO RIDING WHEN YOU'RE DONE MUCKING OUT?
GET OUT IN THE FRESH AIR. PUT THE COLOR BACK IN YOUR CHEEKS.
MPH
ALL RIGHT, GRANNY -- WHAT'S WRONG?
WRONG WITH WHAT, DEAR?
YOU KNOW YOU'RE ONLY SWEET WHEN SOMETHING'S BOTHERING YOU.
SO STOP DIMPLING AT ME, AND TELL ME WHAT'S THE MATTER.
THIS CAME IN THE POST TODAY.
SOMETHING TO DO WITH YOUR YOUNG MAN.

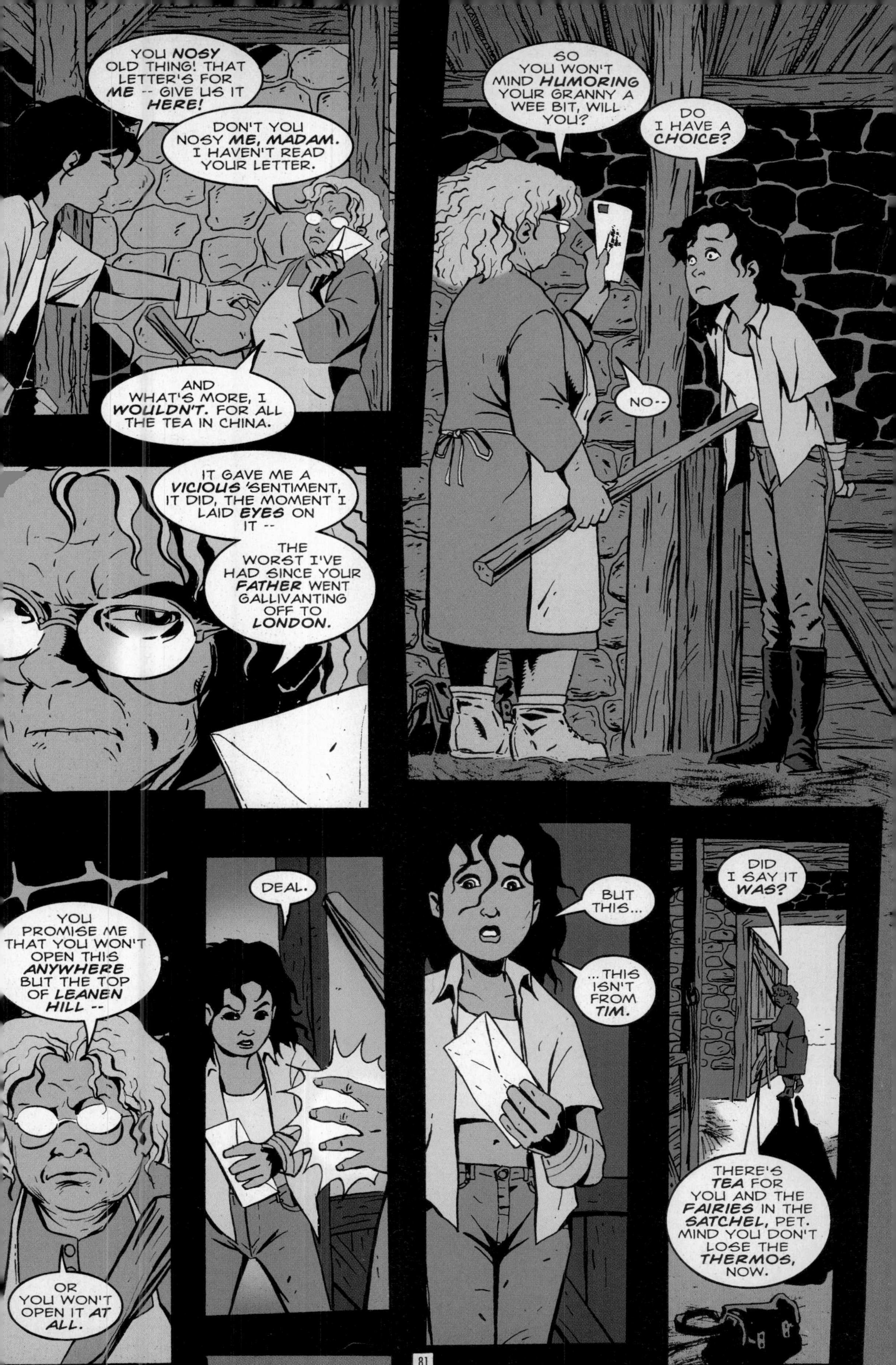
YOU NOSY OLD THING! THAT LETTER'S FOR ME -- GIVE US IT HERE!
DON'T YOU NOSY ME, MADAM. I HAVEN'T READ YOUR LETTER.
AND WHAT'S MORE, I WOULDN'T. FOR ALL THE TEA IN CHINA.
SO YOU WON'T MIND HUMORING YOUR GRANNY A WEE BIT, WILL YOU?
DO I HAVE A CHOICE?
NO--
IT GAVE ME A VICIOUS 'SENTIMENT, IT DID, THE MOMENT I LAID EYES ON IT --
THE WORST I'VE HAD SINCE YOUR FATHER WENT GALLIVANTING OFF TO LONDON.
YOU PROMISE ME THAT YOU WON'T OPEN THIS ANYWHERE BUT THE TOP OF LEANEN HILL --
OR YOU WON'T OPEN IT AT ALL.
DEAL.
BUT THIS...
...THIS ISN'T FROM TIM.
DID I SAY IT WAS?
THERE'S TEA FOR YOU AND THE FAIRIES IN THE SATCHEL, PET. MIND YOU DON'T LOSE THE THERMOS, NOW.

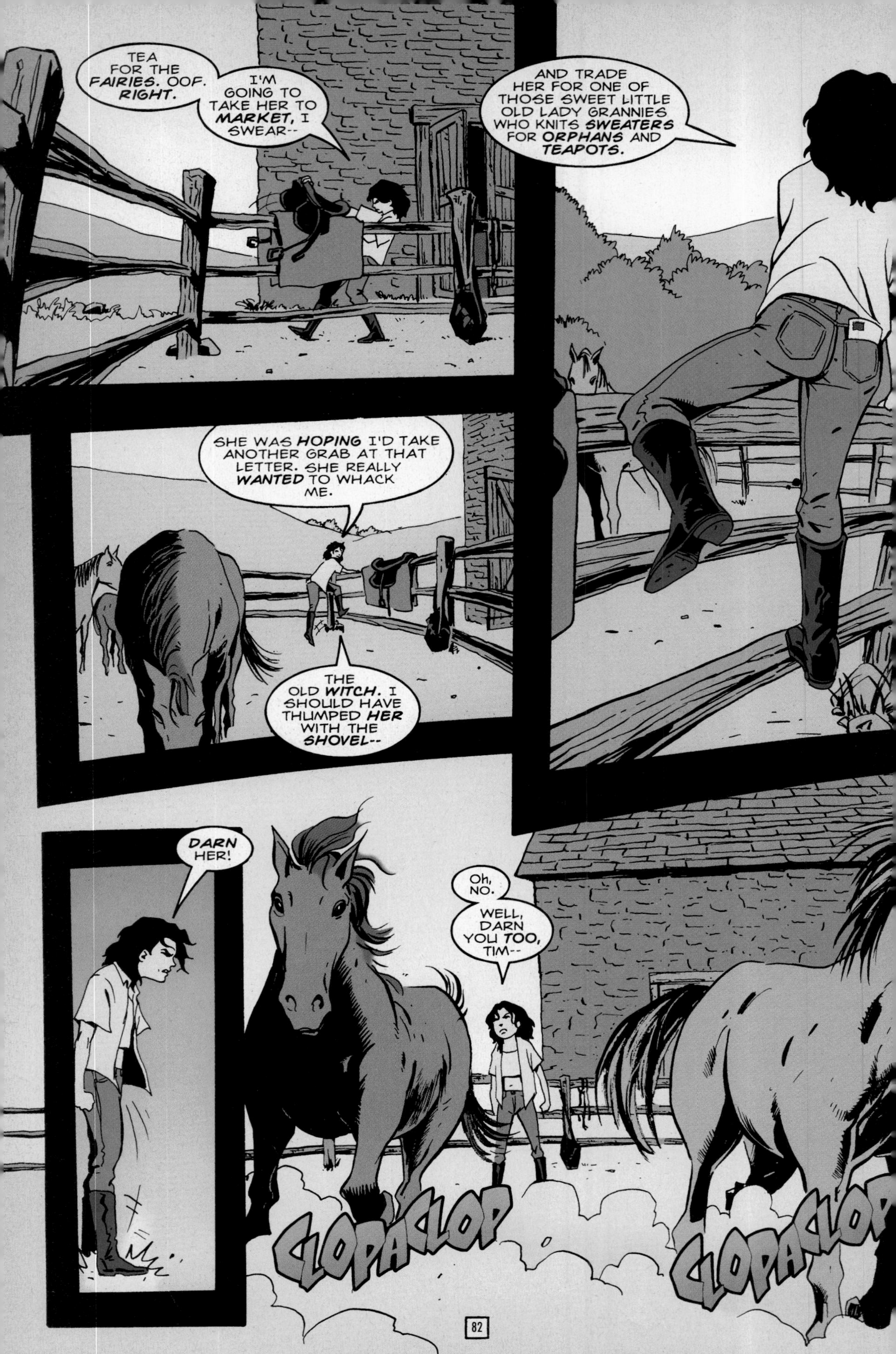
TEA FOR THE FAIRIES. OOF. RIGHT.
I'M GOING TO TAKE HER TO MARKET, I SWEAR--
AND TRADE HER FOR ONE OF THOSE SWEET LITTLE OLD LADY GRANNIES WHO KNITS SWEATERS FOR ORPHANS AND TEAPOTS.
SHE WAS HOPING I'D TAKE ANOTHER GRAB AT THAT LETTER. SHE REALLY WANTED TO WHACK ME.
THE OLD WITCH. I SHOULD HAVE THUMPED HER WITH THE SHOVEL--
DARN HER!
Oh, NO.
WELL, DARN YOU TOO, TIM--
CLOPACLOP
CLOPACLOP

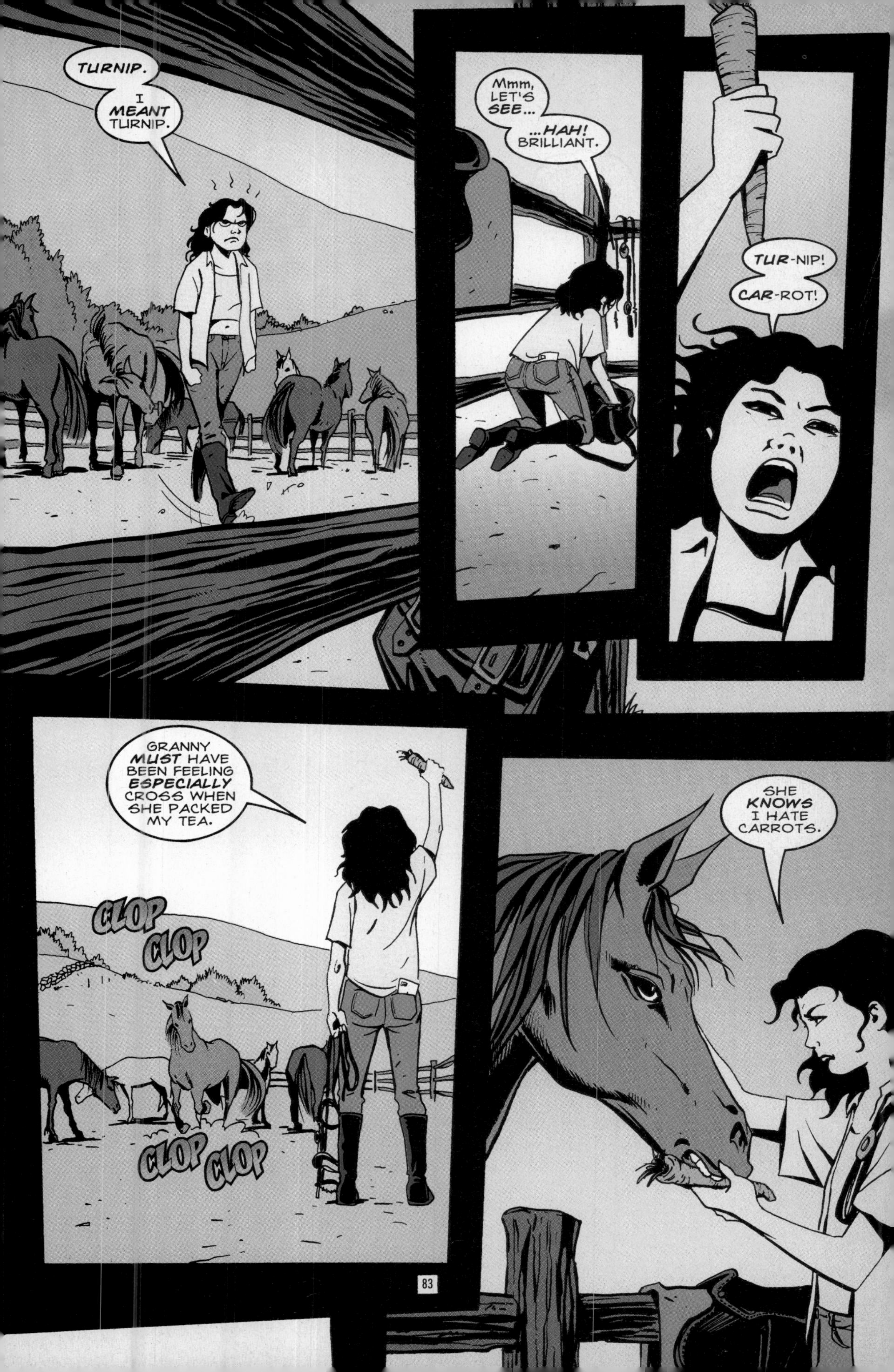

TURNIP.
I MEANT TURNIP.
Mmm, LET'S SEE...
...HAH! BRILLIANT.
TUR-NIP!
CAR-ROT!
GRANNY MUST HAVE BEEN FEELING ESPECIALLY CROSS WHEN SHE PACKED MY TEA.
CLOP
CLOP
CLOP
CLOP
SHE KNOWS I HATE CARROTS.

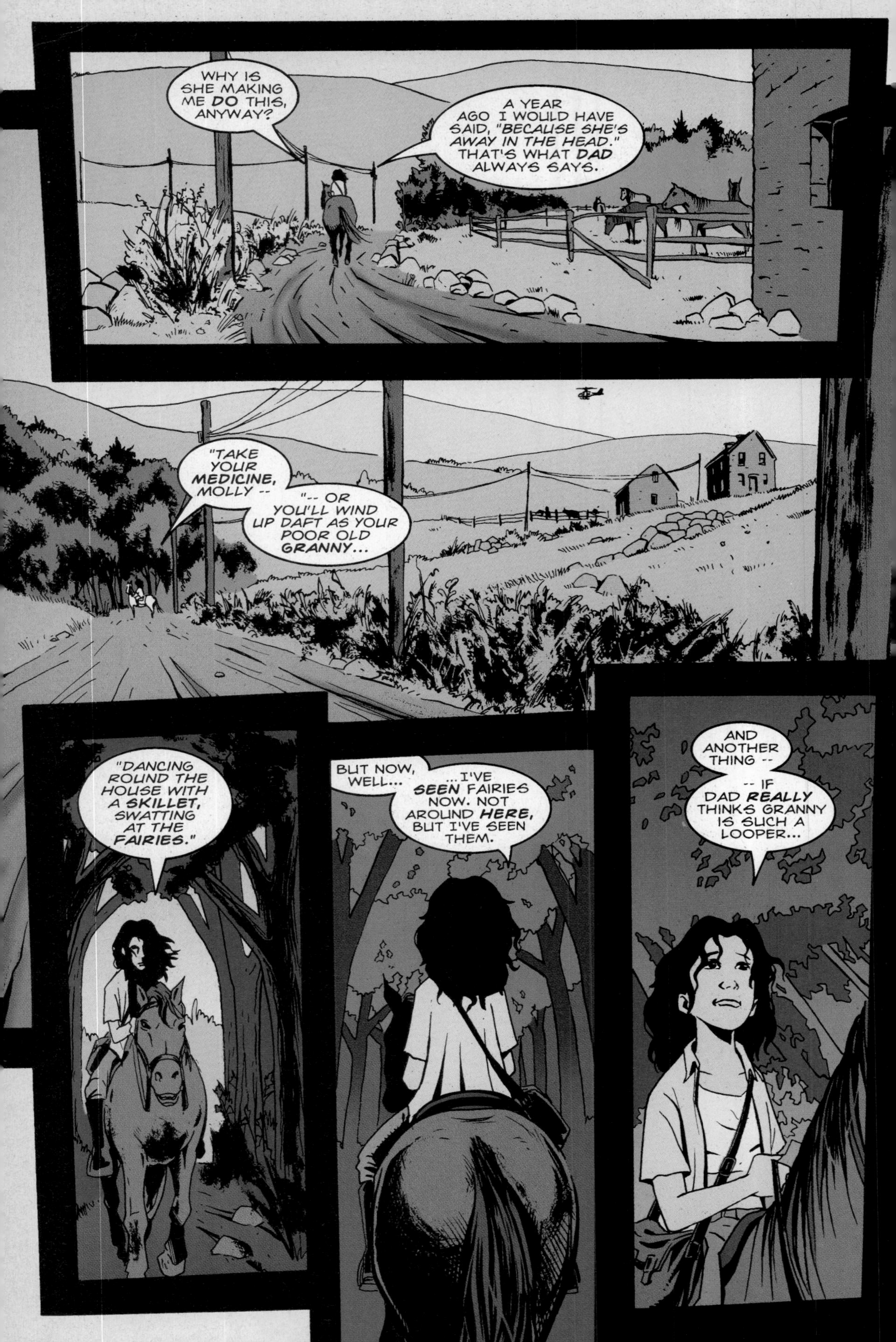
WHY IS SHE MAKING ME DO THIS, ANYWAY?
A YEAR AGO I WOULD HAVE SAID, "BECAUSE SHE'S AWAY IN THE HEAD." THAT'S WHAT DAD ALWAYS SAYS.
"TAKE YOUR MEDICINE, MOLLY --
"-- OR YOU'LL WIND UP DAFT AS YOUR POOR OLD GRANNY...
"DANCING ROUND THE HOUSE WITH A SKILLET, SWATTING AT THE FAIRIES."
BUT NOW, WELL...
...I'VE SEEN FAIRIES NOW. NOT AROUND HERE, BUT I'VE SEEN THEM.
AND ANOTHER THING --
-- IF DAD REALLY THINKS GRANNY IS SUCH A LOOPER...

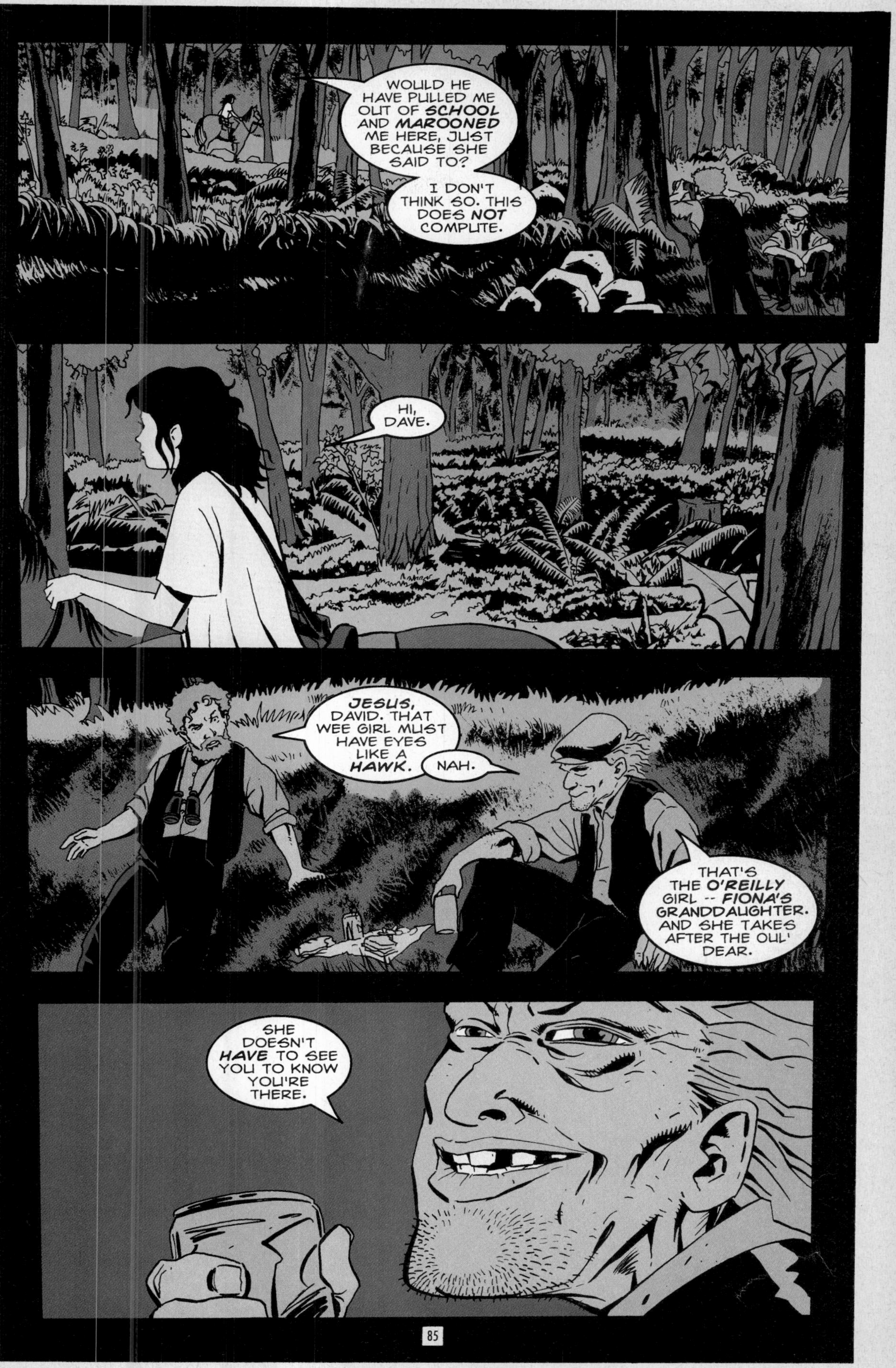
WOULD HE HAVE PULLED ME OUT OF SCHOOL AND MAROONED ME HERE, JUST BECAUSE SHE SAID TO?
I DON'T THINK SO. THIS DOES NOT COMPUTE.
HI, DAVE.
JESUS, DAVID. THAT WEE GIRL MUST HAVE EYES LIKE A HAWK.
NAH.
THAT'S THE O'REILLY GIRL -- FIONA'S GRANDDAUGHTER. AND SHE TAKES AFTER THE OUL' DEAR.
SHE DOESN'T HAVE TO SEE YOU TO KNOW YOU'RE THERE.

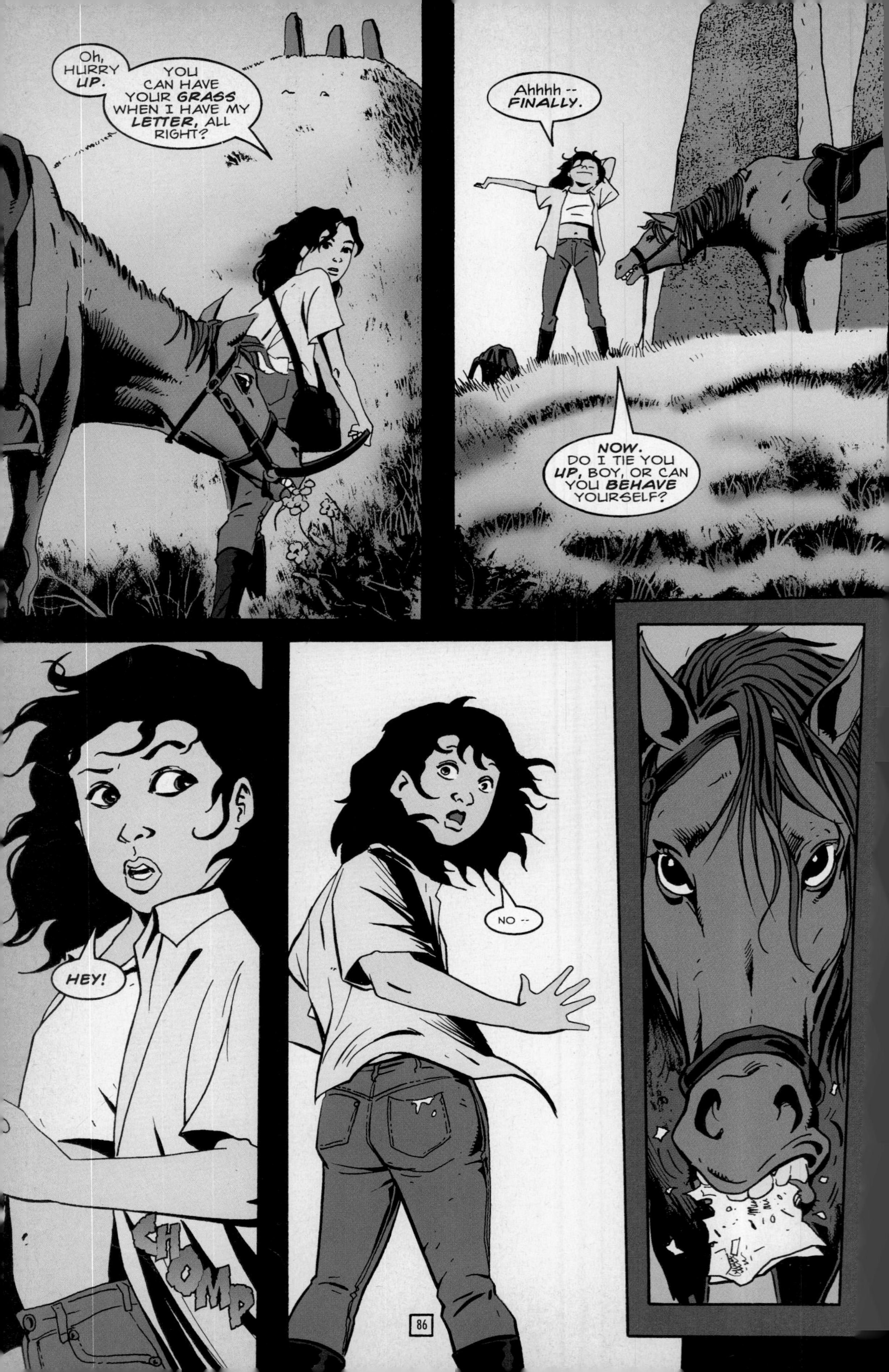

Oh, HURRY UP.
YOU CAN HAVE YOUR GRASS WHEN I HAVE MY LETTER, ALL RIGHT?
Ahhhh -- FINALLY.
NOW. DO I TIE YOU UP, BOY, OR CAN YOU BEHAVE YOURSELF?
HEY!
CHOMP
NO --

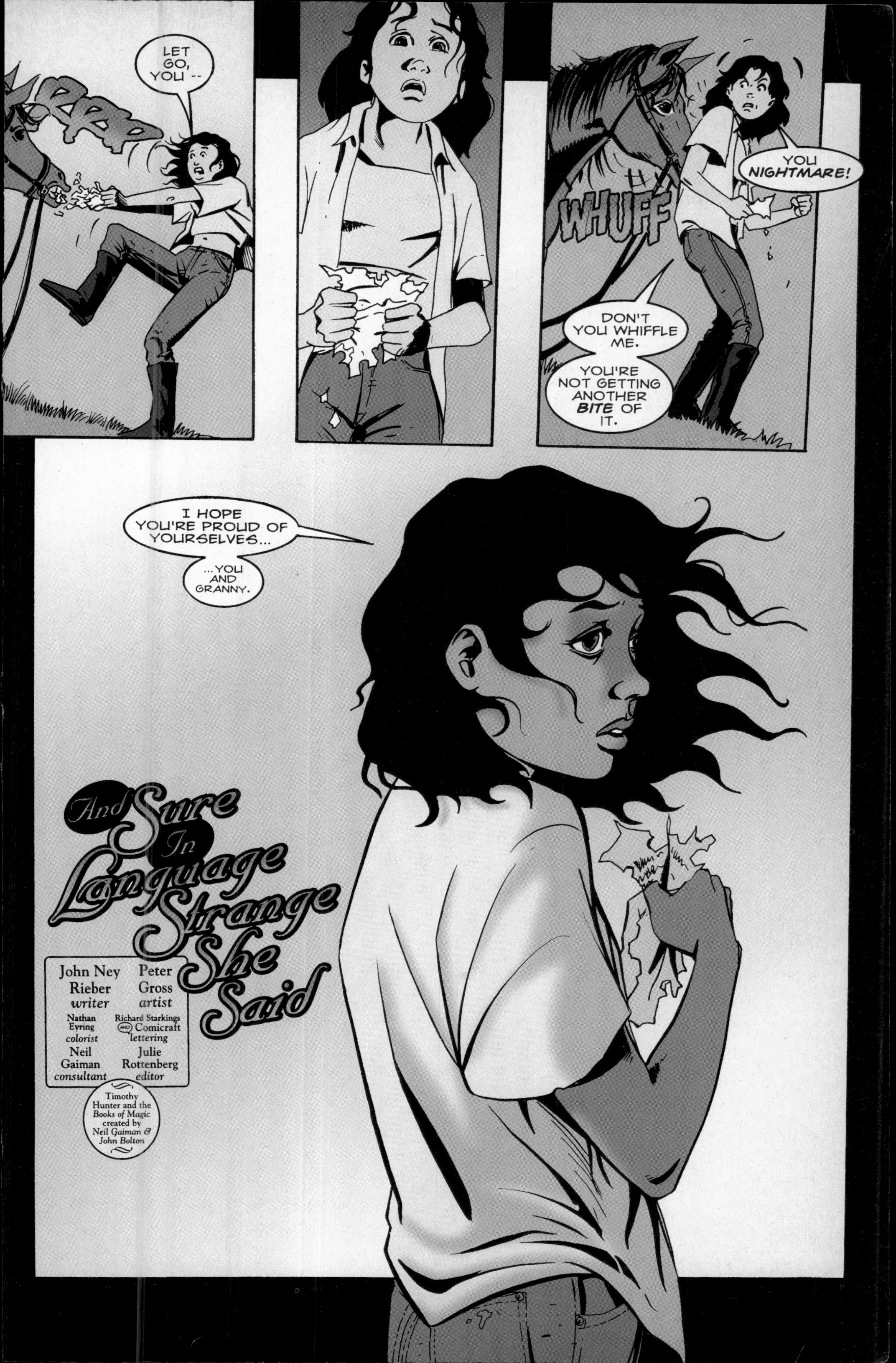
LET GO, YOU --
BRRR
YOU NIGHTMARE!
WHUFF
DON'T YOU WHIFFLE ME.
YOU'RE NOT GETTING ANOTHER BITE OF IT.
I HOPE YOU'RE PROUD OF YOURSELVES...
...YOU AND GRANNY.
And Sure In Language Strange She Said
John Ney Rieber writer
Peter Gross artist
Nathan Eyring colorist
Richard Starkings and Comicraft lettering
Neil Gaiman consultant
Julie Rottenberg editor
Timothy Hunter and the Books of Magic created by Neil Gaiman & John Bolton

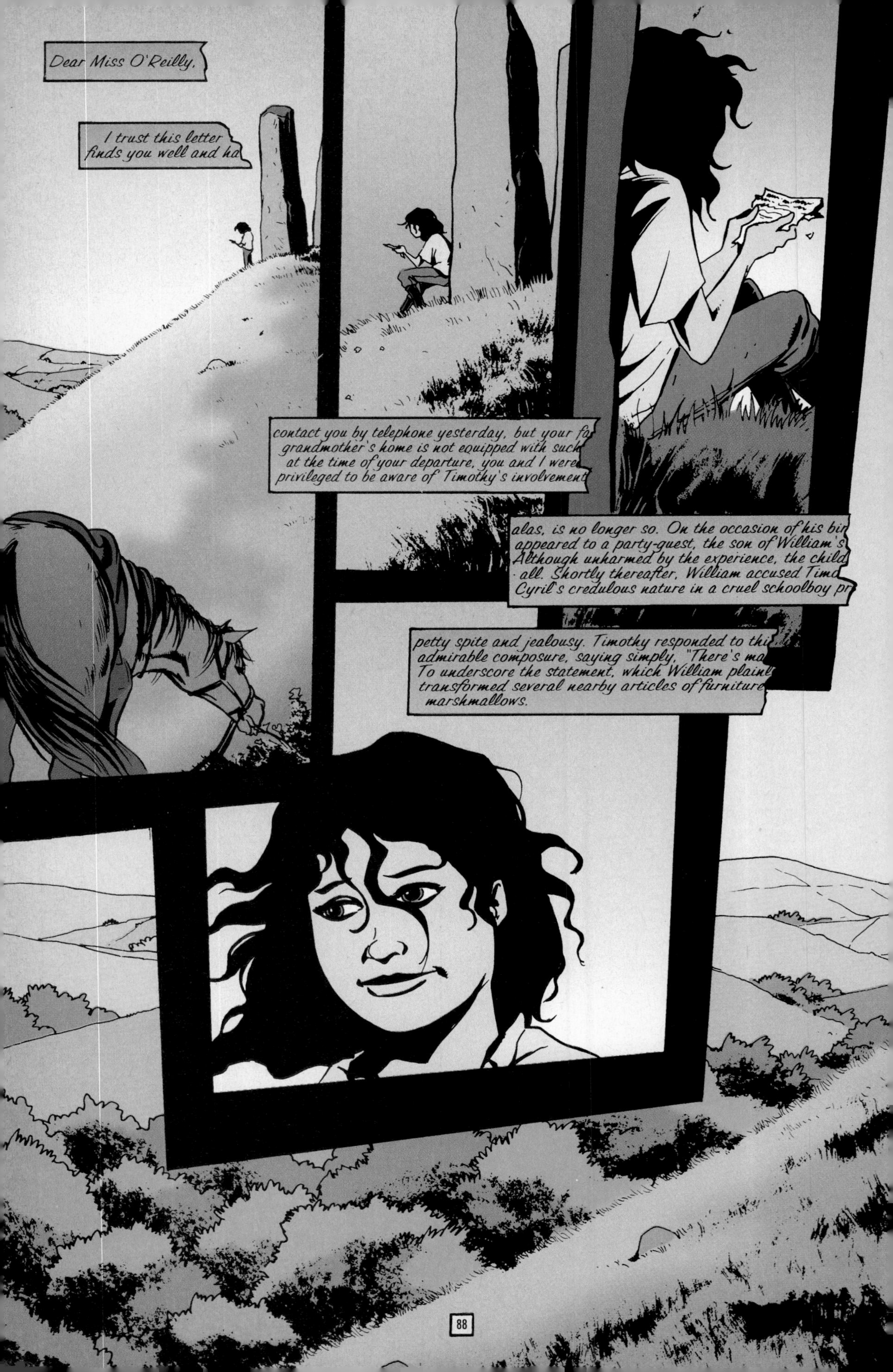
Dear Miss O'Reilly,
I trust this letter finds you well and ha
contact you by telephone yesterday, but your fa grandmother's home is not equipped with such at the time of your departure, you and I were privileged to be aware of Timothy's involvement
alas, is no longer so. On the occasion of his bi appeared to a party-guest, the son of William's Although unharmed by the experience, the child all. Shortly thereafter, William accused Tim Cyril's credulous nature in a cruel schoolboy pr
petty spite and jealousy. Timothy responded to thi admirable composure, saying simply, "There's ma To underscore the statement, which William plain transformed several nearby articles of furniture marshmallows.

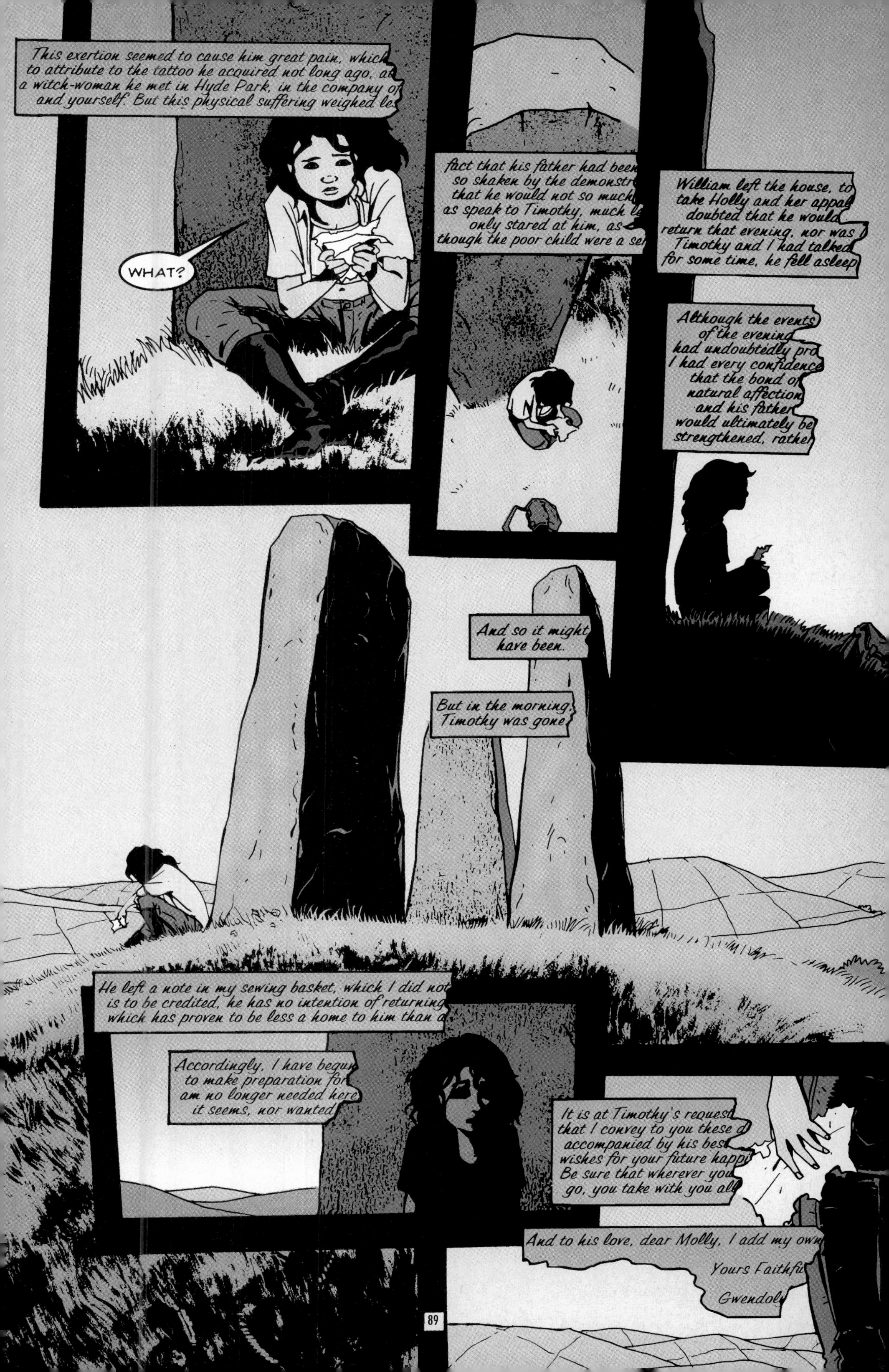
This exertion seemed to cause him great pain, which
to attribute to the tattoo he acquired not long ago, a
a witch-woman he met in Hyde Park, in the company of
and yourself. But this physical suffering weighed le
WHAT?
fact that his father had been
so shaken by the demonstr
that he would not so much
as speak to Timothy, much le
only stared at him, as
though the poor child were a se
William left the house, to
take Holly and her appa
doubted that he would
return that evening, nor was
Timothy and I had talked
for some time, he fell asleep
Although the events
of the evening
had undoubtedly pr
I had every confidence
that the bond of
natural affection
and his father
would ultimately be
strengthened, rathe
And so it might
have been.
But in the morning,
Timothy was gone.
He left a note in my sewing basket, which I did not
is to be credited, he has no intention of returning
which has proven to be less a home to him than a
Accordingly, I have begu
to make preparation fo
am no longer needed here
it seems, nor wanted
It is at Timothy's reques
that I convey to you these
accompanied by his bes
wishes for your future happ
Be sure that wherever you
go, you take with you al
And to his love, dear Molly, I add my own
Yours Faithfu
Gwendol

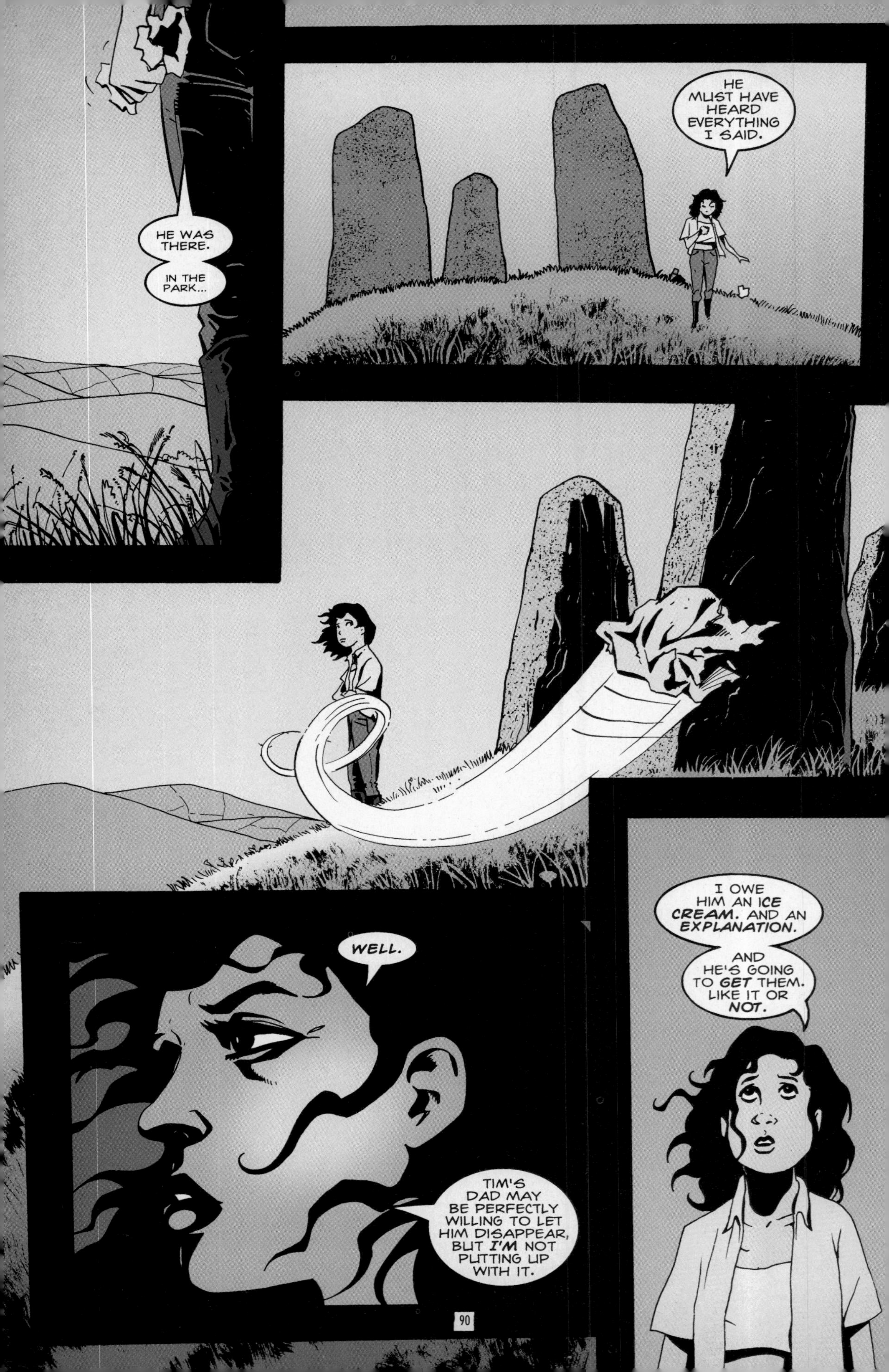
HE WAS THERE.
IN THE PARK...
HE MUST HAVE HEARD EVERYTHING I SAID.
WELL.
TIM'S DAD MAY BE PERFECTLY WILLING TO LET HIM DISAPPEAR, BUT I'M NOT PUTTING UP WITH IT.
I OWE HIM AN ICE CREAM. AND AN EXPLANATION.
AND HE'S GOING TO GET THEM. LIKE IT OR NOT.

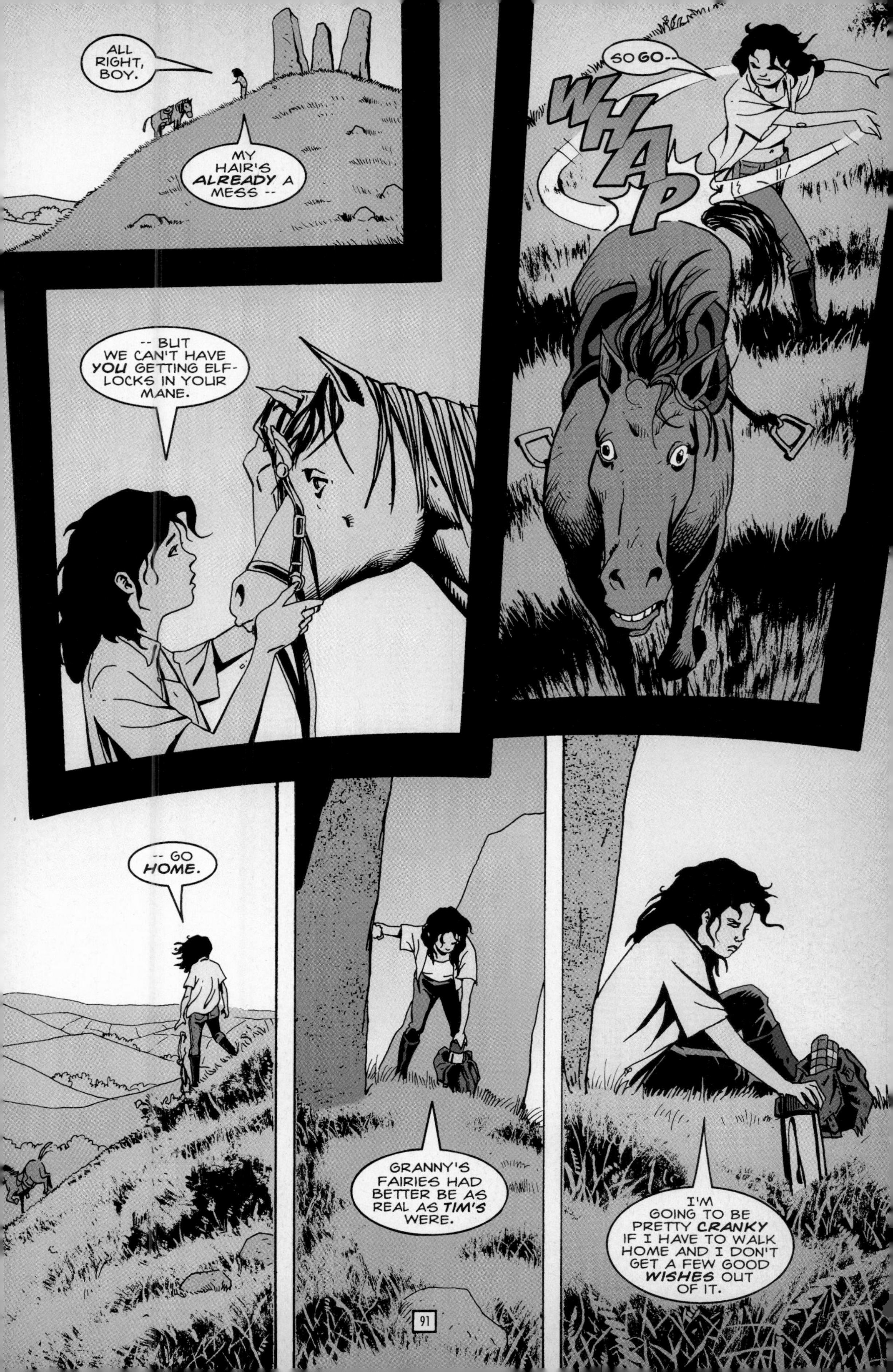
ALL RIGHT, BOY.
MY HAIR'S ALREADY A MESS --
-- BUT WE CAN'T HAVE YOU GETTING ELF-LOCKS IN YOUR MANE.
SO GO--
WHAP
-- GO HOME.
GRANNY'S FAIRIES HAD BETTER BE AS REAL AS TIM'S WERE.
I'M GOING TO BE PRETTY CRANKY IF I HAVE TO WALK HOME AND I DON'T GET A FEW GOOD WISHES OUT OF IT.

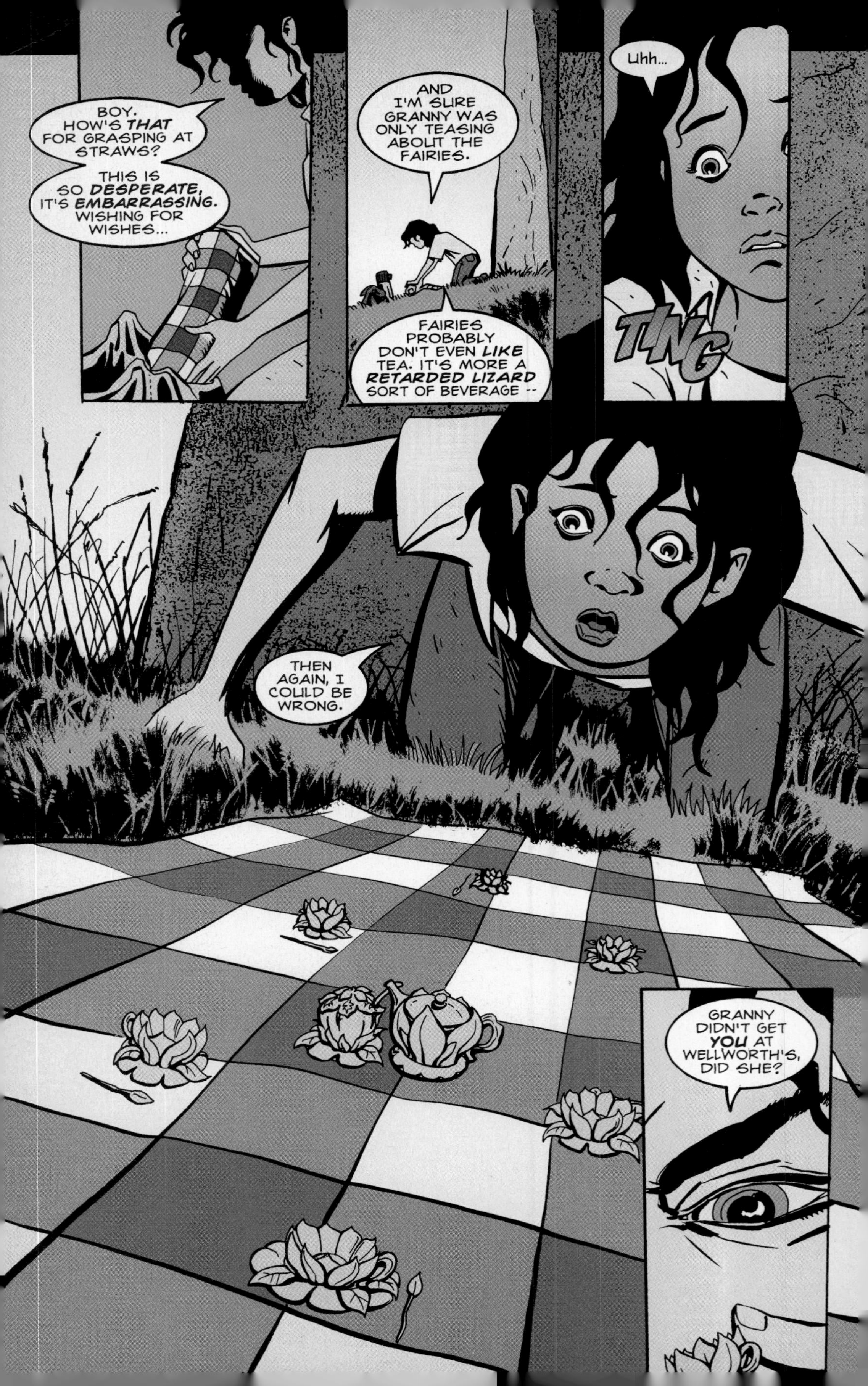

BOY. HOW'S *THAT* FOR GRASPING AT STRAWS?
THIS IS SO *DESPERATE*, IT'S *EMBARRASSING*. WISHING FOR WISHES...
AND I'M SURE GRANNY WAS ONLY TEASING ABOUT THE FAIRIES.
FAIRIES PROBABLY DON'T EVEN *LIKE* TEA. IT'S MORE A *RETARDED LIZARD* SORT OF BEVERAGE --
Uhh...
TING
THEN AGAIN, I COULD BE WRONG.
GRANNY DIDN'T GET *YOU* AT WELLWORTH'S, DID SHE?

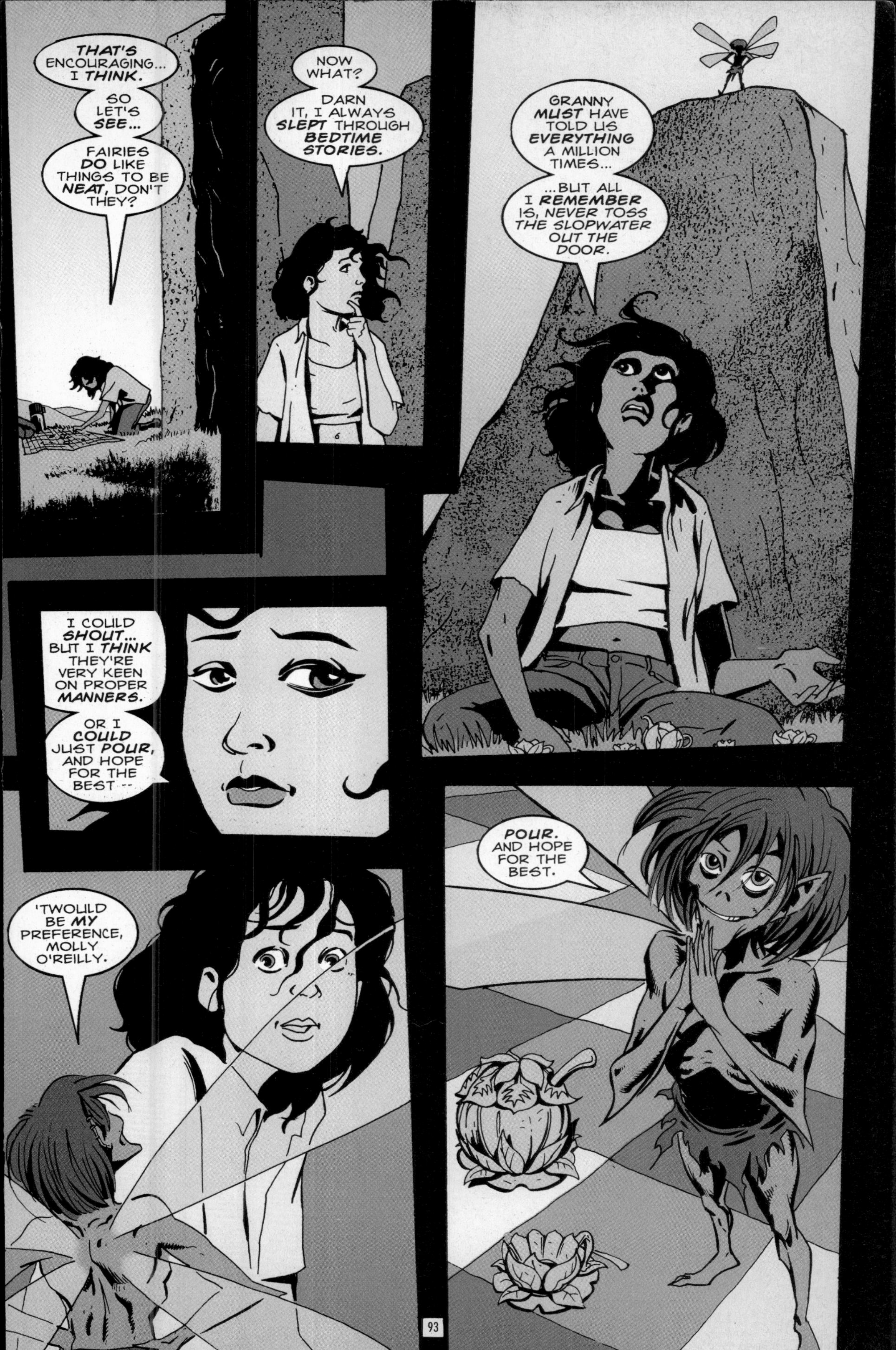
THAT'S ENCOURAGING... I THINK.
SO LET'S SEE...
FAIRIES DO LIKE THINGS TO BE NEAT, DON'T THEY?
NOW WHAT?
DARN IT, I ALWAYS SLEPT THROUGH BEDTIME STORIES.
GRANNY MUST HAVE TOLD US EVERYTHING A MILLION TIMES...
...BUT ALL I REMEMBER IS, NEVER TOSS THE SLOPWATER OUT THE DOOR.
I COULD SHOUT... BUT I THINK THEY'RE VERY KEEN ON PROPER MANNERS.
OR I COULD JUST POUR, AND HOPE FOR THE BEST --
POUR. AND HOPE FOR THE BEST.
'TWOULD BE MY PREFERENCE, MOLLY O'REILLY.

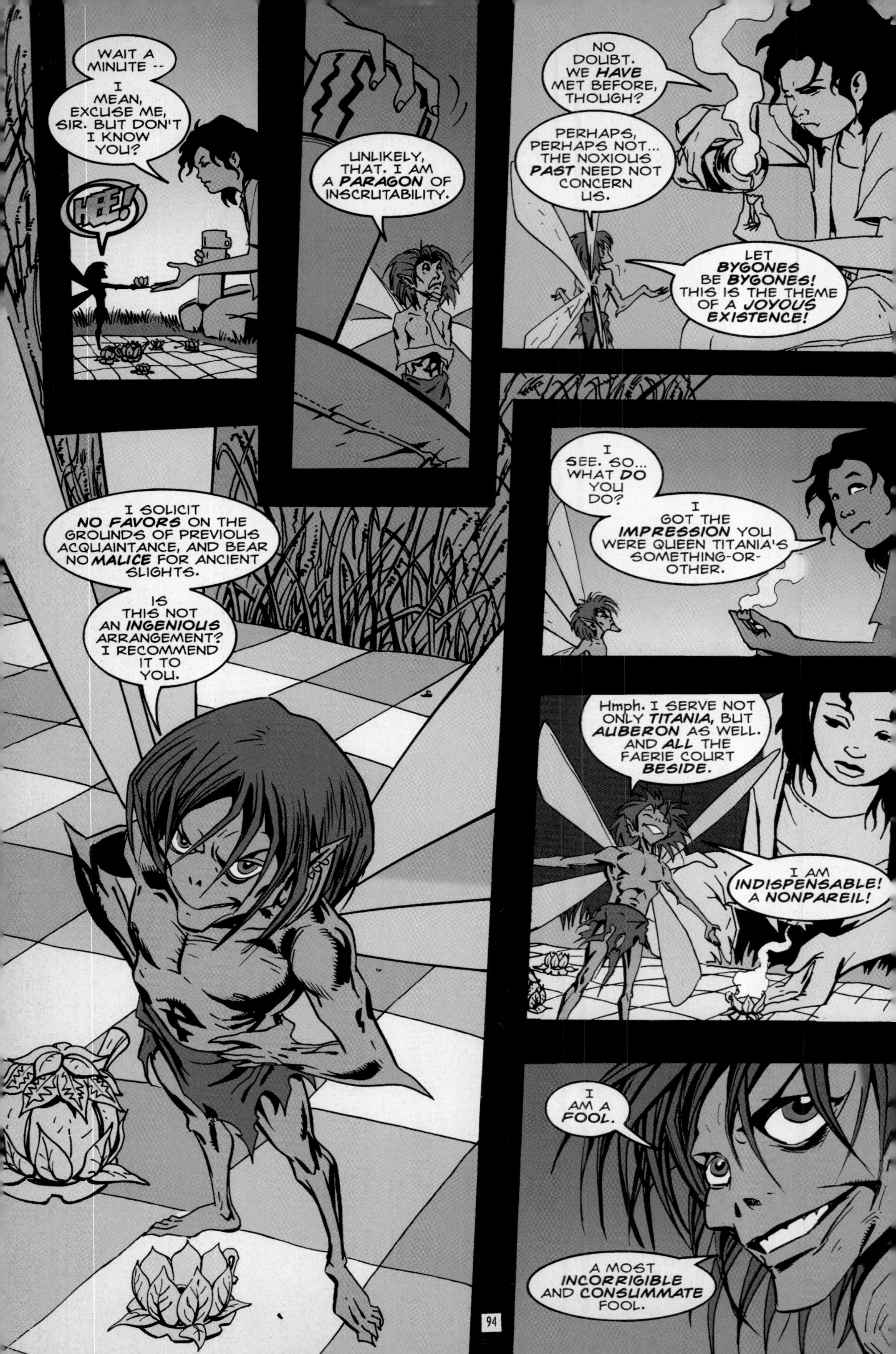

WAIT A MINUTE -- I MEAN, EXCUSE ME, SIR. BUT DON'T I KNOW YOU?
HEE!
UNLIKELY, THAT. I AM A PARAGON OF INSCRUTABILITY.
NO DOUBT. WE HAVE MET BEFORE, THOUGH?
PERHAPS, PERHAPS NOT... THE NOXIOUS PAST NEED NOT CONCERN US.
LET BYGONES BE BYGONES! THIS IS THE THEME OF A JOYOUS EXISTENCE!
I SOLICIT NO FAVORS ON THE GROUNDS OF PREVIOUS ACQUAINTANCE, AND BEAR NO MALICE FOR ANCIENT SLIGHTS.
IS THIS NOT AN INGENIOUS ARRANGEMENT? I RECOMMEND IT TO YOU.
I SEE. SO... WHAT DO YOU DO?
I GOT THE IMPRESSION YOU WERE QUEEN TITANIA'S SOMETHING-OR-OTHER.
Hmph. I SERVE NOT ONLY TITANIA, BUT AUBERON AS WELL. AND ALL THE FAERIE COURT BESIDE.
I AM INDISPENSABLE! A NONPAREIL!
I AM A FOOL.
A MOST INCORRIGIBLE AND CONSUMMATE FOOL.

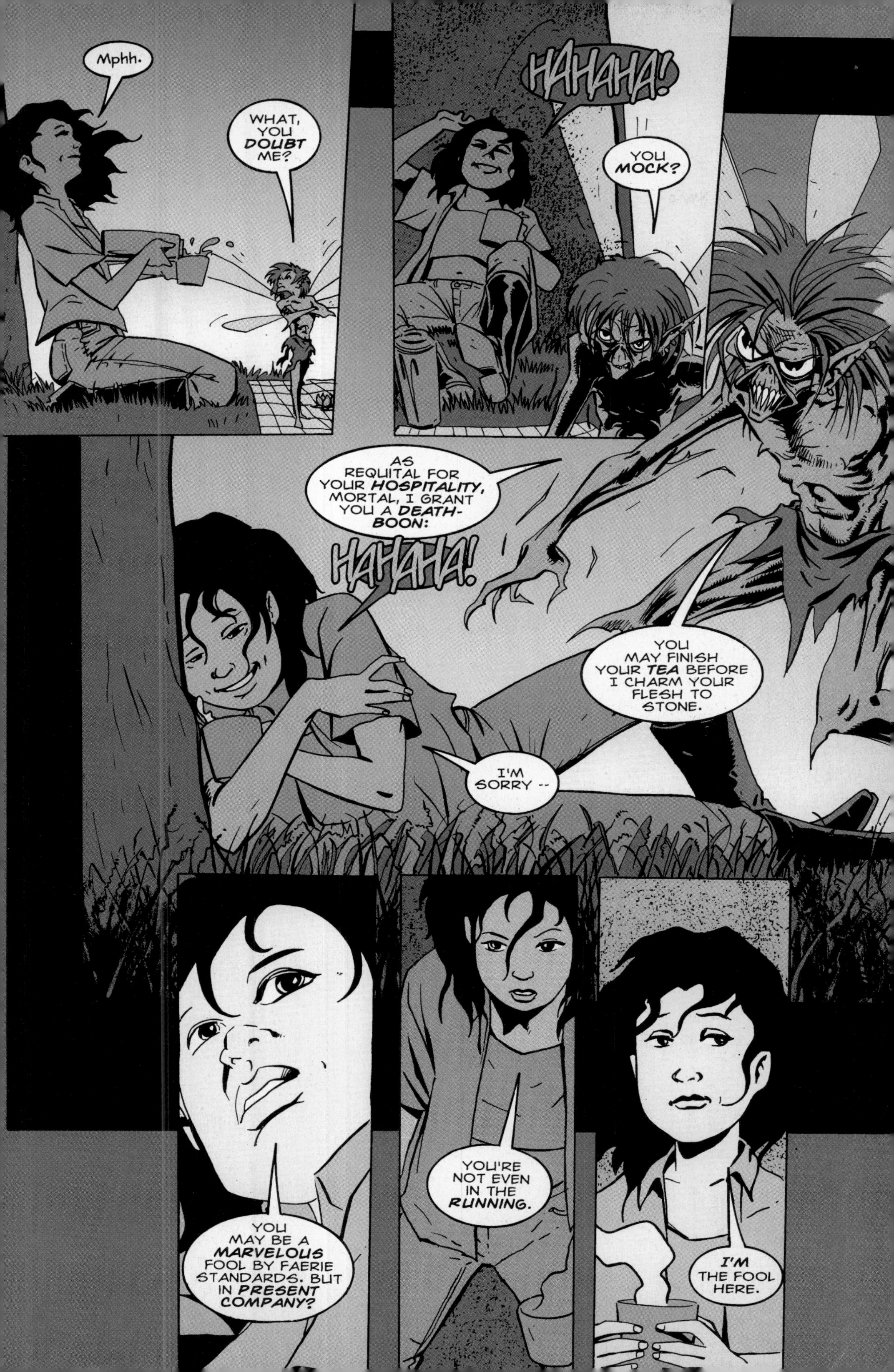
Mphh.
WHAT, YOU DOUBT ME?
HAHAHA!
YOU MOCK?
AS REQUITAL FOR YOUR HOSPITALITY, MORTAL, I GRANT YOU A DEATH-BOON:
HAHAHA!
YOU MAY FINISH YOUR TEA BEFORE I CHARM YOUR FLESH TO STONE.
I'M SORRY --
YOU MAY BE A MARVELOUS FOOL BY FAERIE STANDARDS. BUT IN PRESENT COMPANY?
YOU'RE NOT EVEN IN THE RUNNING.
I'M THE FOOL HERE.

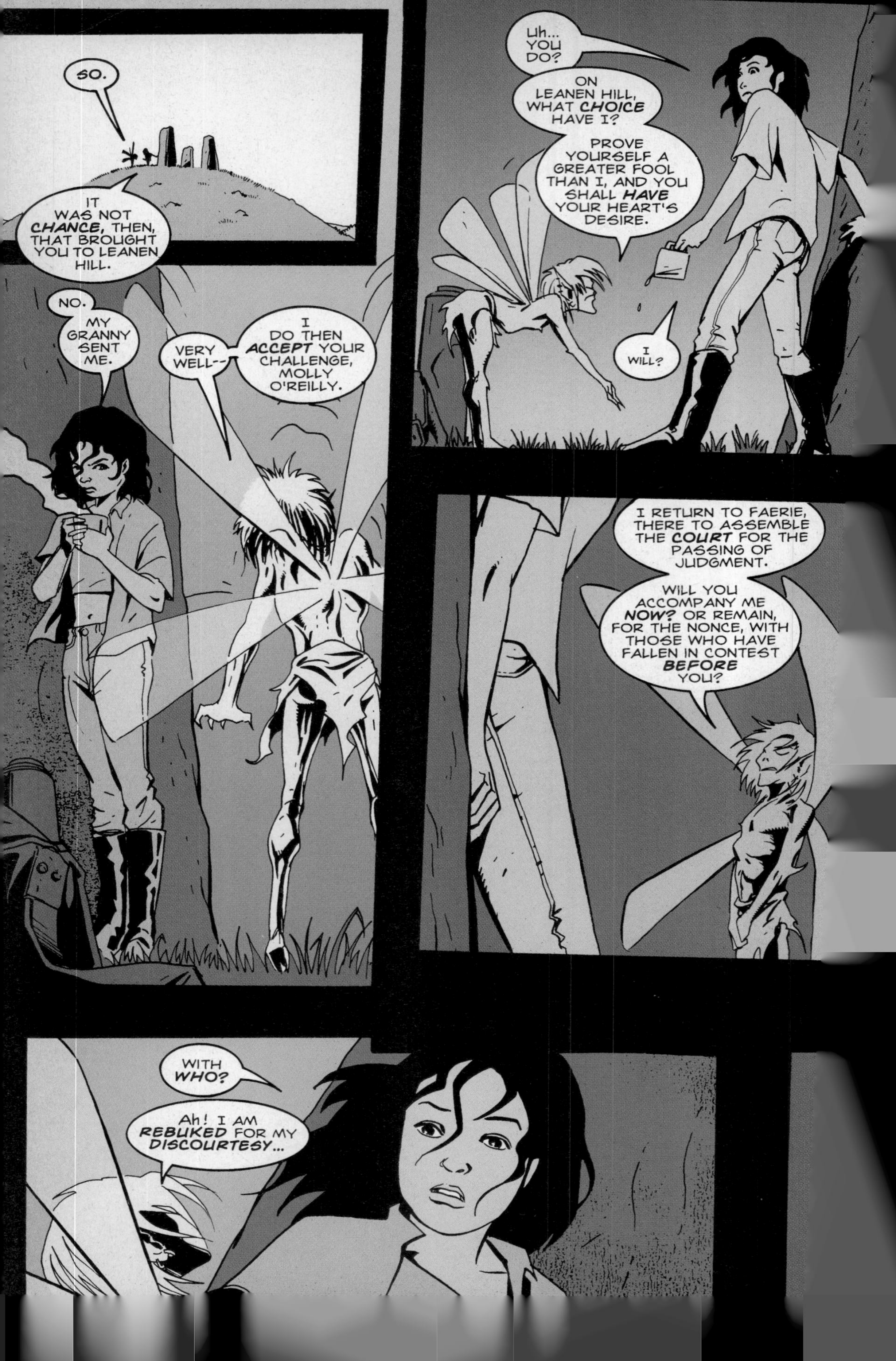
SO.
IT WAS NOT CHANCE, THEN, THAT BROUGHT YOU TO LEANEN HILL.
NO.
MY GRANNY SENT ME.
VERY WELL--
I DO THEN ACCEPT YOUR CHALLENGE, MOLLY O'REILLY.
Uh... YOU DO?
ON LEANEN HILL, WHAT CHOICE HAVE I?
PROVE YOURSELF A GREATER FOOL THAN I, AND YOU SHALL HAVE YOUR HEART'S DESIRE.
I WILL?
I RETURN TO FAERIE, THERE TO ASSEMBLE THE COURT FOR THE PASSING OF JUDGMENT.
WILL YOU ACCOMPANY ME NOW? OR REMAIN, FOR THE NONCE, WITH THOSE WHO HAVE FALLEN IN CONTEST BEFORE YOU?
WITH WHO?
Ah! I AM REBUKED FOR MY DISCOURTESY...

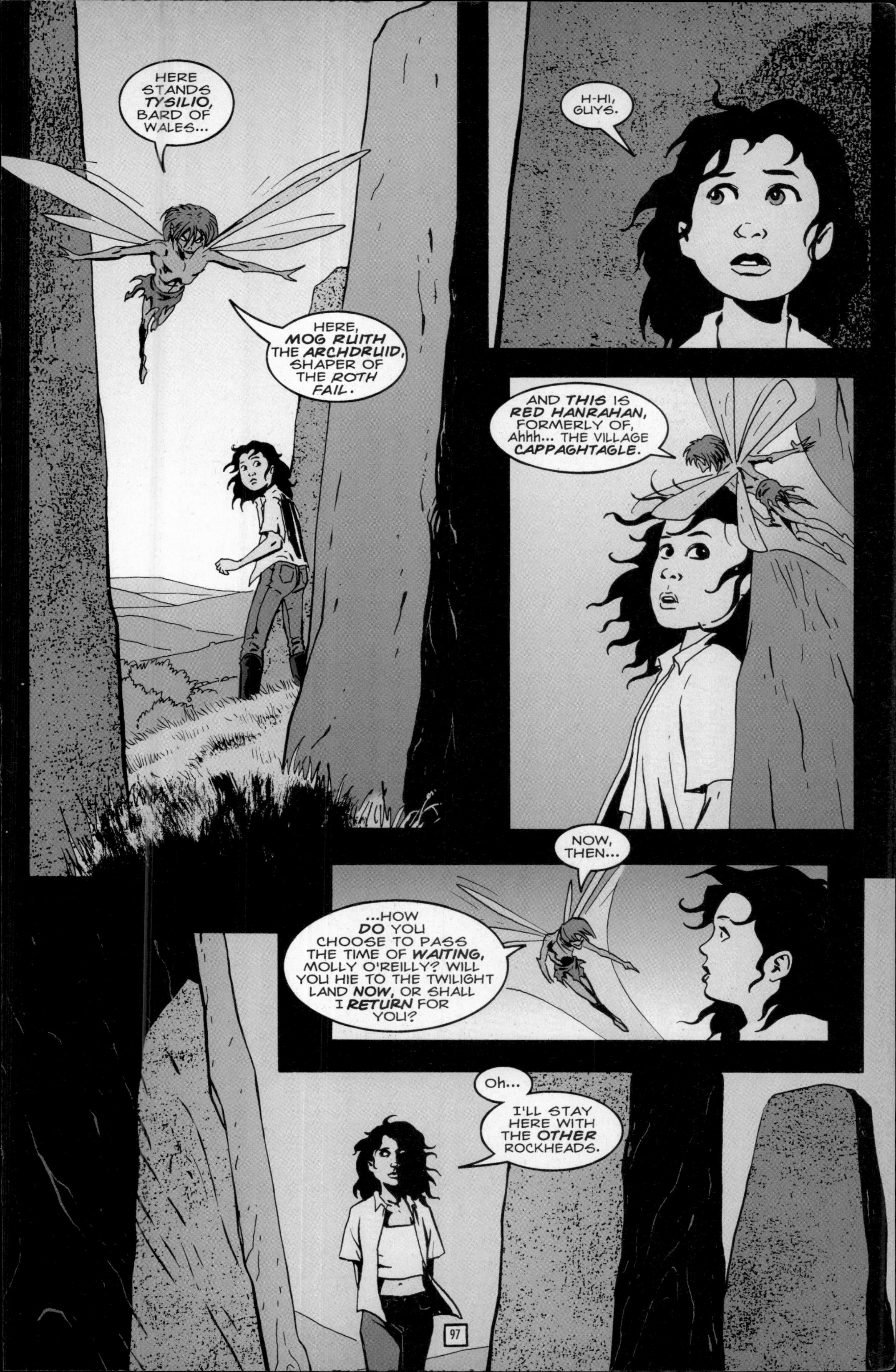
HERE STANDS TYSILIO, BARD OF WALES...
HERE, MOG RUITH THE ARCHDRUID, SHAPER OF THE ROTH FAIL.
H-HI, GUYS.
AND THIS IS RED HANRAHAN, FORMERLY OF, Ahhh... THE VILLAGE CAPPAGHTAGLE.
NOW, THEN...
...HOW DO YOU CHOOSE TO PASS THE TIME OF WAITING, MOLLY O'REILLY? WILL YOU HIE TO THE TWILIGHT LAND NOW, OR SHALL I RETURN FOR YOU?
Oh...
I'LL STAY HERE WITH THE OTHER ROCKHEADS.

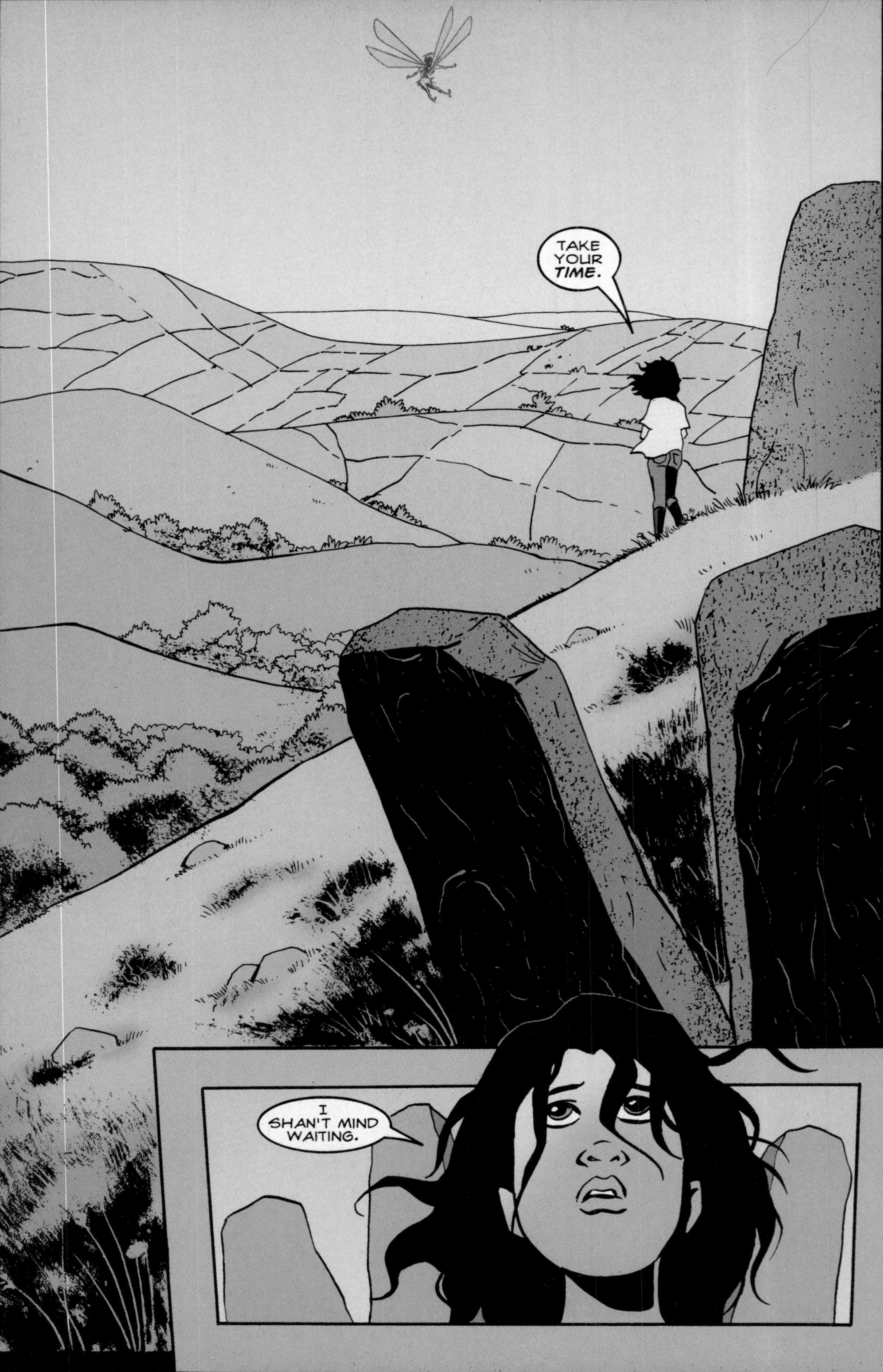

TAKE YOUR TIME.
I SHAN'T MIND WAITING.

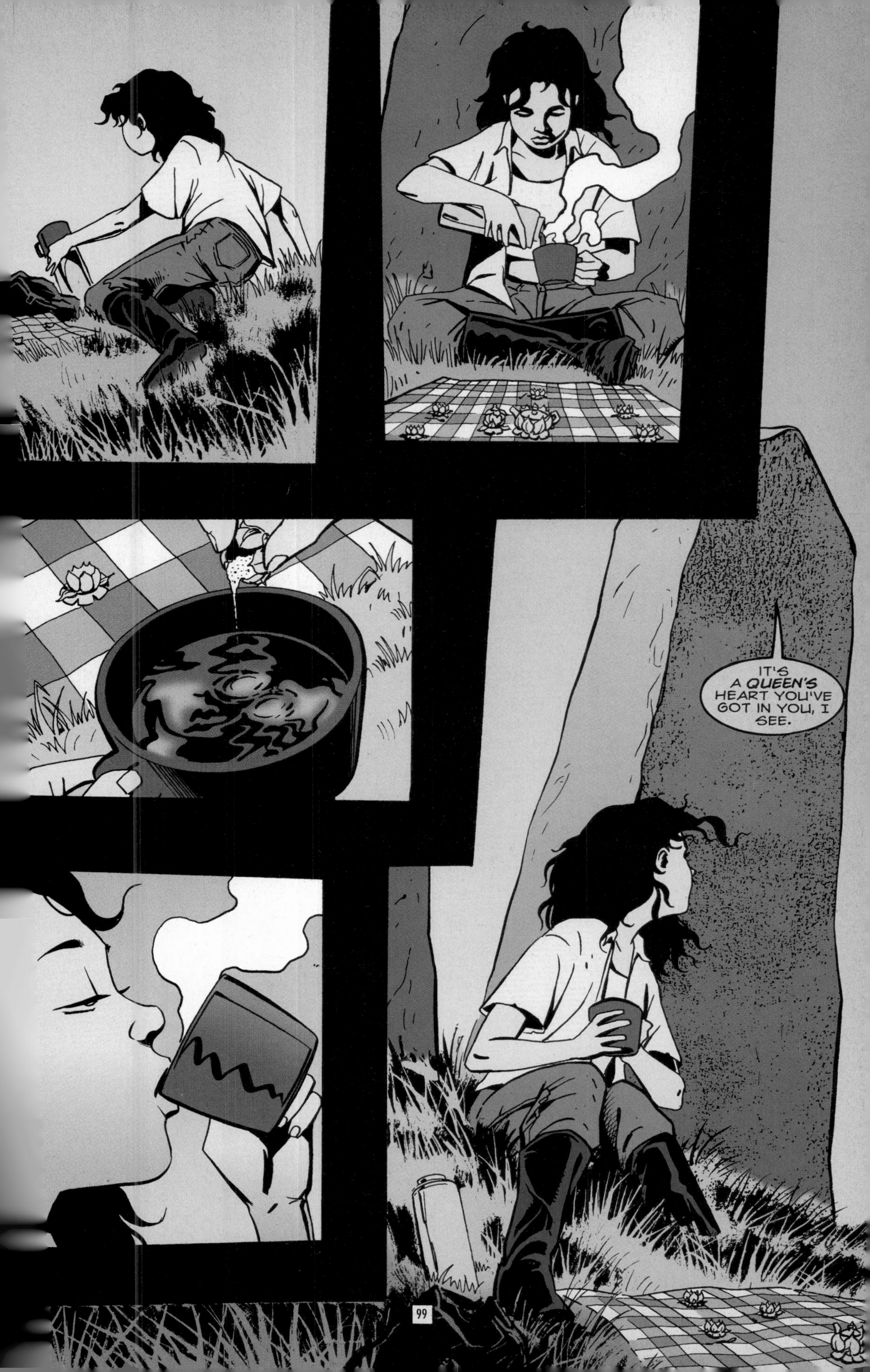
IT'S A QUEEN'S HEART YOU'VE GOT IN YOU, I SEE.

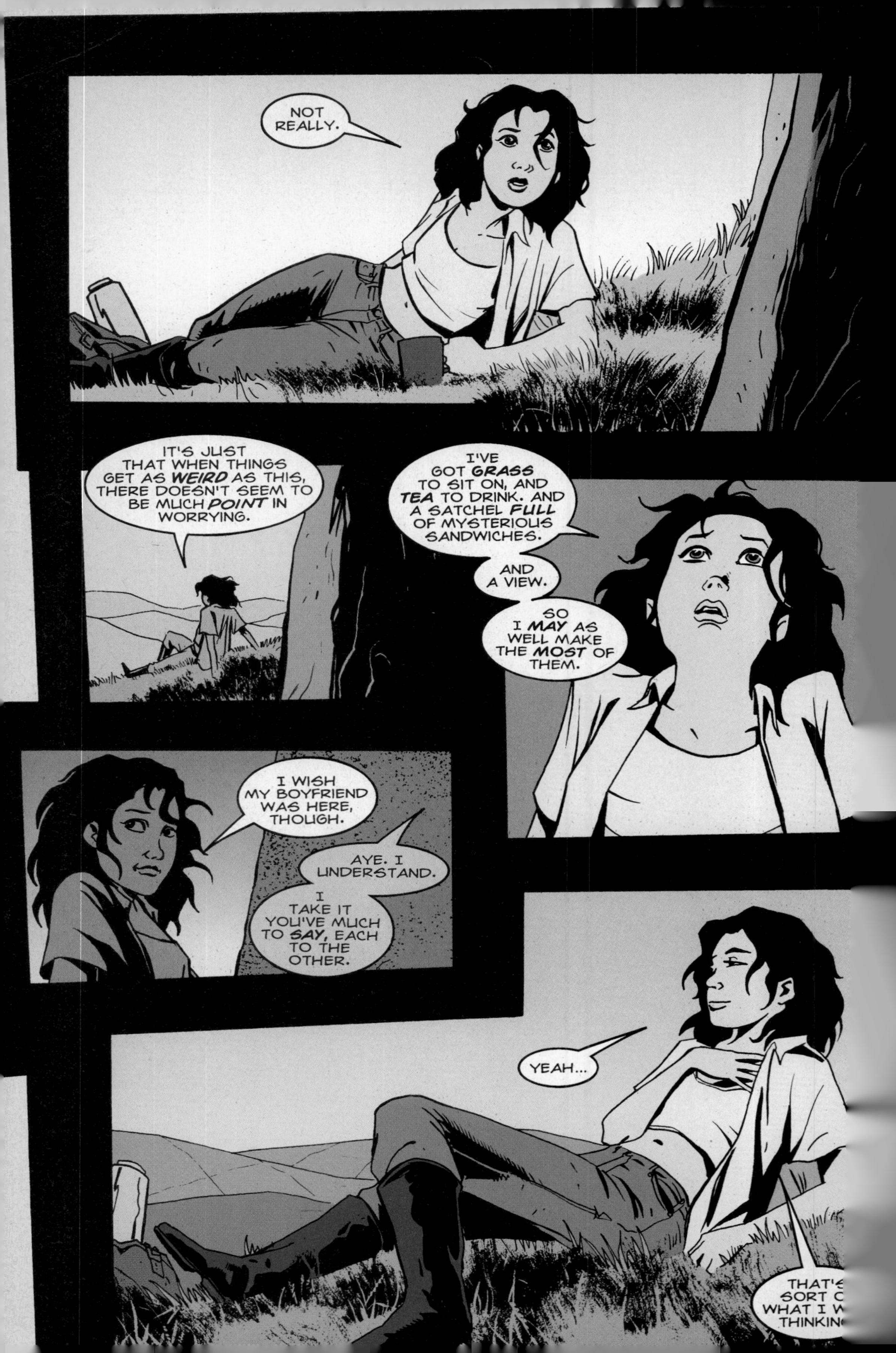
NOT REALLY.
IT'S JUST THAT WHEN THINGS GET AS WEIRD AS THIS, THERE DOESN'T SEEM TO BE MUCH POINT IN WORRYING.
I'VE GOT GRASS TO SIT ON, AND TEA TO DRINK. AND A SATCHEL FULL OF MYSTERIOUS SANDWICHES.
AND A VIEW.
SO I MAY AS WELL MAKE THE MOST OF THEM.
I WISH MY BOYFRIEND WAS HERE, THOUGH.
AYE. I UNDERSTAND.
I TAKE IT YOU'VE MUCH TO SAY, EACH TO THE OTHER.
YEAH...

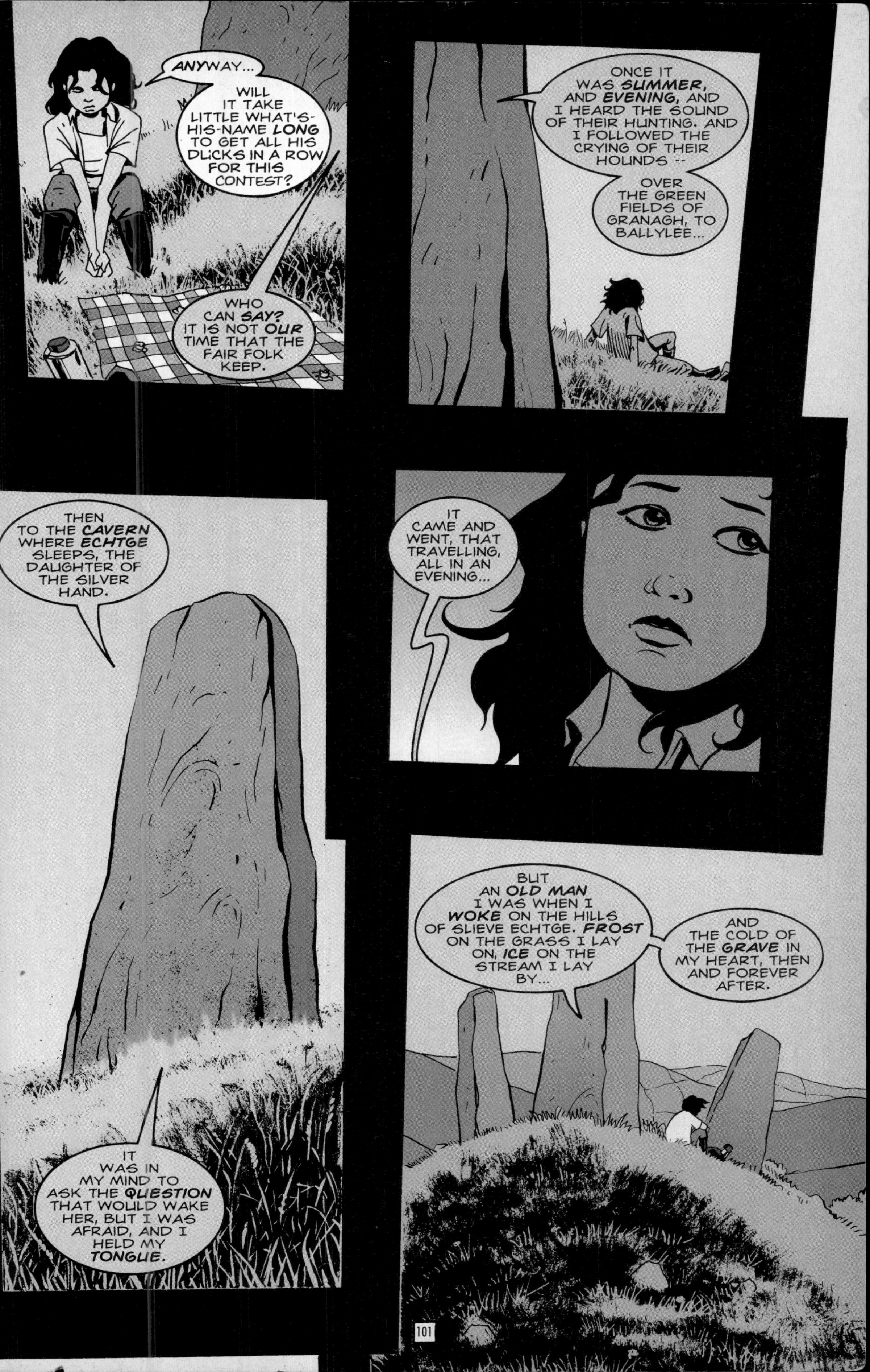

ANYWAY...
WILL IT TAKE LITTLE WHAT'S-HIS-NAME LONG TO GET ALL HIS DUCKS IN A ROW FOR THIS CONTEST?
WHO CAN SAY? IT IS NOT OUR TIME THAT THE FAIR FOLK KEEP.
ONCE IT WAS SUMMER, AND EVENING, AND I HEARD THE SOUND OF THEIR HUNTING. AND I FOLLOWED THE CRYING OF THEIR HOUNDS --
OVER THE GREEN FIELDS OF GRANAGH, TO BALLYLEE...
THEN TO THE CAVERN WHERE ECHTGE SLEEPS, THE DAUGHTER OF THE SILVER HAND.
IT WAS IN MY MIND TO ASK THE QUESTION THAT WOULD WAKE HER, BUT I WAS AFRAID, AND I HELD MY TONGUE.
IT CAME AND WENT, THAT TRAVELLING, ALL IN AN EVENING...
BUT AN OLD MAN I WAS WHEN I WOKE ON THE HILLS OF SLIEVE ECHTGE. FROST ON THE GRASS I LAY ON, ICE ON THE STREAM I LAY BY...
AND THE COLD OF THE GRAVE IN MY HEART, THEN AND FOREVER AFTER.

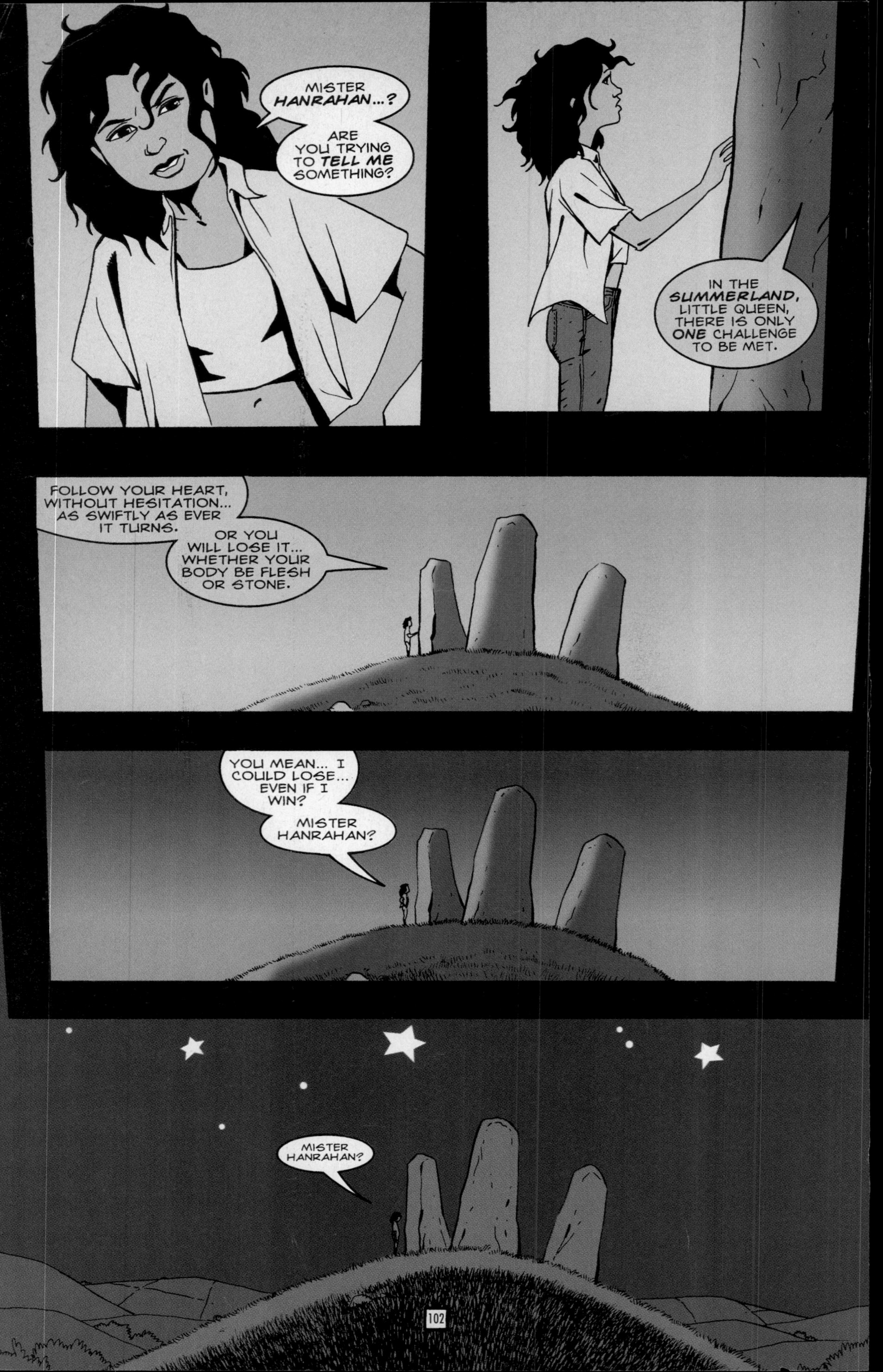
MISTER HANRAHAN...?
ARE YOU TRYING TO TELL ME SOMETHING?
IN THE SUMMERLAND, LITTLE QUEEN, THERE IS ONLY ONE CHALLENGE TO BE MET.
FOLLOW YOUR HEART, WITHOUT HESITATION... AS SWIFTLY AS EVER IT TURNS.
OR YOU WILL LOSE IT... WHETHER YOUR BODY BE FLESH OR STONE.
YOU MEAN... I COULD LOSE... EVEN IF I WIN?
MISTER HANRAHAN?
MISTER HANRAHAN?

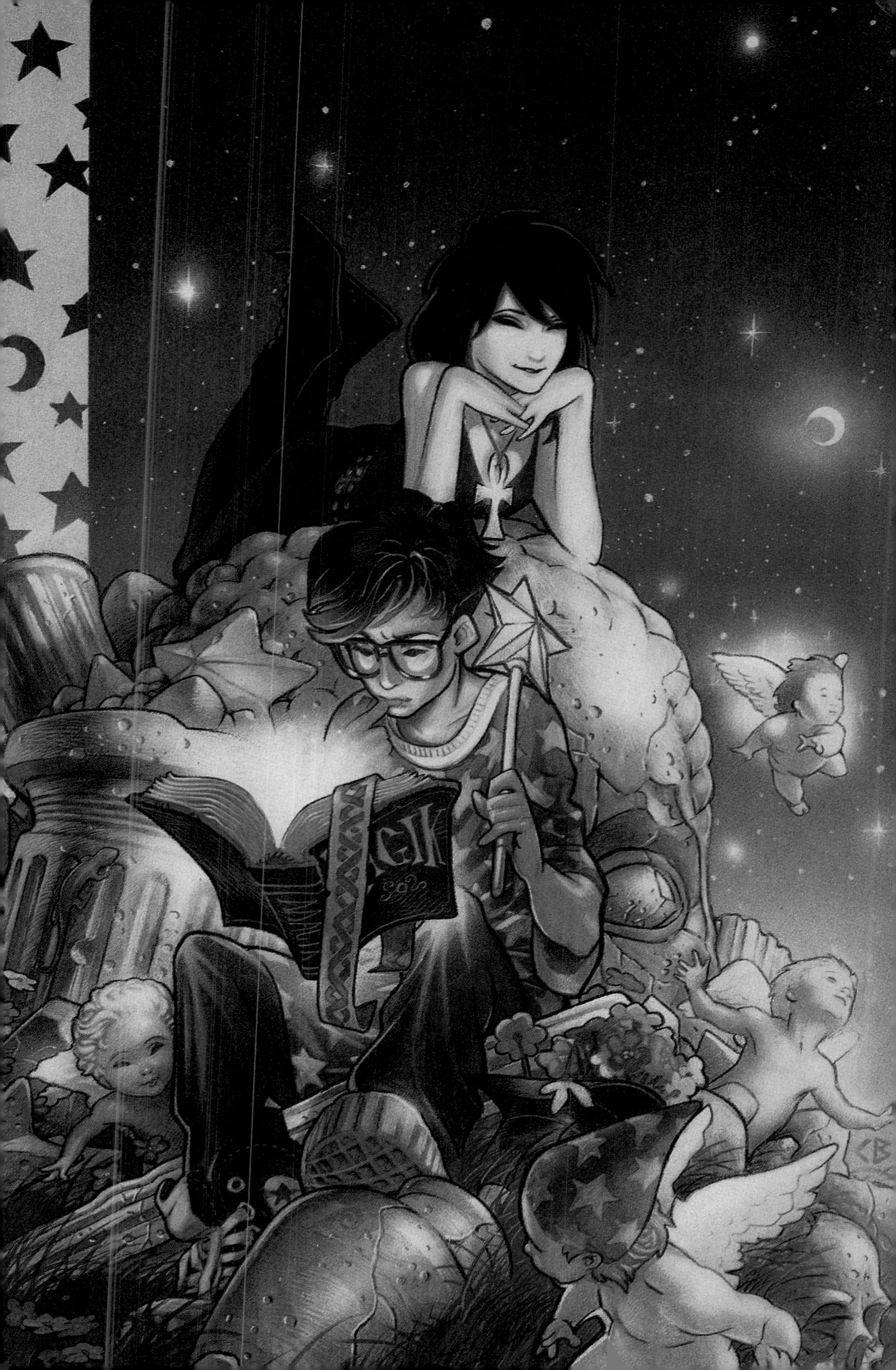

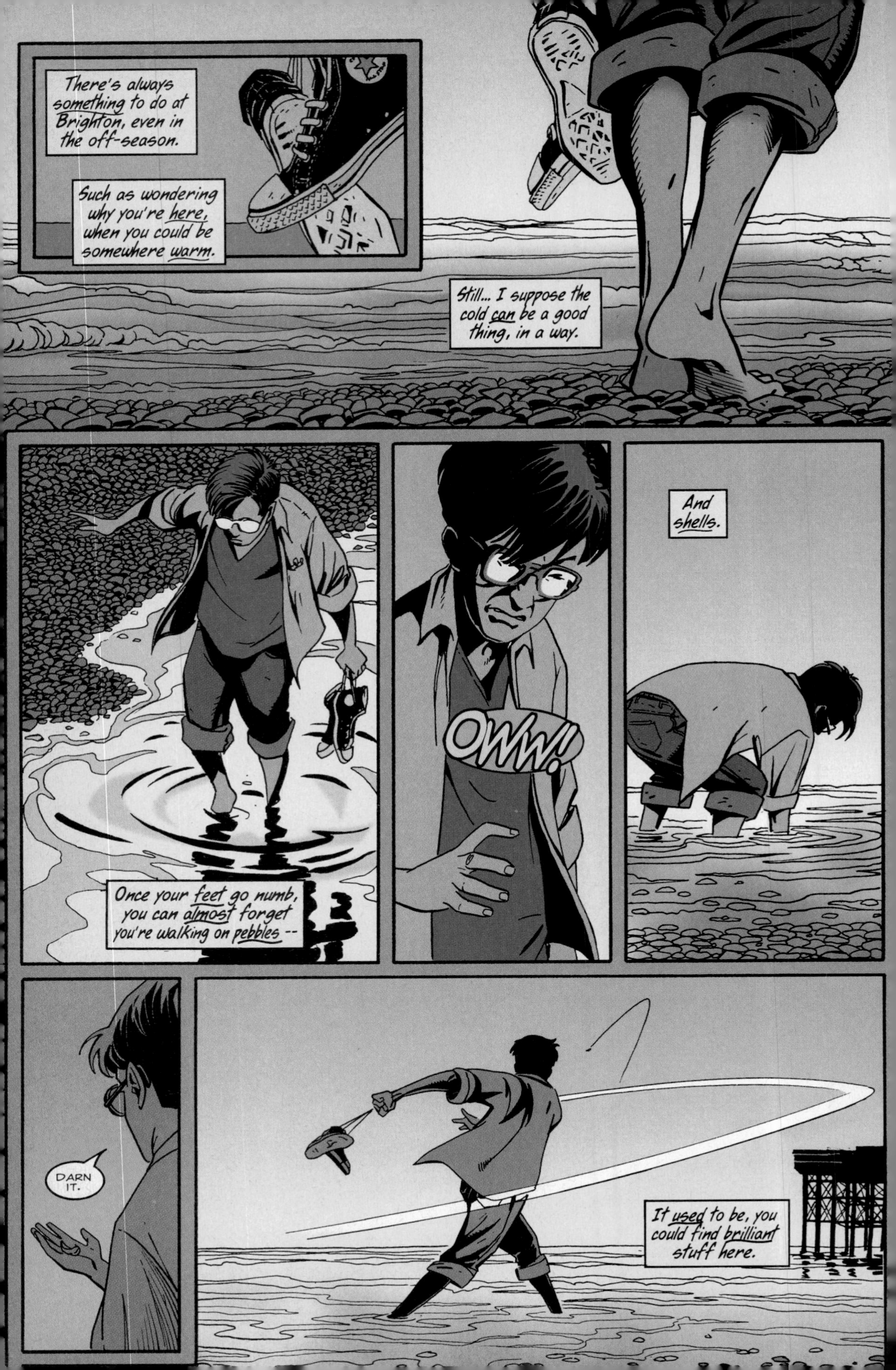
There's always something to do at Brighton, even in the off-season.
Such as wondering why you're here, when you could be somewhere warm.
Still... I suppose the cold can be a good thing, in a way.
Once your feet go numb, you can almost forget you're walking on pebbles --
OWW!
And shells.
DARN IT.
It used to be, you could find brilliant stuff here.

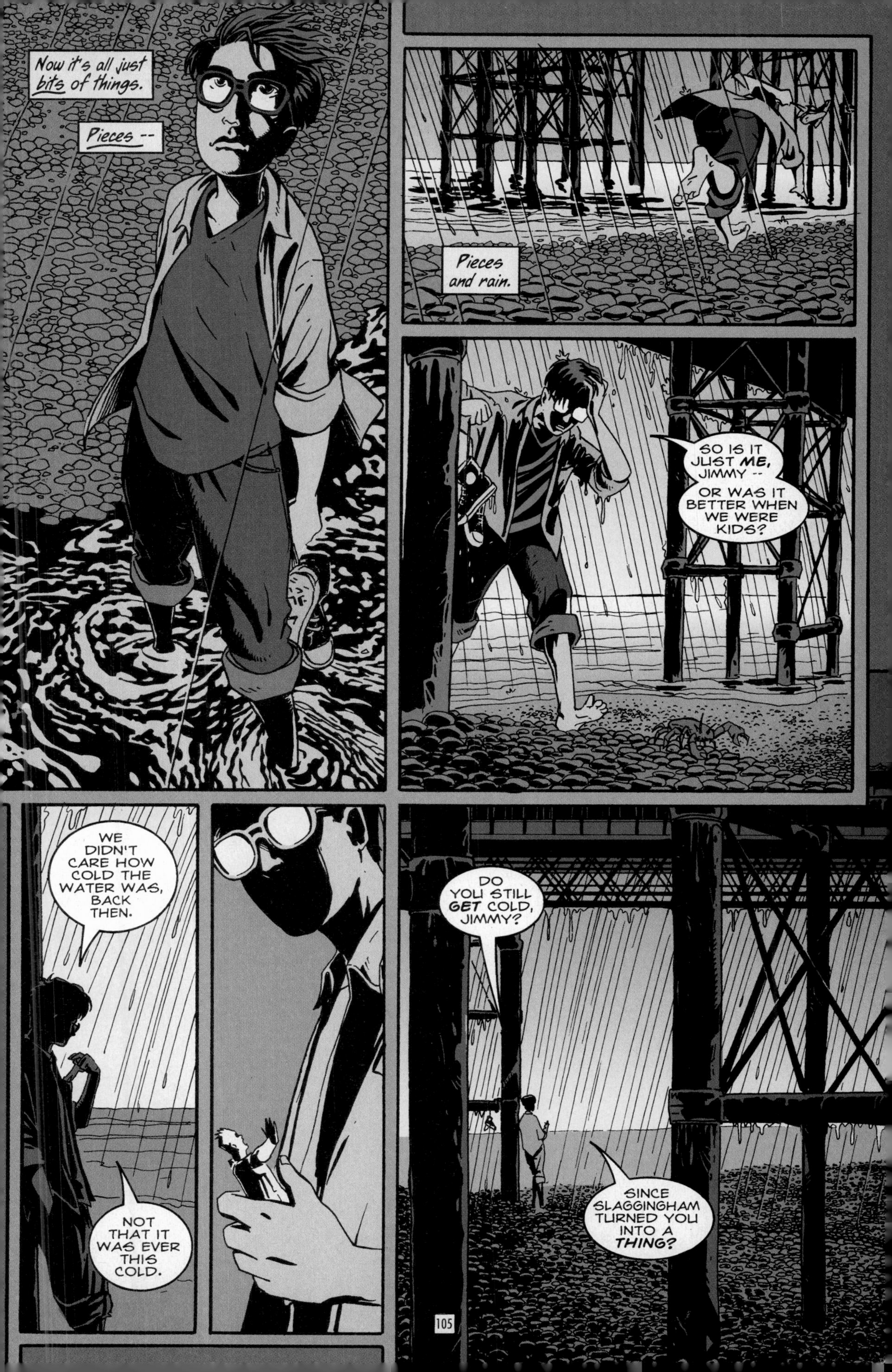
Now it's all just bits of things.
Pieces --
Pieces and rain.
SO IS IT JUST ME, JIMMY --
OR WAS IT BETTER WHEN WE WERE KIDS?
WE DIDN'T CARE HOW COLD THE WATER WAS, BACK THEN.
NOT THAT IT WAS EVER THIS COLD.
DO YOU STILL GET COLD, JIMMY?
SINCE SLAGGINGHAM TURNED YOU INTO A THING?

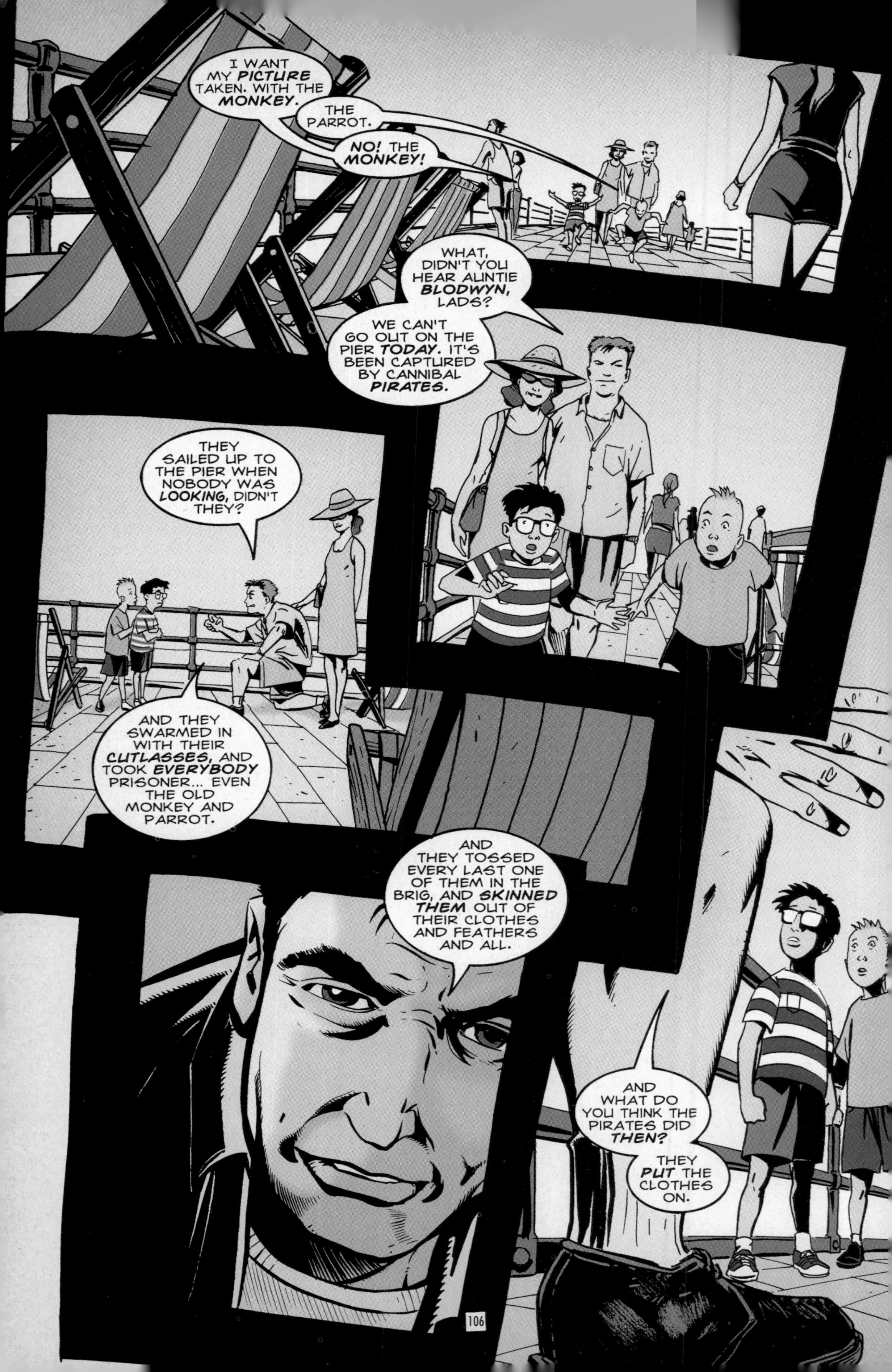
I WANT MY PICTURE TAKEN. WITH THE MONKEY.
THE PARROT.
NO! THE MONKEY!
WHAT, DIDN'T YOU HEAR AUNTIE BLODWYN, LADS?
WE CAN'T GO OUT ON THE PIER TODAY. IT'S BEEN CAPTURED BY CANNIBAL PIRATES.
THEY SAILED UP TO THE PIER WHEN NOBODY WAS LOOKING, DIDN'T THEY?
AND THEY SWARMED IN WITH THEIR CUTLASSES, AND TOOK EVERYBODY PRISONER... EVEN THE OLD MONKEY AND PARROT.
AND THEY TOSSED EVERY LAST ONE OF THEM IN THE BRIG, AND SKINNED THEM OUT OF THEIR CLOTHES AND FEATHERS AND ALL.
AND WHAT DO YOU THINK THE PIRATES DID THEN?
THEY PUT THE CLOTHES ON.

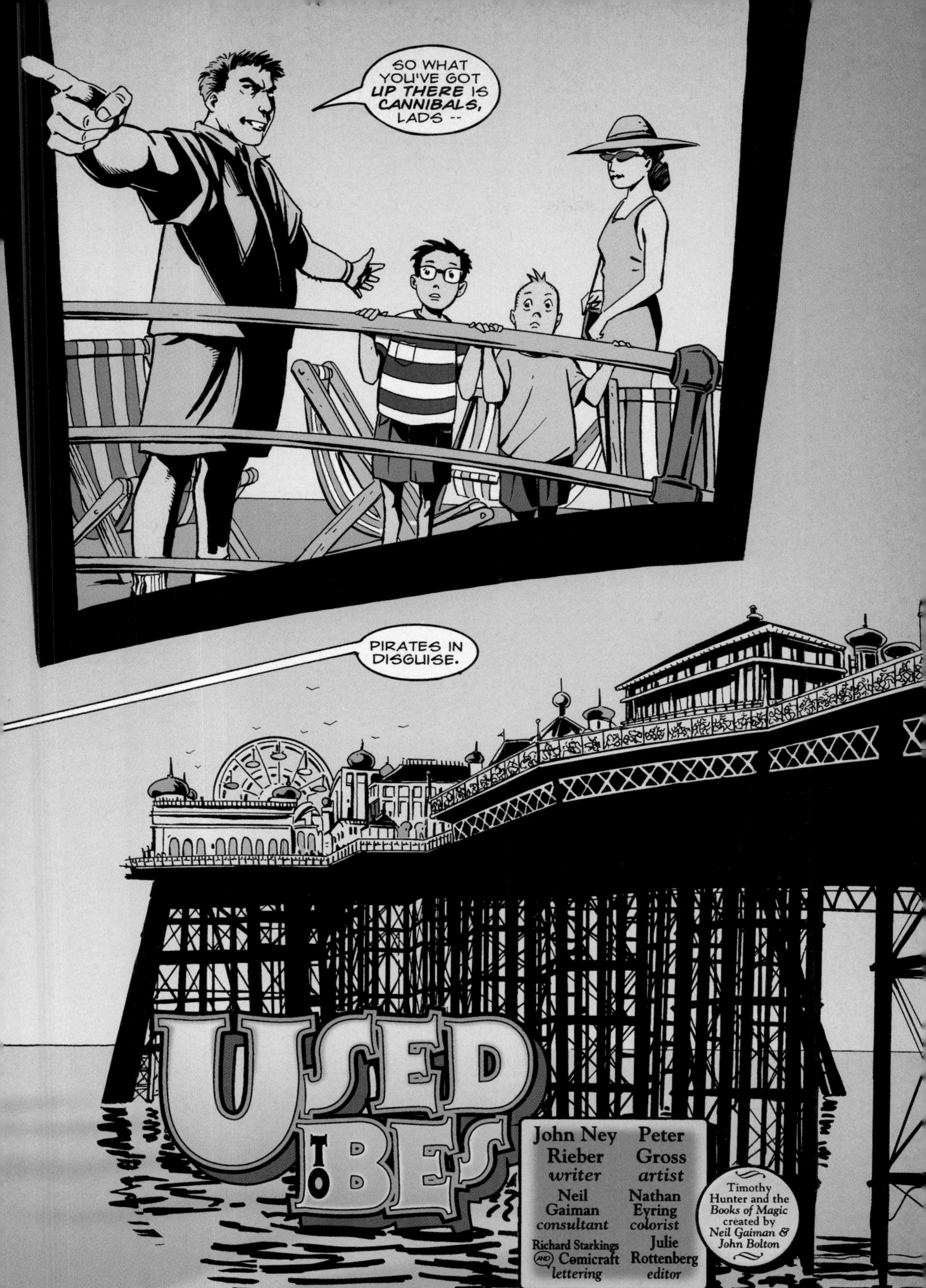

SO WHAT YOU'VE GOT UP THERE IS CANNIBALS, LADS --
PIRATES IN DISGUISE.
USED TO BES
John Ney Rieber writer
Peter Gross artist
Neil Gaiman consultant
Nathan Eyring colorist
Richard Starkings AND Comicraft lettering
Julie Rottenberg editor
Timothy Hunter and the Books of Magic created by Neil Gaiman & John Bolton

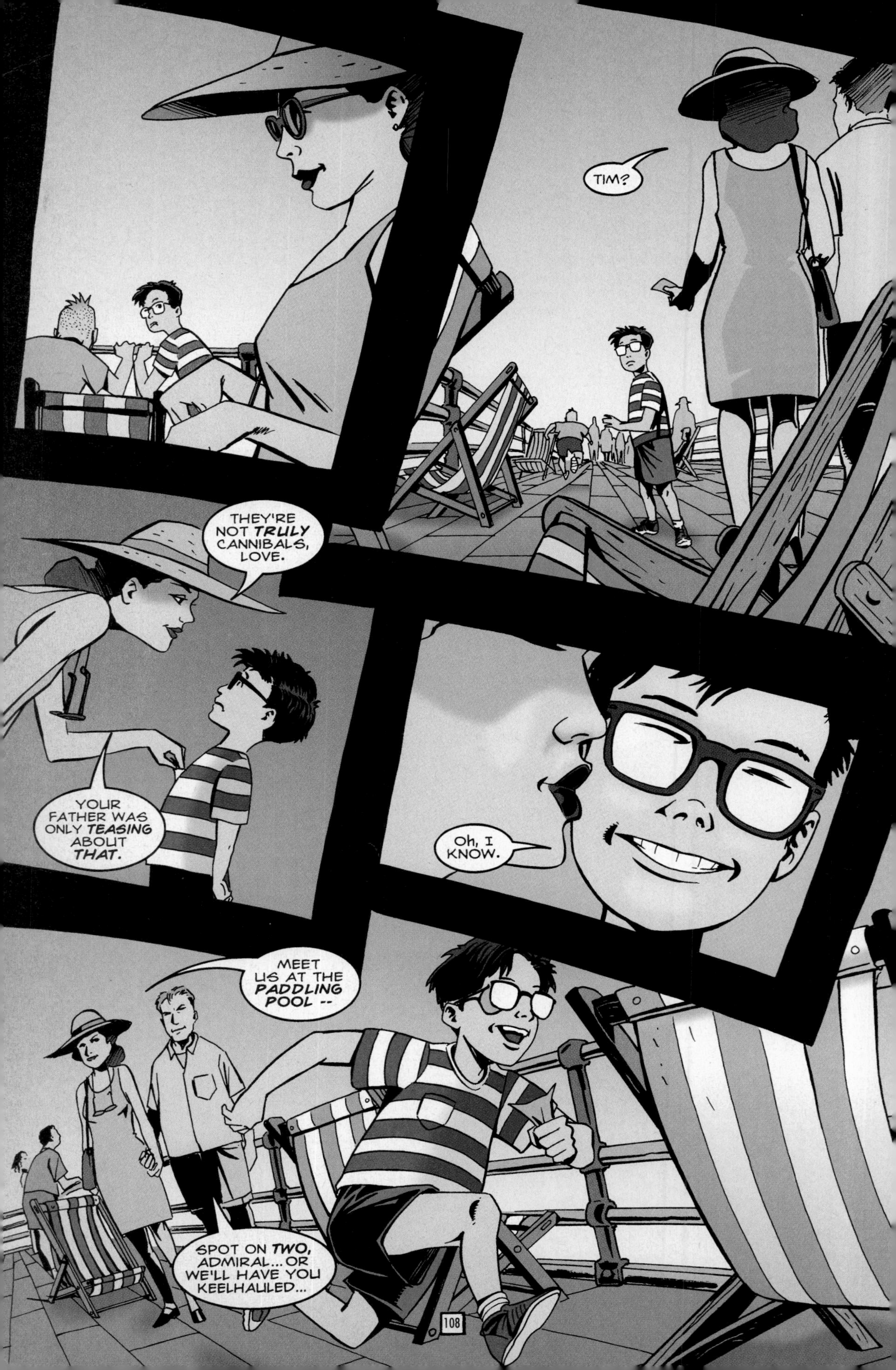
TIM?
THEY'RE NOT TRULY CANNIBALS, LOVE.
YOUR FATHER WAS ONLY TEASING ABOUT THAT.
Oh, I KNOW.
MEET US AT THE PADDLING POOL --
SPOT ON TWO, ADMIRAL... OR WE'LL HAVE YOU KEELHAULED...

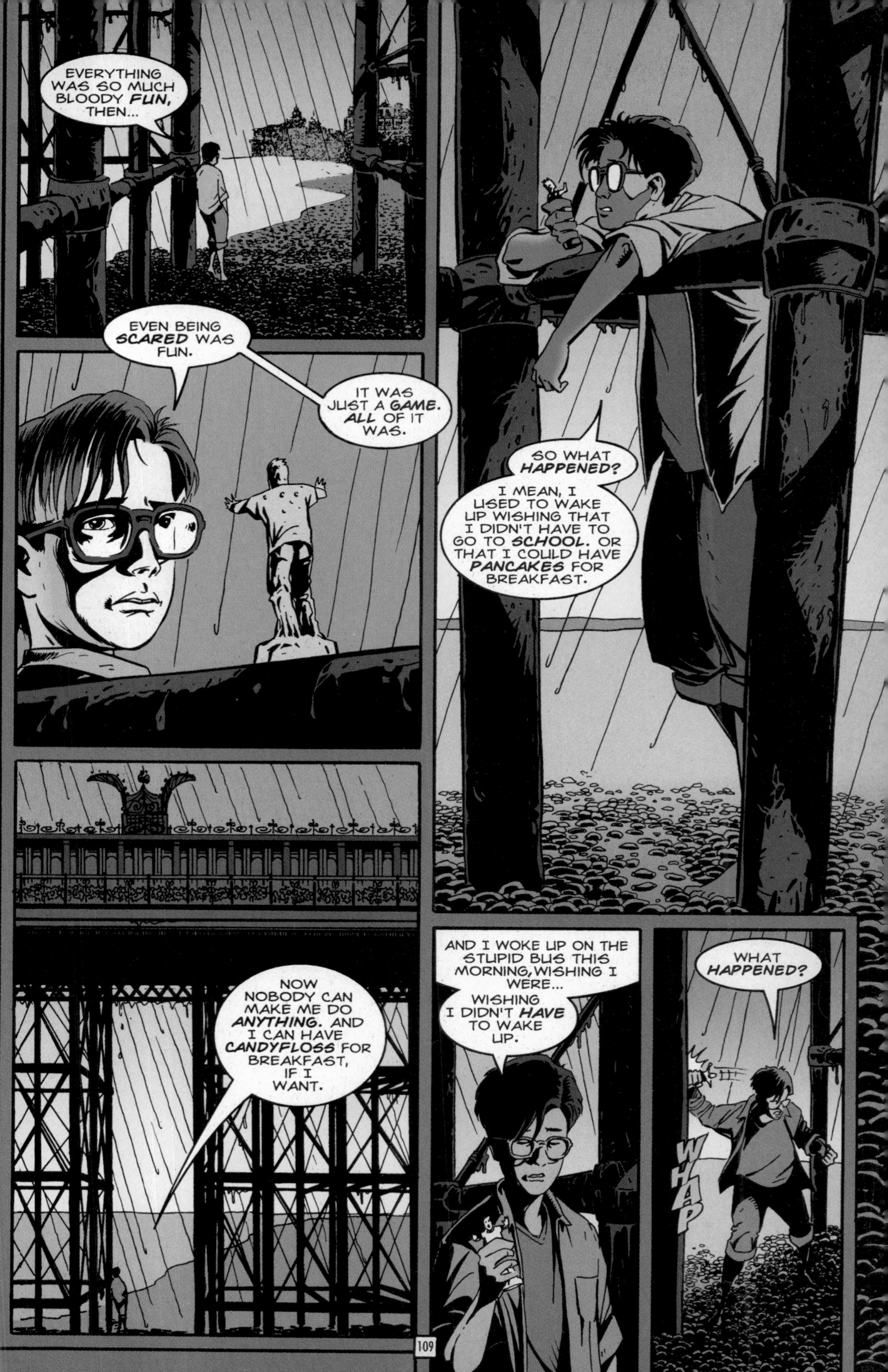
EVERYTHING WAS SO MUCH BLOODY FUN, THEN...
EVEN BEING SCARED WAS FUN.
IT WAS JUST A GAME. ALL OF IT WAS.
SO WHAT HAPPENED?
I MEAN, I USED TO WAKE UP WISHING THAT I DIDN'T HAVE TO GO TO SCHOOL. OR THAT I COULD HAVE PANCAKES FOR BREAKFAST.
NOW NOBODY CAN MAKE ME DO ANYTHING. AND I CAN HAVE CANDYFLOSS FOR BREAKFAST, IF I WANT.
AND I WOKE UP ON THE STUPID BUS THIS MORNING, WISHING I WERE...
WISHING I DIDN'T HAVE TO WAKE UP.
WHAT HAPPENED?
WHAP

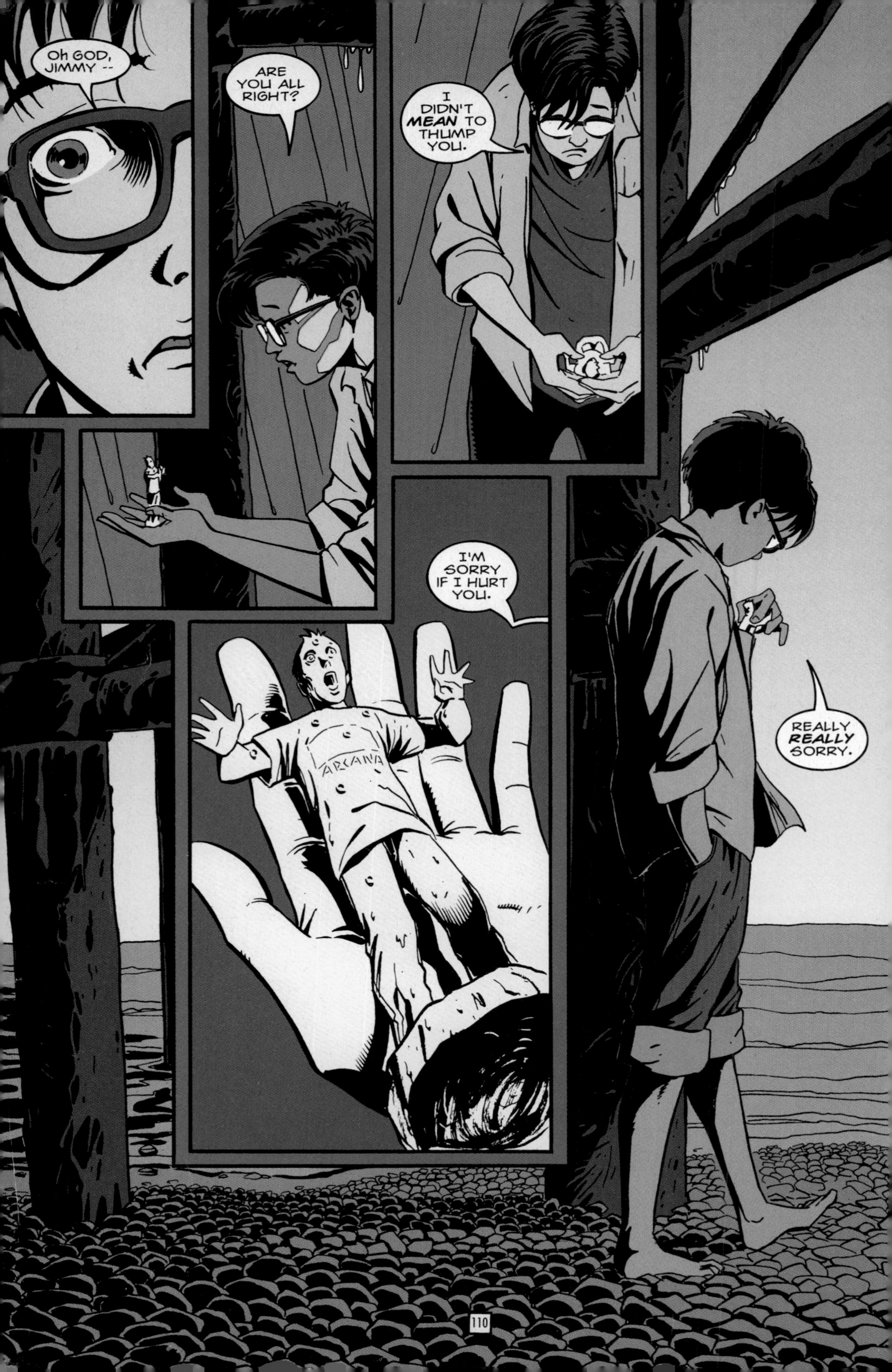

Oh GOD, JIMMY --
ARE YOU ALL RIGHT?
I DIDN'T **MEAN** TO THUMP YOU.
I'M SORRY IF I HURT YOU.
ARKANA
REALLY **REALLY** SORRY.

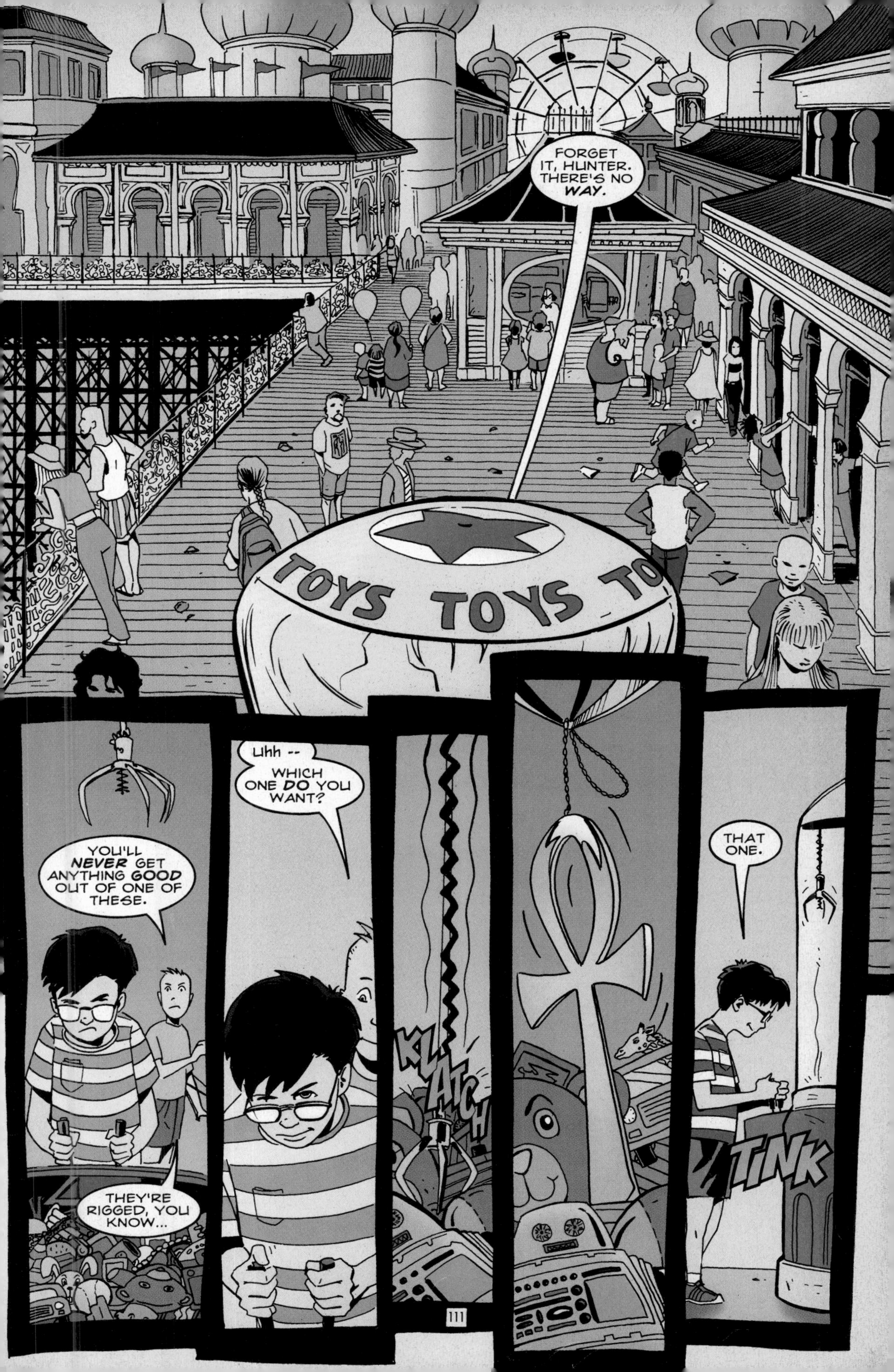
FORGET IT, HUNTER. THERE'S NO WAY.
TOYS TOYS TO
YOU'LL NEVER GET ANYTHING GOOD OUT OF ONE OF THESE.
THEY'RE RIGGED, YOU KNOW...
uhh --
WHICH ONE DO YOU WANT?
KLATCH
THAT ONE.
TINK

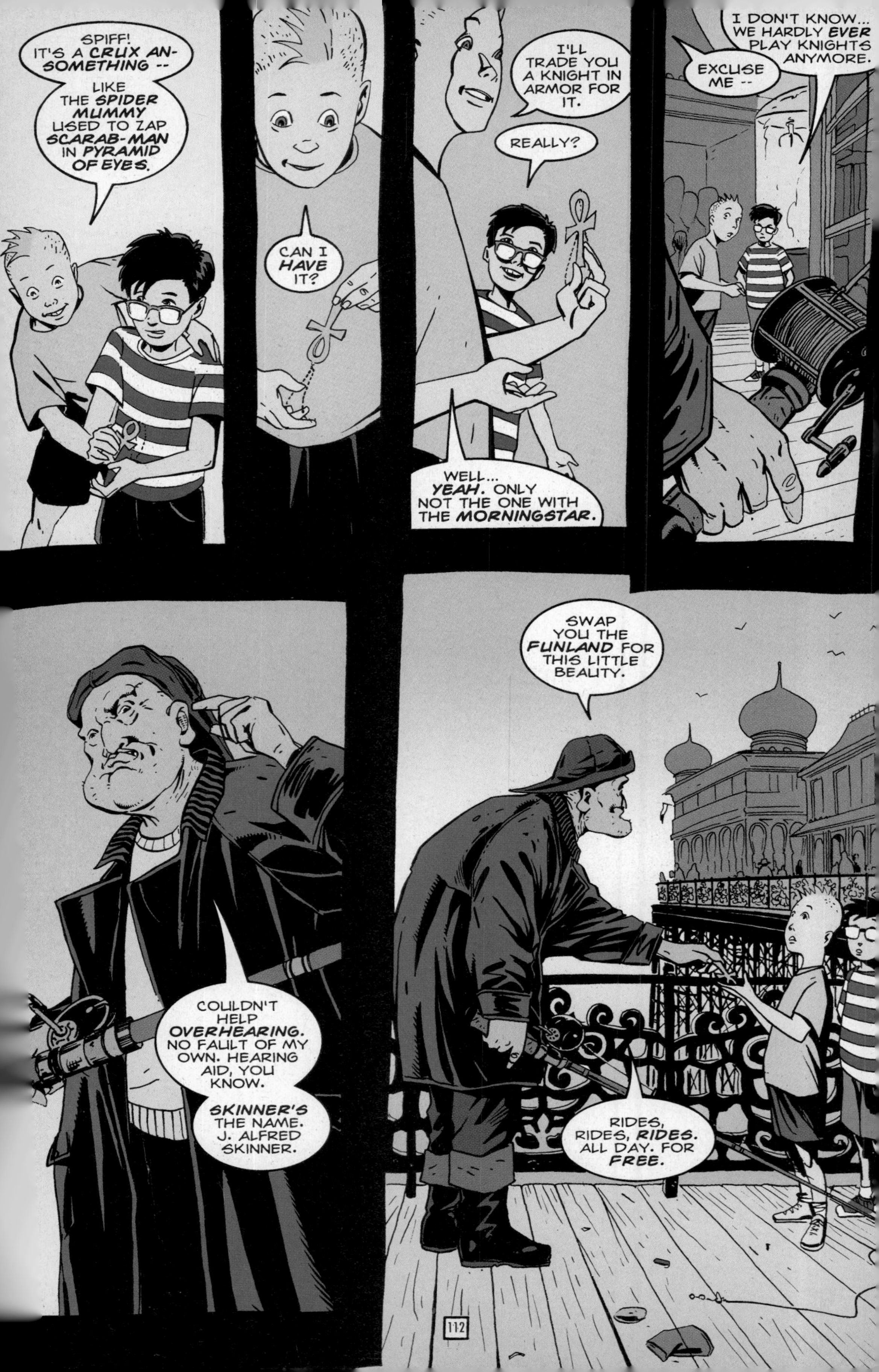
SPIFF! IT'S A CRUX AN-SOMETHING -- LIKE THE SPIDER MUMMY USED TO ZAP SCARAB-MAN IN PYRAMID OF EYES.
CAN I HAVE IT?
I'LL TRADE YOU A KNIGHT IN ARMOR FOR IT.
REALLY?
WELL... YEAH. ONLY NOT THE ONE WITH THE MORNINGSTAR.
I DON'T KNOW... WE HARDLY EVER PLAY KNIGHTS ANYMORE.
EXCUSE ME --
COULDN'T HELP OVERHEARING. NO FAULT OF MY OWN. HEARING AID, YOU KNOW.
SKINNER'S THE NAME. J. ALFRED SKINNER.
SWAP YOU THE FUNLAND FOR THIS LITTLE BEAUTY.
RIDES, RIDES, RIDES. ALL DAY. FOR FREE.

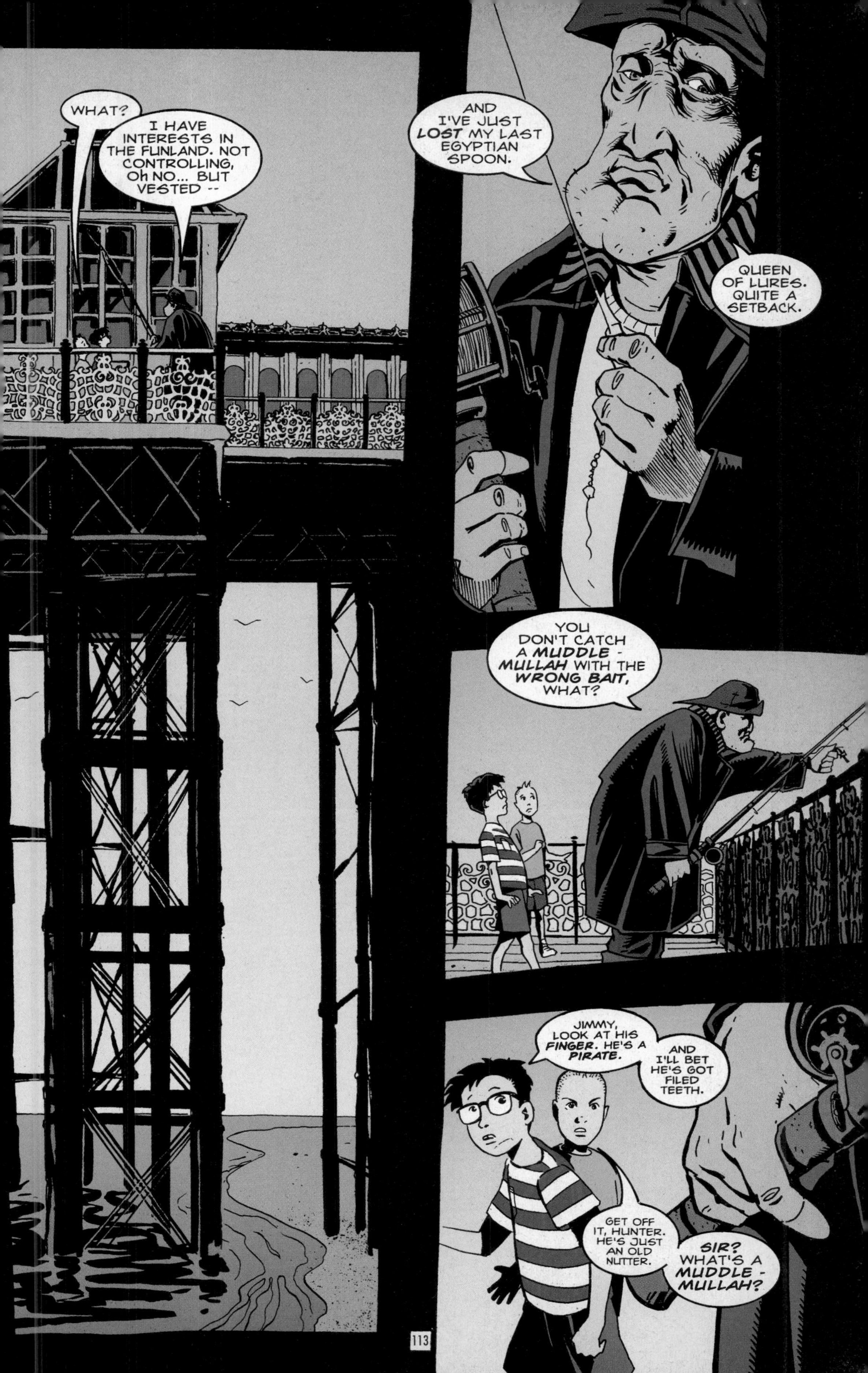
WHAT?
I HAVE INTERESTS IN THE FUNLAND. NOT CONTROLLING, Oh NO... BUT VESTED --
AND I'VE JUST LOST MY LAST EGYPTIAN SPOON.
QUEEN OF LURES. QUITE A SETBACK.
YOU DON'T CATCH A MUDDLE-MULLAH WITH THE WRONG BAIT, WHAT?
JIMMY, LOOK AT HIS FINGER. HE'S A PIRATE.
AND I'LL BET HE'S GOT FILED TEETH.
GET OFF IT, HUNTER. HE'S JUST AN OLD NUTTER.
SIR? WHAT'S A MUDDLE-MULLAH?

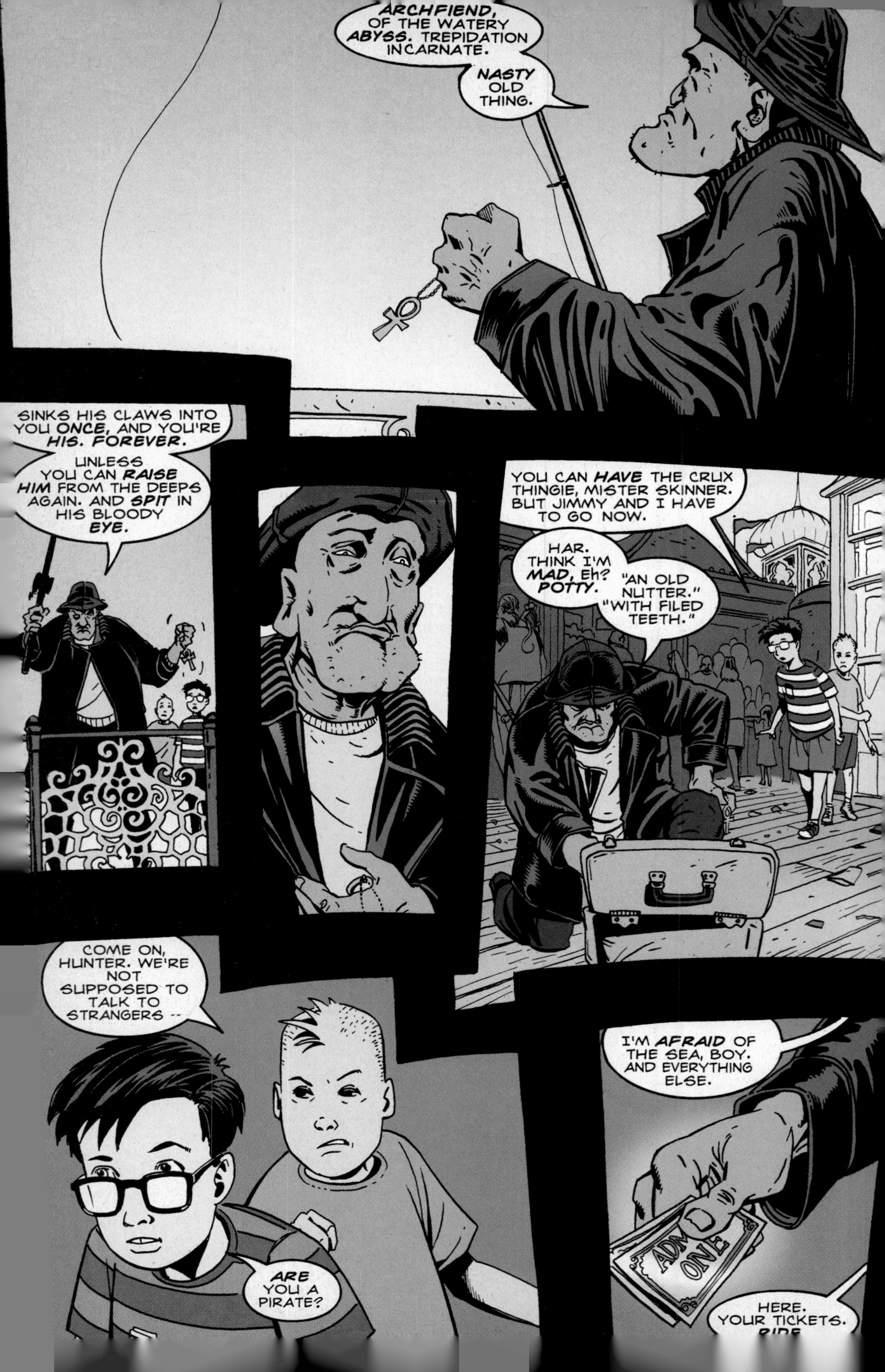
ARCHFIEND, OF THE WATERY ABYSS. TREPIDATION INCARNATE.
NASTY OLD THING.
SINKS HIS CLAWS INTO YOU ONCE, AND YOU'RE HIS. FOREVER.
UNLESS YOU CAN RAISE HIM FROM THE DEEPS AGAIN. AND SPIT IN HIS BLOODY EYE.
YOU CAN HAVE THE CRUX THINGIE, MISTER SKINNER. BUT JIMMY AND I HAVE TO GO NOW.
HAR. THINK I'M MAD, Eh? POTTY.
"AN OLD NUTTER." "WITH FILED TEETH."
COME ON, HUNTER. WE'RE NOT SUPPOSED TO TALK TO STRANGERS --
ARE YOU A PIRATE?
I'M AFRAID OF THE SEA, BOY. AND EVERYTHING ELSE.
ADMIT ONE
HERE. YOUR TICKETS.

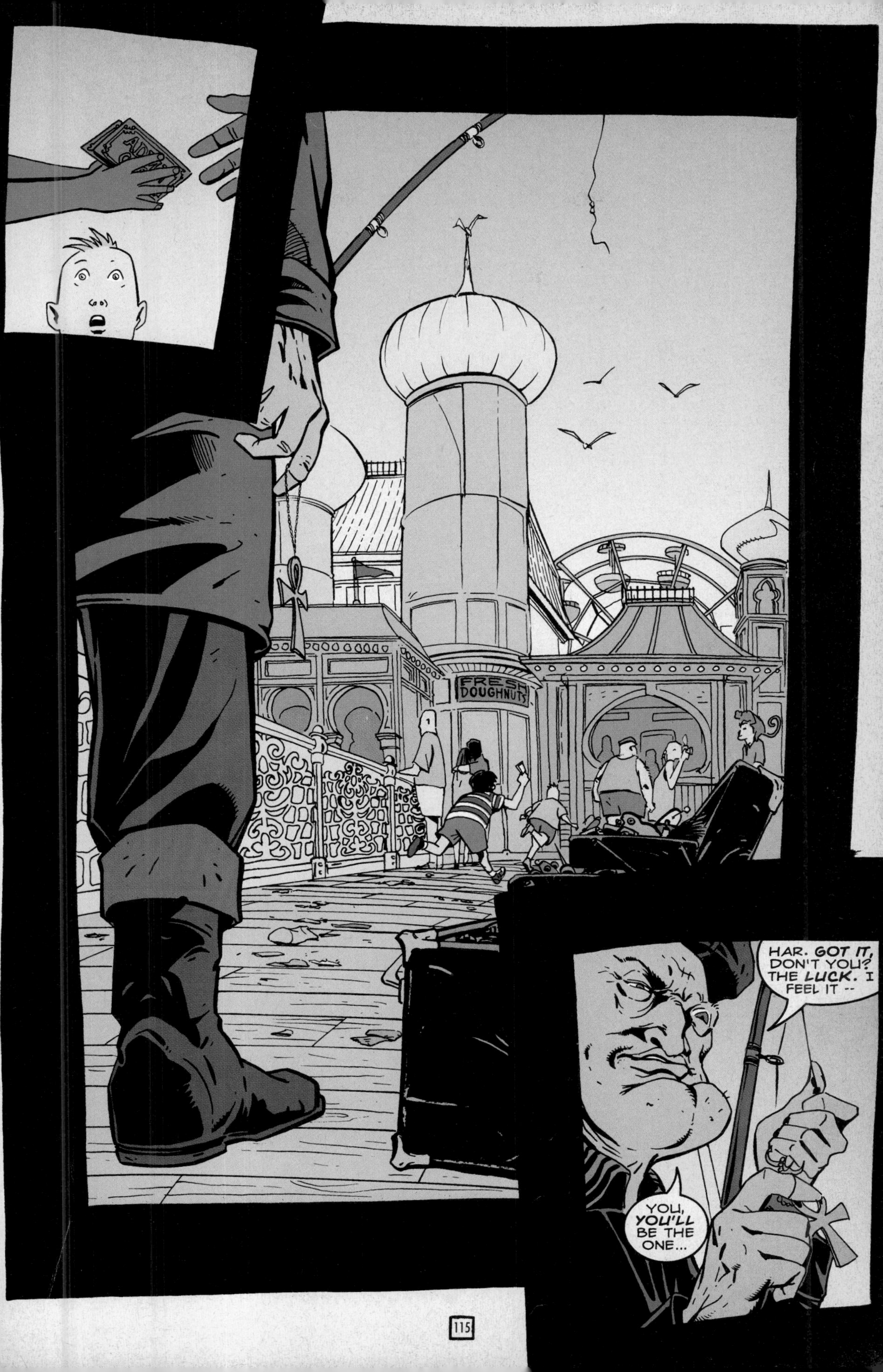
FRESH DOUGHNUTS
HAR. GOT IT, DON'T YOU? THE LUCK. I FEEL IT --
YOU, YOU'LL BE THE ONE...

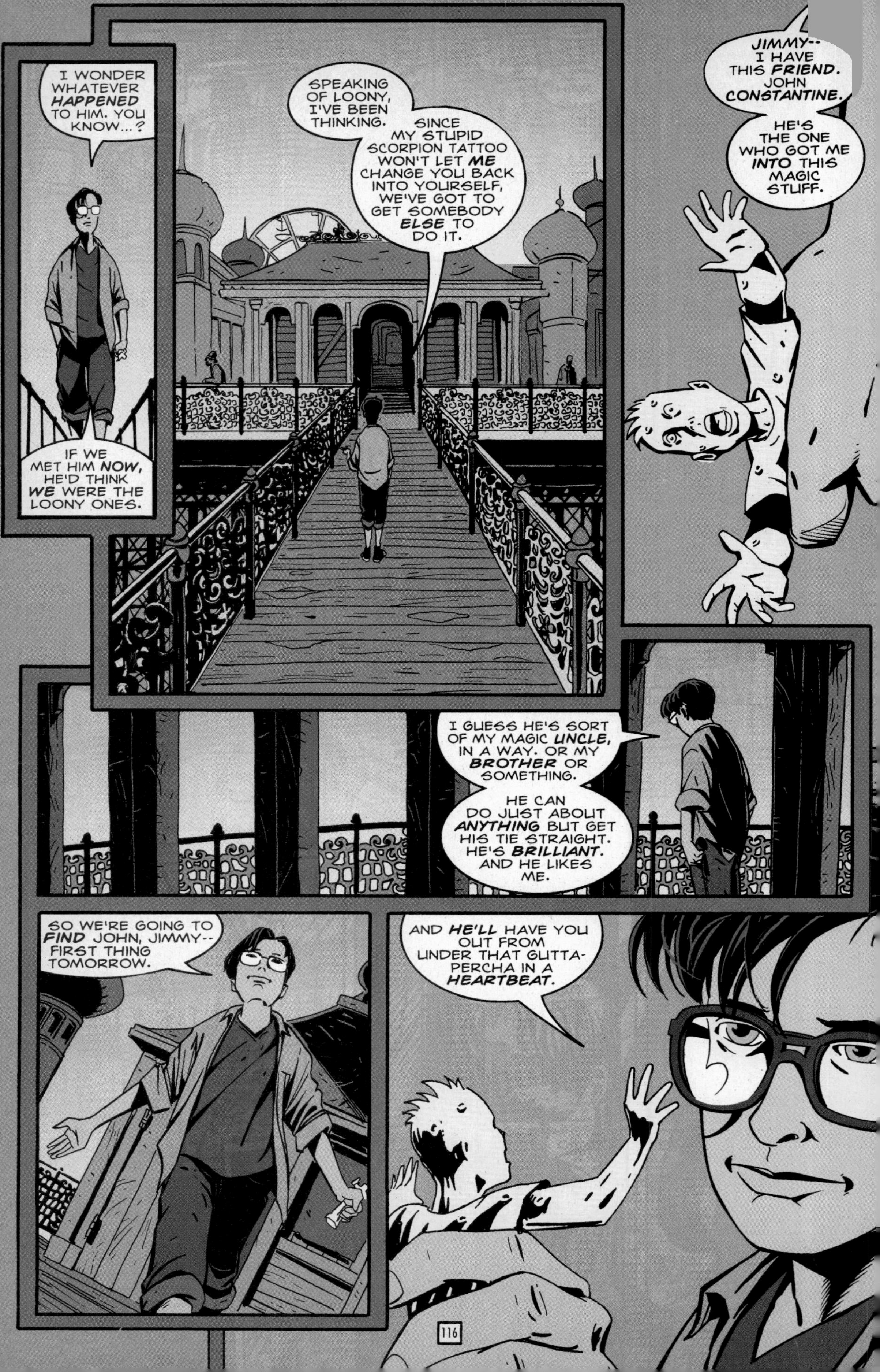
I WONDER WHATEVER HAPPENED TO HIM. YOU KNOW...?
IF WE MET HIM NOW, HE'D THINK WE WERE THE LOONY ONES.
SPEAKING OF LOONY, I'VE BEEN THINKING.
SINCE MY STUPID SCORPION TATTOO WON'T LET ME CHANGE YOU BACK INTO YOURSELF, WE'VE GOT TO GET SOMEBODY ELSE TO DO IT.
JIMMY-- I HAVE THIS FRIEND. JOHN CONSTANTINE.
HE'S THE ONE WHO GOT ME INTO THIS MAGIC STUFF.
I GUESS HE'S SORT OF MY MAGIC UNCLE, IN A WAY. OR MY BROTHER OR SOMETHING.
HE CAN DO JUST ABOUT ANYTHING BUT GET HIS TIE STRAIGHT. HE'S BRILLIANT. AND HE LIKES ME.
SO WE'RE GOING TO FIND JOHN, JIMMY-- FIRST THING TOMORROW.
AND HE'LL HAVE YOU OUT FROM UNDER THAT GUTTA-PERCHA IN A HEARTBEAT.

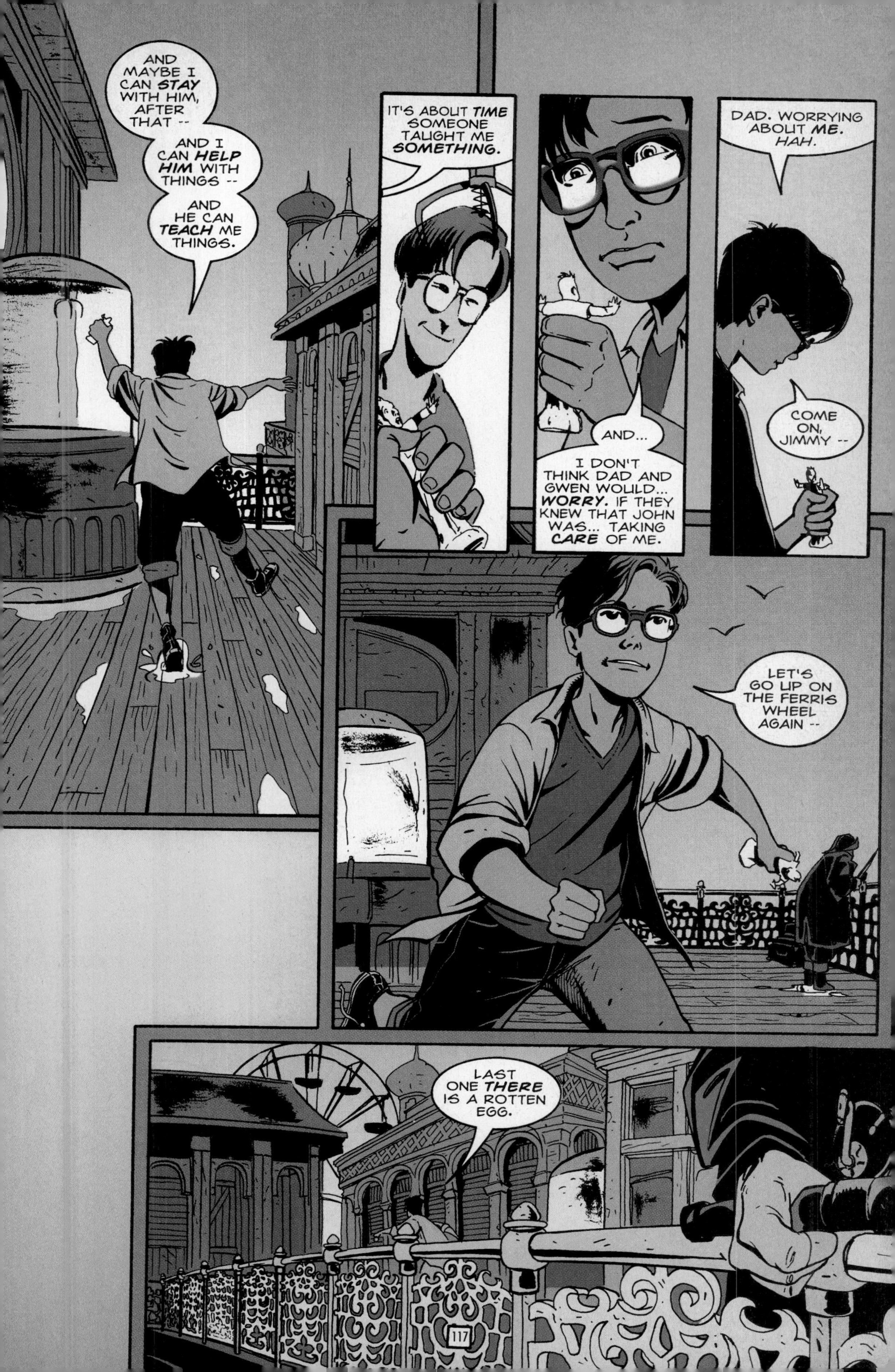
AND MAYBE I CAN STAY WITH HIM, AFTER THAT --
AND I CAN HELP HIM WITH THINGS --
AND HE CAN TEACH ME THINGS.
IT'S ABOUT TIME SOMEONE TAUGHT ME SOMETHING.
AND...
I DON'T THINK DAD AND GWEN WOULD... WORRY. IF THEY KNEW THAT JOHN WAS... TAKING CARE OF ME.
DAD. WORRYING ABOUT ME. HAH.
COME ON, JIMMY --
LET'S GO UP ON THE FERRIS WHEEL AGAIN --
LAST ONE THERE IS A ROTTEN EGG.

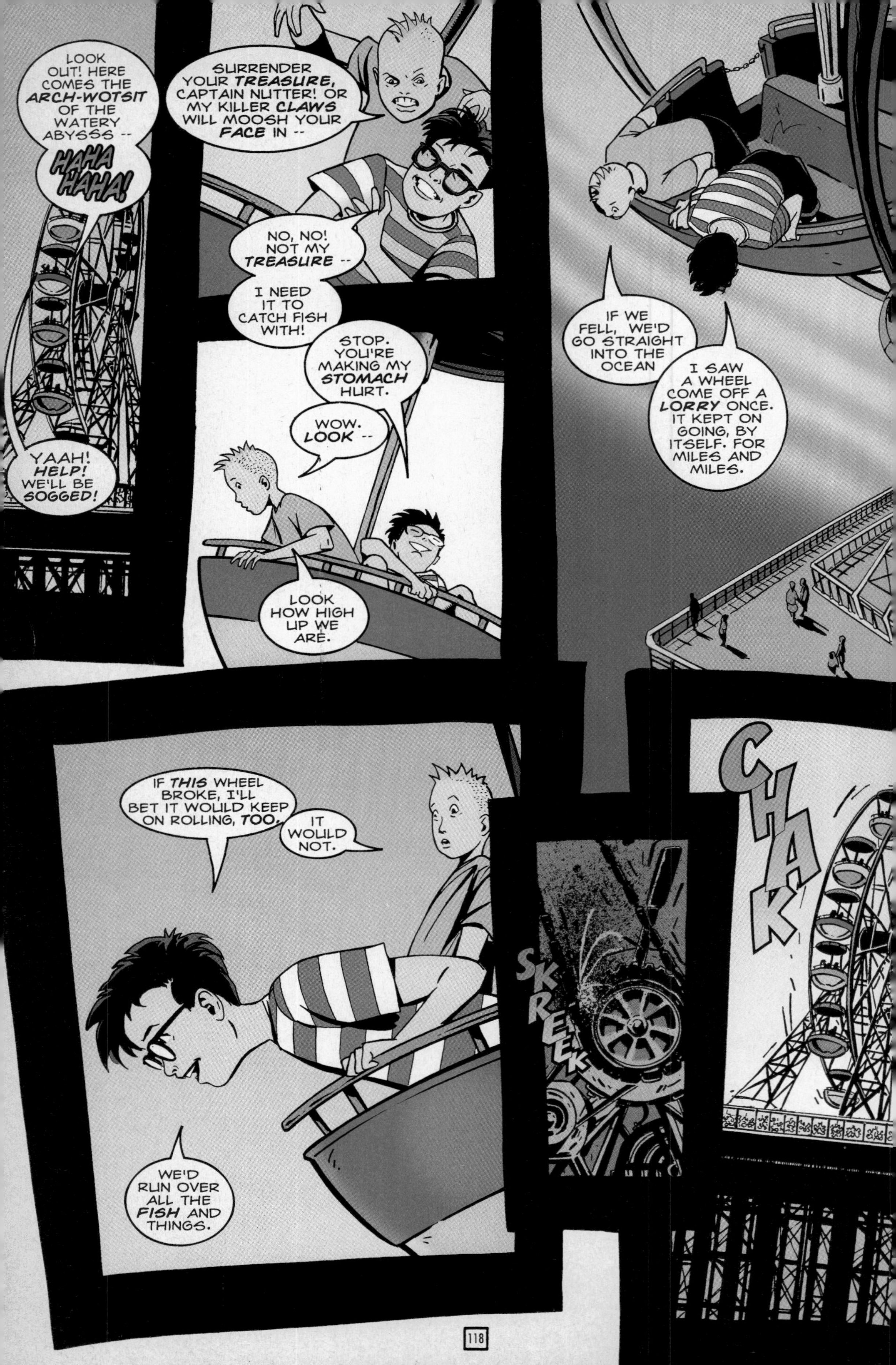

LOOK OUT! HERE COMES THE ARCH-WOTSIT OF THE WATERY ABYSSS --
HAHA HAHA!
YAAH! HELP! WE'LL BE SOGGED!
SURRENDER YOUR TREASURE, CAPTAIN NUTTER! OR MY KILLER CLAWS WILL MOOSH YOUR FACE IN --
NO, NO! NOT MY TREASURE --
I NEED IT TO CATCH FISH WITH!
STOP. YOU'RE MAKING MY STOMACH HURT.
WOW. LOOK --
LOOK HOW HIGH UP WE ARE.
IF WE FELL, WE'D GO STRAIGHT INTO THE OCEAN
I SAW A WHEEL COME OFF A LORRY ONCE. IT KEPT ON GOING, BY ITSELF. FOR MILES AND MILES.
IF THIS WHEEL BROKE, I'LL BET IT WOULD KEEP ON ROLLING, TOO.
IT WOULD NOT.
WE'D RUN OVER ALL THE FISH AND THINGS.
SKREEEK
CHAK

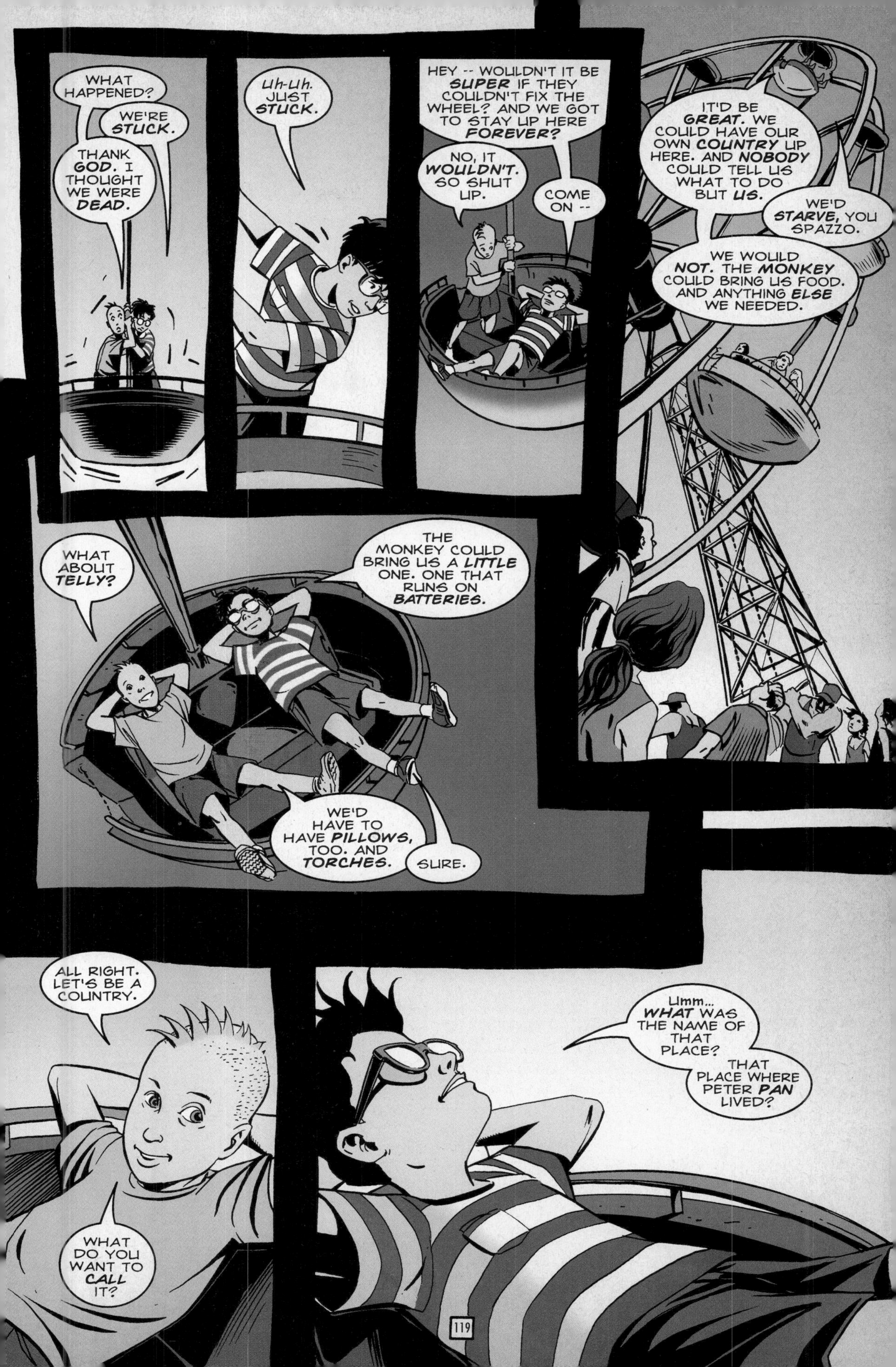

WHAT HAPPENED?
WE'RE STUCK.
THANK GOD. I THOUGHT WE WERE DEAD.
Uh-uh. JUST STUCK.
HEY -- WOULDN'T IT BE SUPER IF THEY COULDN'T FIX THE WHEEL? AND WE GOT TO STAY UP HERE FOREVER?
NO, IT WOULDN'T. SO SHUT UP.
COME ON --
IT'D BE GREAT. WE COULD HAVE OUR OWN COUNTRY UP HERE. AND NOBODY COULD TELL US WHAT TO DO BUT US.
WE'D STARVE, YOU SPAZZO.
WE WOULD NOT. THE MONKEY COULD BRING US FOOD. AND ANYTHING ELSE WE NEEDED.
WHAT ABOUT TELLY?
THE MONKEY COULD BRING US A LITTLE ONE. ONE THAT RUNS ON BATTERIES.
WE'D HAVE TO HAVE PILLOWS, TOO. AND TORCHES.
SURE.
ALL RIGHT. LET'S BE A COUNTRY.
WHAT DO YOU WANT TO CALL IT?
Umm... WHAT WAS THE NAME OF THAT PLACE?
THAT PLACE WHERE PETER PAN LIVED?

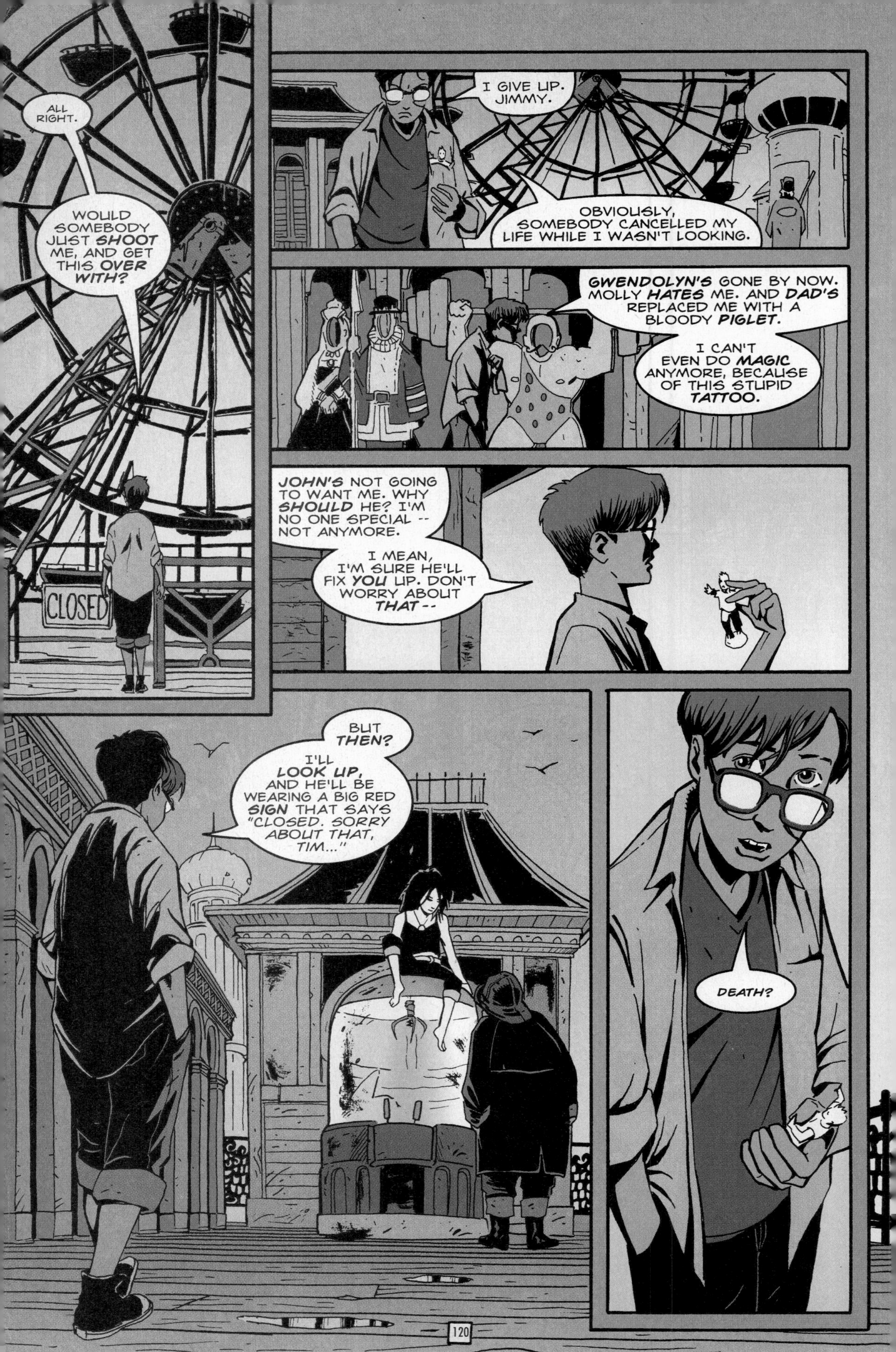
ALL RIGHT.
WOULD SOMEBODY JUST SHOOT ME, AND GET THIS OVER WITH?
CLOSED
I GIVE UP. JIMMY.
OBVIOUSLY, SOMEBODY CANCELLED MY LIFE WHILE I WASN'T LOOKING.
GWENDOLYN'S GONE BY NOW. MOLLY HATES ME. AND DAD'S REPLACED ME WITH A BLOODY PIGLET.
I CAN'T EVEN DO MAGIC ANYMORE, BECAUSE OF THIS STUPID TATTOO.
JOHN'S NOT GOING TO WANT ME. WHY SHOULD HE? I'M NO ONE SPECIAL -- NOT ANYMORE.
I MEAN, I'M SURE HE'LL FIX YOU UP. DON'T WORRY ABOUT THAT --
BUT THEN?
I'LL LOOK UP, AND HE'LL BE WEARING A BIG RED SIGN THAT SAYS "CLOSED. SORRY ABOUT THAT, TIM..."
DEATH?

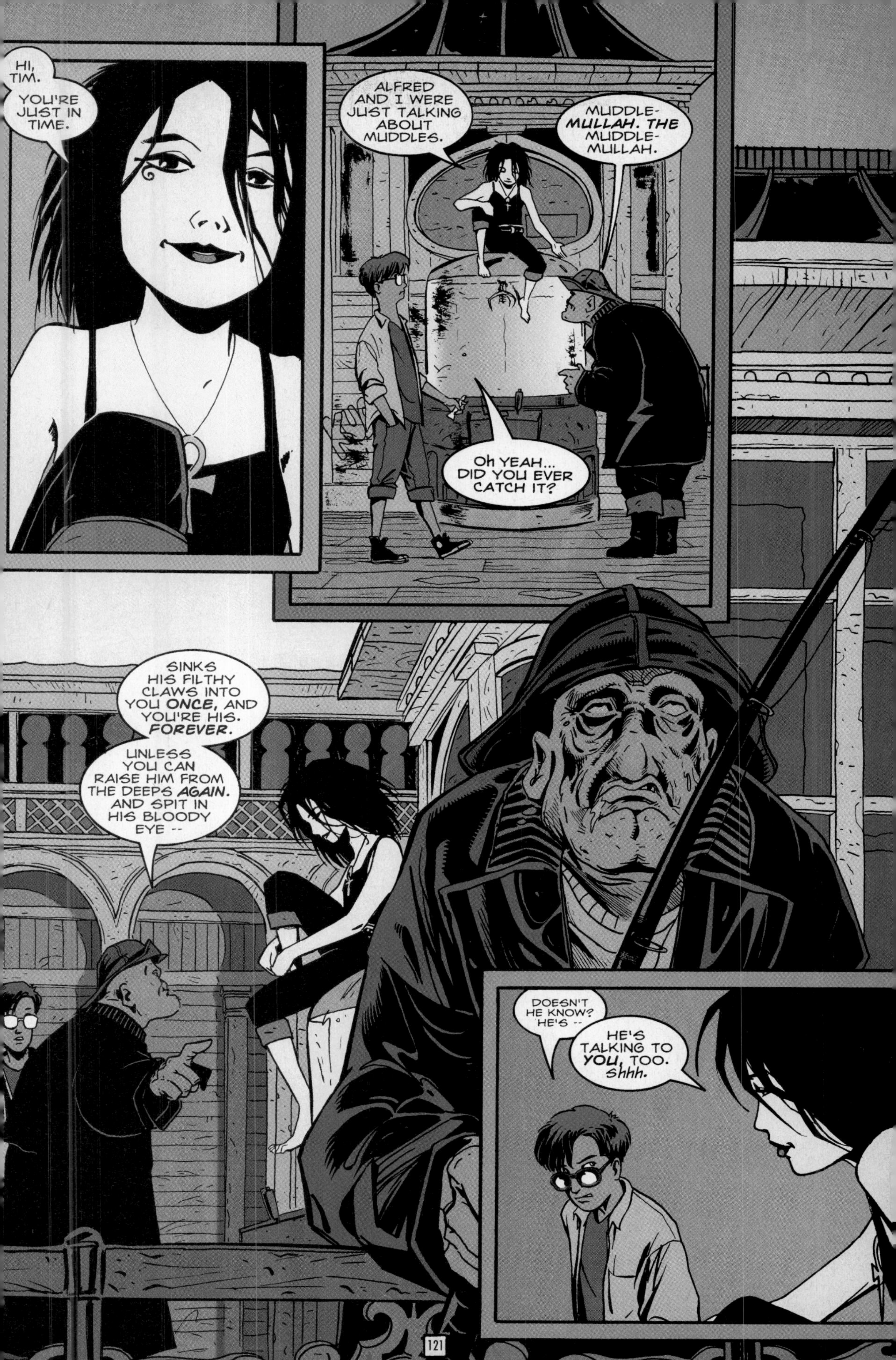
HI, TIM.
YOU'RE JUST IN TIME.
ALFRED AND I WERE JUST TALKING ABOUT MUDDLES.
MUDDLE-MULLAH. THE MUDDLE-MULLAH.
Oh YEAH... DID YOU EVER CATCH IT?
SINKS HIS FILTHY CLAWS INTO YOU ONCE, AND YOU'RE HIS. FOREVER.
UNLESS YOU CAN RAISE HIM FROM THE DEEPS AGAIN. AND SPIT IN HIS BLOODY EYE --
DOESN'T HE KNOW? HE'S --
HE'S TALKING TO YOU, TOO. shhh.

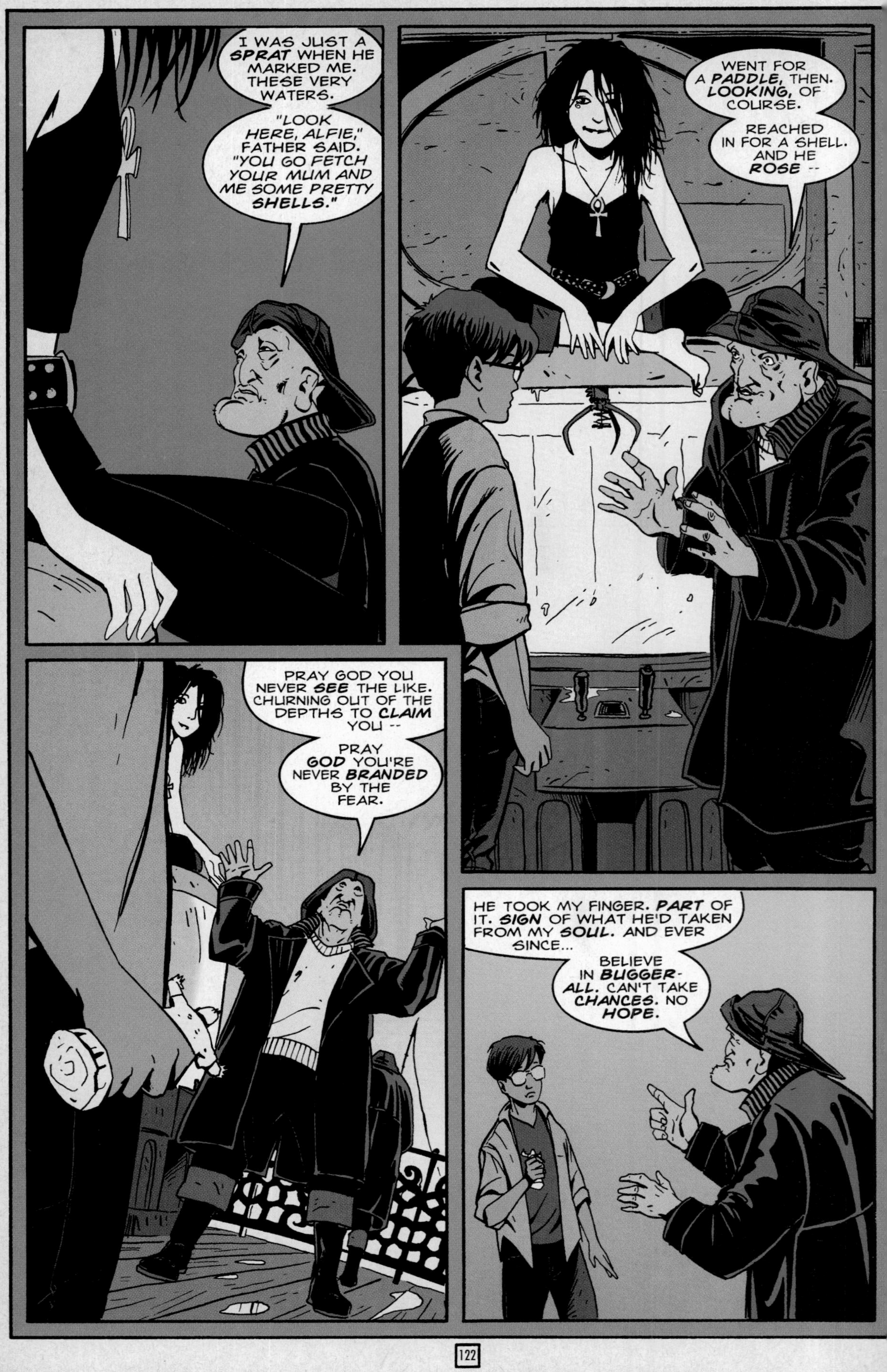
I WAS JUST A SPRAT WHEN HE MARKED ME. THESE VERY WATERS.
"LOOK HERE, ALFIE," FATHER SAID. "YOU GO FETCH YOUR MUM AND ME SOME PRETTY SHELLS."
WENT FOR A PADDLE, THEN. LOOKING, OF COURSE.
REACHED IN FOR A SHELL. AND HE ROSE --
PRAY GOD YOU NEVER SEE THE LIKE. CHURNING OUT OF THE DEPTHS TO CLAIM YOU --
PRAY GOD YOU'RE NEVER BRANDED BY THE FEAR.
HE TOOK MY FINGER. PART OF IT. SIGN OF WHAT HE'D TAKEN FROM MY SOUL. AND EVER SINCE...
BELIEVE IN BUGGER-ALL. CAN'T TAKE CHANCES. NO HOPE.

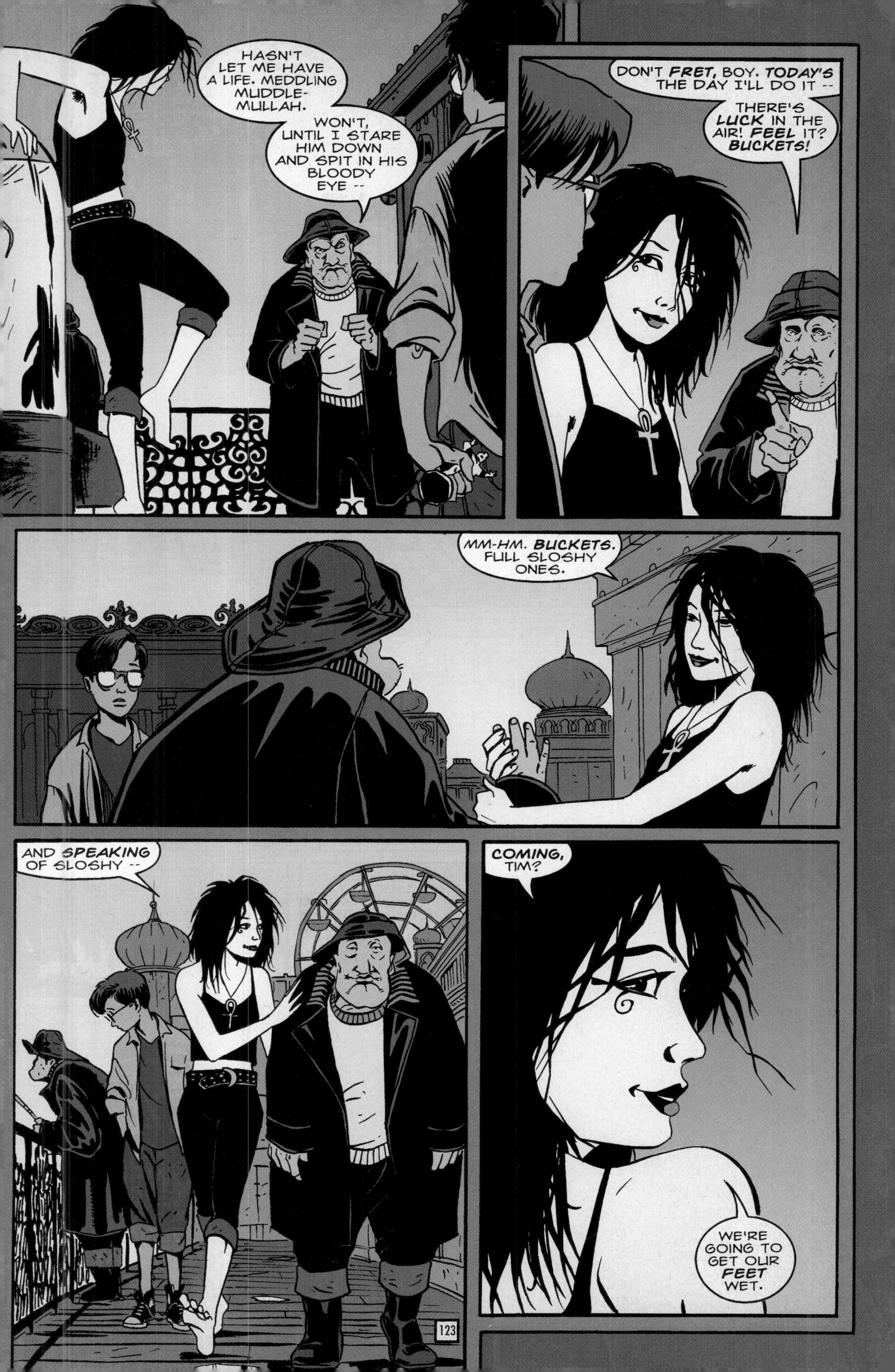
HASN'T LET ME HAVE A LIFE. MEDDLING MUDDLE-MULLAH.
WON'T, UNTIL I STARE HIM DOWN AND SPIT IN HIS BLOODY EYE --
DON'T FRET, BOY. TODAY'S THE DAY I'LL DO IT --
THERE'S LUCK IN THE AIR! FEEL IT? BUCKETS!
MM-HM. BUCKETS. FULL SLOSHY ONES.
AND SPEAKING OF SLOSHY --
COMING, TIM?
WE'RE GOING TO GET OUR FEET WET.

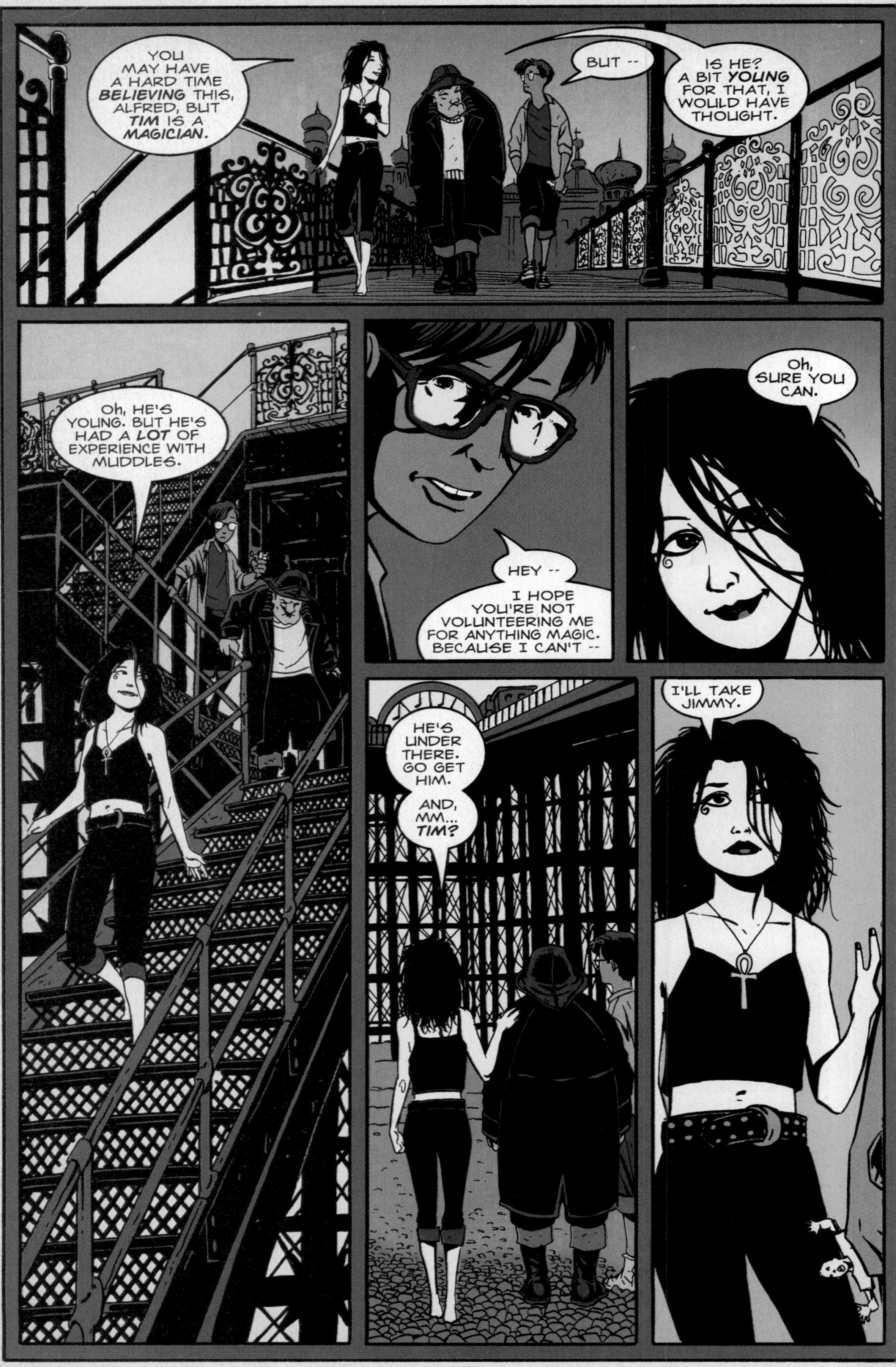
YOU MAY HAVE A HARD TIME BELIEVING THIS, ALFRED, BUT TIM IS A MAGICIAN.
BUT --
IS HE? A BIT YOUNG FOR THAT, I WOULD HAVE THOUGHT.
Oh, HE'S YOUNG. BUT HE'S HAD A LOT OF EXPERIENCE WITH MUDDLES.
HEY --
I HOPE YOU'RE NOT VOLUNTEERING ME FOR ANYTHING MAGIC. BECAUSE I CAN'T --
Oh, SURE YOU CAN.
HE'S UNDER THERE. GO GET HIM.
AND, MM... TIM?
I'LL TAKE JIMMY.

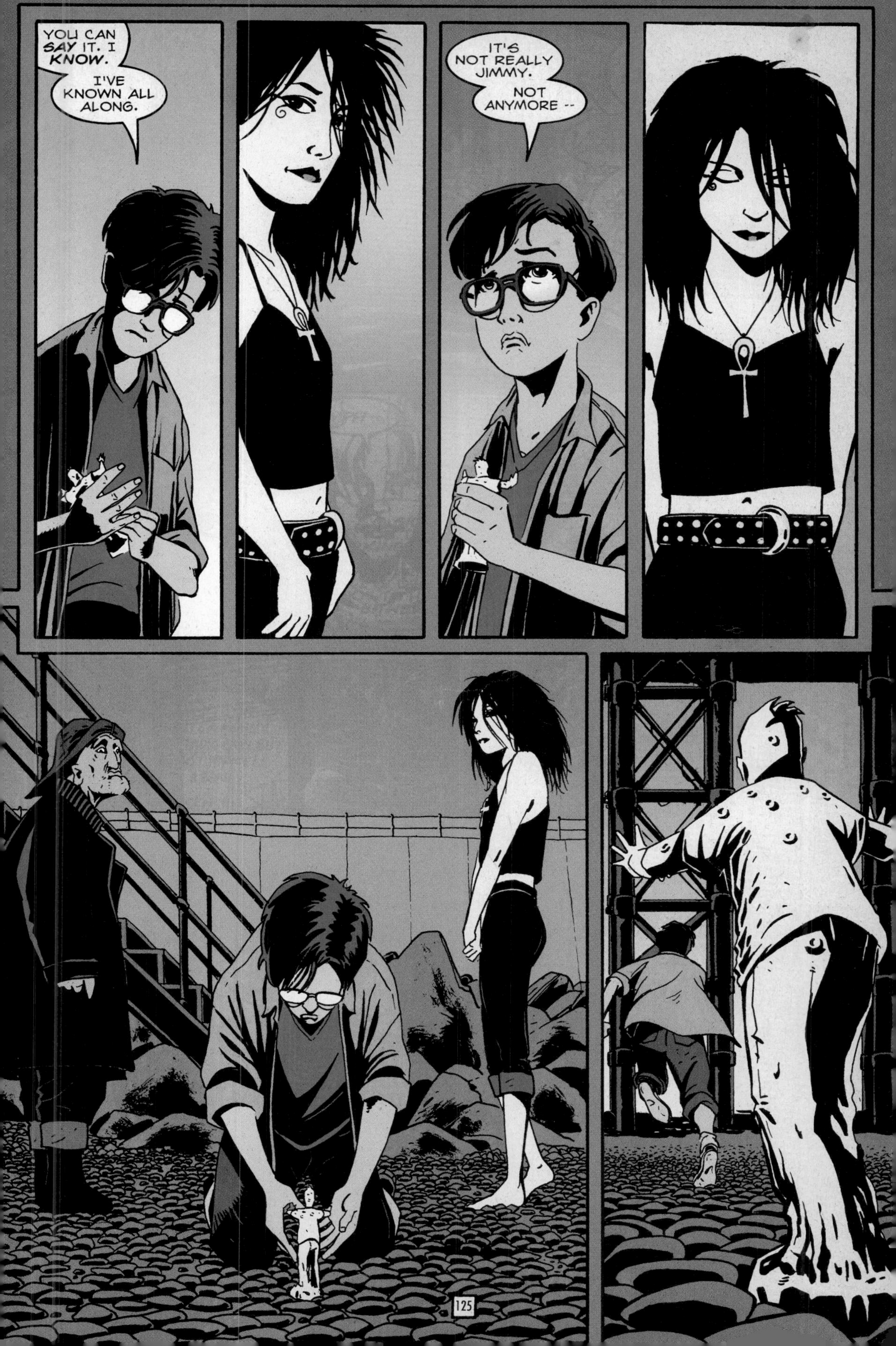
YOU CAN SAY IT. I KNOW.
I'VE KNOWN ALL ALONG.
IT'S NOT REALLY JIMMY.
NOT ANYMORE --

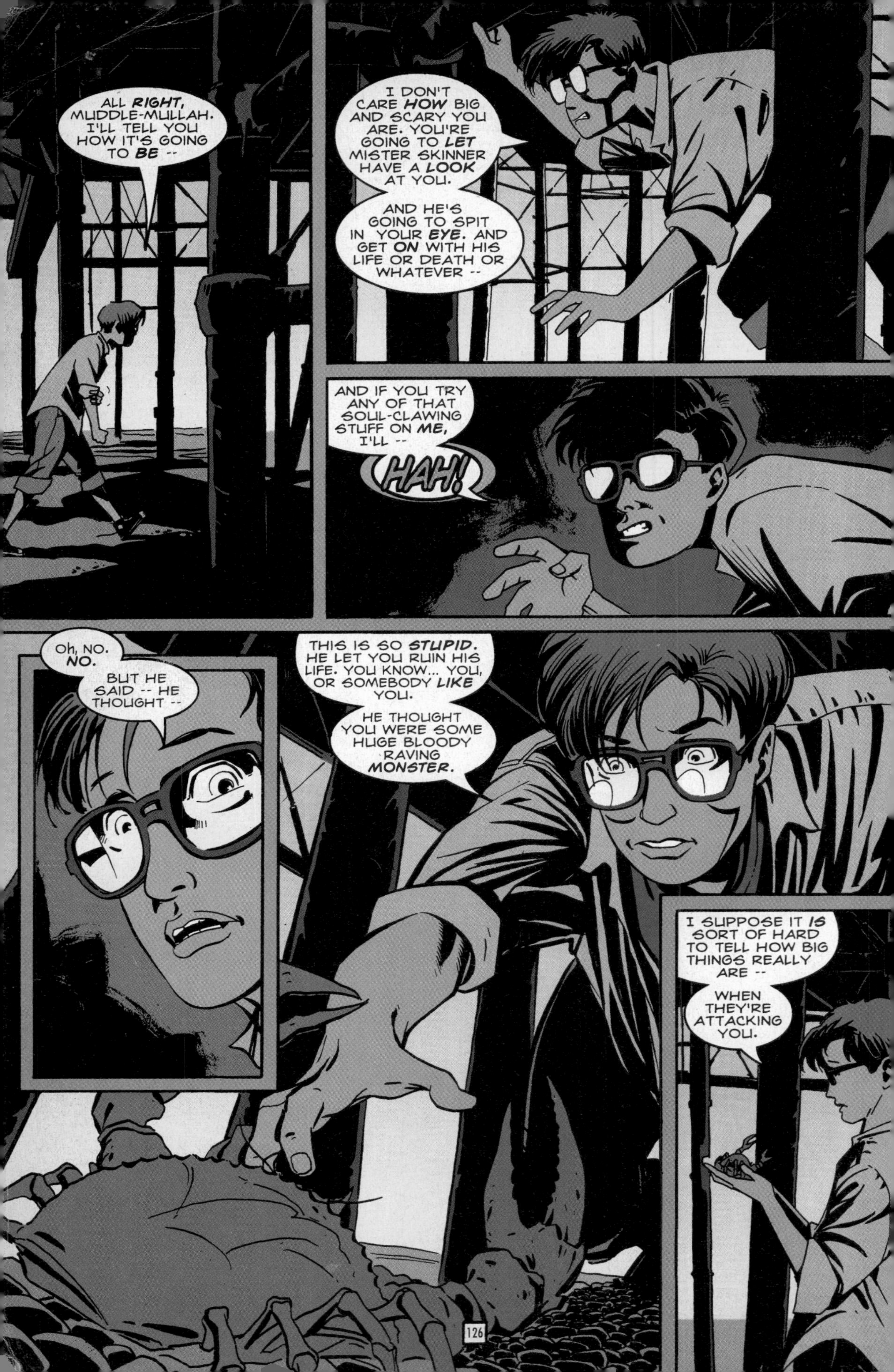
ALL RIGHT, MUDDLE-MULLAH. I'LL TELL YOU HOW IT'S GOING TO BE --
I DON'T CARE HOW BIG AND SCARY YOU ARE. YOU'RE GOING TO LET MISTER SKINNER HAVE A LOOK AT YOU.
AND HE'S GOING TO SPIT IN YOUR EYE. AND GET ON WITH HIS LIFE OR DEATH OR WHATEVER --
AND IF YOU TRY ANY OF THAT SOUL-CLAWING STUFF ON ME, I'LL --
HAH!
Oh, NO. NO.
BUT HE SAID -- HE THOUGHT --
THIS IS SO STUPID. HE LET YOU RUIN HIS LIFE. YOU KNOW... YOU, OR SOMEBODY LIKE YOU.
HE THOUGHT YOU WERE SOME HUGE BLOODY RAVING MONSTER.
I SUPPOSE IT IS SORT OF HARD TO TELL HOW BIG THINGS REALLY ARE --
WHEN THEY'RE ATTACKING YOU.

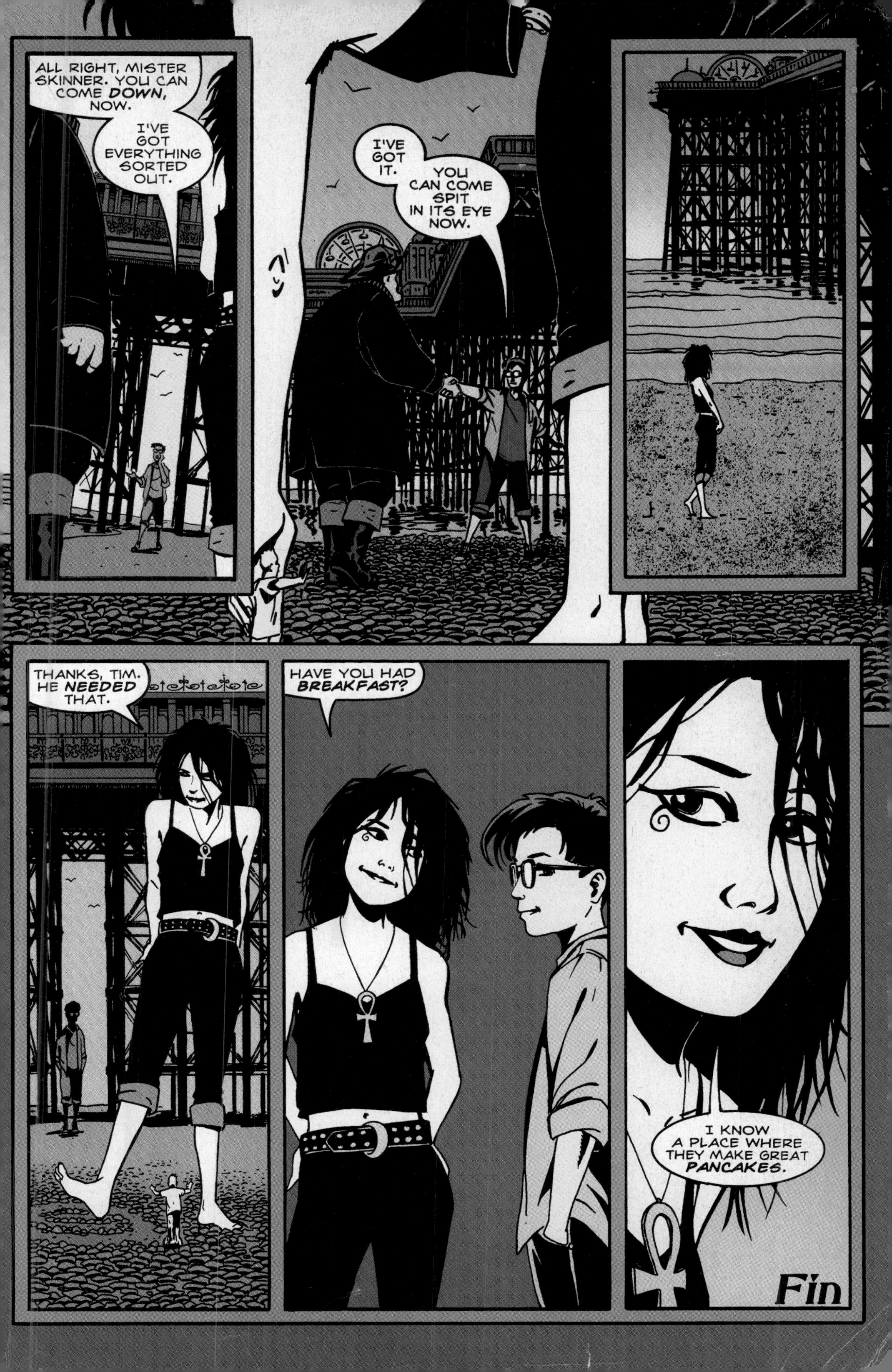
ALL RIGHT, MISTER SKINNER. YOU CAN COME DOWN, NOW.
I'VE GOT EVERYTHING SORTED OUT.
I'VE GOT IT.
YOU CAN COME SPIT IN ITS EYE NOW.
THANKS, TIM. HE NEEDED THAT.
HAVE YOU HAD BREAKFAST?
I KNOW A PLACE WHERE THEY MAKE GREAT PANCAKES.
Fin

Look For These Other Vertigo Books:

All VERTIGO backlist books are suggested for mature readers

Graphic Novels

DHAMPIRE: STILLBORN
Nancy A. Collins/Paul Lee

DOG MOON
Robert Hunter/Tim Truman

MENZ INSANA
Christopher Fowler/John Bolton

MERCY
J. M. DeMatteis/Paul Johnson

MR. PUNCH
Neil Gaiman/Dave McKean

THE MYSTERY PLAY
Grant Morrison/Jon J Muth

TELL ME, DARK
Karl Wagner/Kent Williams

VERTIGO VÉRITÉ:
SEVEN MILES A SECOND
David Wojnarowicz/
James Romberger

VERTIGO VOICES:
THE EATERS
Peter Milligan/Dean Ormston

Collections

ANIMAL MAN
Grant Morrison/Chas Truog/
Tom Grummett/Doug Hazlewood

BLACK ORCHID
Neil Gaiman/Dave McKean

THE BOOKS OF MAGIC
Neil Gaiman/John Bolton/
Scott Hampton/Charles Vess/
Paul Johnson

THE BOOKS OF MAGIC:
BINDINGS
John Ney Rieber/Gary Amaro/
Peter Gross

THE BOOKS OF MAGIC:
SUMMONINGS
John Ney Rieber/Peter Gross/
Peter Snejbjerg/Gary Amaro/
Dick Giordano

THE BOOKS OF MAGIC:
RECKONINGS
John Ney Rieber/Peter Snejbjerg/
Peter Gross/John Ridgway

BREATHTAKER
Mark Wheatley/Marc Hempel

DEATH:
THE HIGH COST OF LIVING
Neil Gaiman/Chris Bachalo/
Mark Buckingham

DEATH:
THE TIME OF YOUR LIFE
Neil Gaiman/Chris Bachalo/
Mark Buckingham/
Mark Pennington

DOOM PATROL: CRAWLING
FROM THE WRECKAGE
Grant Morrison/Richard Case/
various

ENIGMA
Peter Milligan/Duncan Fegredo

HELLBLAZER:
ORIGINAL SINS
Jamie Delano/John Ridgway/
various

HELLBLAZER:
DANGEROUS HABITS
Garth Ennis/William Simpson/
various

HELLBLAZER:
FEAR AND LOATHING
Garth Ennis/Steve Dillon

HOUSE OF SECRETS:
FOUNDATION
Steven T. Seagle/
Teddy Kristiansen

THE INVISIBLES: SAY YOU
WANT A REVOLUTION
Grant Morrison/Steve Yeowell/
Jill Thompson/Dennis Cramer

JONAH HEX:
TWO-GUN MOJO
Joe R. Lansdale/Tim
Truman/Sam Glanzman

PREACHER: GONE TO TEXAS
Garth Ennis/Steve Dillon

PREACHER: UNTIL THE END
OF THE WORLD
Garth Ennis/Steve Dillon

PREACHER:
PROUD AMERICANS
Garth Ennis/Steve Dillon

SAGA OF THE
SWAMP THING
Alan Moore/Steve Bissette/
John Totleben

THE SYSTEM
Peter Kuper

TERMINAL CITY
Dean Motter/Michael Lark

TRUE FAITH
Garth Ennis/Warren Pleece

V FOR VENDETTA
Alan Moore/David Lloyd

VAMPS
Elaine Lee/William Simpson

WITCHCRAFT
James Robinson/Peter Snejbjerg/
Michael Zulli/Steve Yeowell/
Teddy Kristiansen

The Sandman Library

THE SANDMAN:
PRELUDES & NOCTURNES
Neil Gaiman/Sam Kieth/
Mike Dringenberg/
Malcolm Jones III

THE SANDMAN:
THE DOLL'S HOUSE
Neil Gaiman/Mike Dringenberg/
Malcolm Jones III/Chris Bachalo/
Michael Zulli/Steve Parkhouse

THE SANDMAN:
DREAM COUNTRY
Neil Gaiman/Kelley Jones/
Charles Vess/Colleen Doran/
Malcolm Jones III

THE SANDMAN:
SEASON OF MISTS
Neil Gaiman/Kelley Jones/
Mike Dringenberg/
Malcolm Jones III/various

THE SANDMAN:
A GAME OF YOU
Neil Gaiman/Shawn McManus/
various

THE SANDMAN:
FABLES AND REFLECTIONS
Neil Gaiman/various artists

THE SANDMAN:
BRIEF LIVES
Neil Gaiman/Jill Thompson/
Vince Locke

THE SANDMAN:
WORLDS' END
Neil Gaiman/various artists

THE SANDMAN:
THE KINDLY ONES
Neil Gaiman/Marc Hempel/
Richard Case/various

THE SANDMAN:
THE WAKE
Neil Gaiman/Michael Zulli/
Jon J Muth/Charles Vess

DUST COVERS-
THE COLLECTED
SANDMAN COVERS
1989-1997
Dave McKean/Neil Gaiman

Other Collections of Interest

CAMELOT 3000
Mike W. Barr/Brian Bolland

RONIN
Frank Miller

WATCHMEN
Alan Moore/Dave Gibbons

*For the nearest comics
shop carrying collected
editions and monthly
titles from DC Comics,
call 1-888-COMIC BOOK.*